DOMESTIC GEESE

Chris Ashton

The Crowood Press

First published in 1999 by
The Crowood Press Ltd
Ramsbury, Marlborough
Wiltshire SN8 2HR

www.crowood.com

This impression 2006

British Library Cataloguing-in-Publication Data
A catalogue record for this book is available from the British
Library

ISBN 1 86126 271 X
EAN 978 1 86126 271 4

Printed and bound in Great Britain by
CPI Bath

Contents ──────────────

Introduction ————

FIRST IMPRESSIONS

Geese have a fierce reputation. They rule the farmyard, terrorize the postman and deter burglars, and they saved Rome from the Goths. It is strange that I ever had geese because this reputation used to intimidate me. I vividly remember looking at grandma's encyclopaedia at the age of five, seeing the painting of the white geese on the Capitol, and comparing them with the farmyard gander. Geese were clearly not to be trifled with.

Not surprisingly, this is how most people still view these gregarious birds. On the farm or smallholding of twenty years ago or more, geese were not pets; they had to manage for themselves. With a strong protective instinct towards their offspring, ganders will take on allcomers in the breeding and rearing season,

when everything on the farm, from dogs to vehicles, is viewed as a threat. Like ducklings, goslings are preyed upon by other birds, cats, dogs and rats, and they need a lot of help if they are to survive.

I can still remember visiting a neighbouring farm when we lived in Leek. I was less than four years old, and I had never noticed that the farm had a pair of geese, because most of the time the birds were out grazing. In April, however, they stayed closer to the yard. Mother had brought some shopping and crossed the flagstones towards the back door, holding my hand. It was the breeding season and the goose was well out of the way, sitting on her eggs, but the gander was bored. There is nothing to do while the goose sits, so two intruders were probably interesting game. With a flurry of raised wings, the gander's feet came slapping across

Opposite:
Fig 1 The Greylag, ancestor of our European Domestic Geese

Fig 2 Tig with the goslings – the first two are joined by three more. The original Buff Back goslings are about 7 weeks old, and have not quite got their first complete set of feathers

Fig 3 The birthday presents at about 7 weeks old

the yard from the sheds as he set about the job of seeing us off.

Fortunately, my mother had a spare arm to lift me off my feet. Children's faces and ganders' beaks are at the same height and geese know they can get the better of small annoyances. But I was lucky. The shopping basket proved the main attraction, first as a focus for his aggression, and then to be probed for the contents. I could feel the power of his beak and neck as he searched around the basket for bread.

The farm's goslings were a different matter. They were brought in for the night, to escape the rats, and warmed in the box by the farmhouse kitchen range. The box of yellow fluff was soft, and the goslings talked. They sat cupped in our hands and went to sleep with soft, contented trills.

Thirty years later, the magic worked again, this time on my daughter. Two fluffy farm goslings were her birthday present, intended by the farmer for us to rear for Christmas eating. The first mistake was to give them names, the second to rear them partly indoors. They ran around in the house in the evening and went out to the coop to graze while we were at work in the day.

Fourteen years later, one 'gosling' was still mothering a dozen adopted goslings a year;

her sister had died of natural causes several years after the intended Christmas dinner. The initial appeal of those goslings for us had determined their, and our, future. This introduction convinced us that we were interested in geese as a hobby. The birds were useful pets; they grazed the grass so it needed cutting less often, and they provided hours of amusement for us and for our visitors. The last thing we wanted was a flock of tame commercial cross-breeds for Christmas, so we embarked on pure-bred geese.

DOMESTICATION

It is generally accepted that, in North Africa and Europe, the goose was domesticated from the Greylag. Not only does the species have a wide range, but it is also more tolerant of disturbance by man than many others. Greylags are the most adaptable of European geese in their food requirements, and will nest closer to man than other species. One population breeds in Iceland and over-winters in Britain, whilst another group breeding in Scandinavia and central Europe overwinters in southern Europe and North Africa. According to Owen (1977), the species used to breed in the East Anglian

Iceland

Norway

Small resident
population in
the Hebrides

Overwintering
in Scotland

Overwintering
in the
Netherlands

Overwintering
in Spain in the
Marismas of the
Guadalquivir

Eastern Algeria
and Tunisia
overwintering

Former breeding sites in the Fens of East Anglia (★) and the Netherlands (◆) before the marshes were drained
Migration routes

Fig 4 Breeding areas and migration patterns of the Greylag goose.
The range of this species as a resident is less extensive than formerly
because of habitat destruction. Most birds are now migratory and
breed in Iceland, Scandinavia and Central Europe

Fig 5 Greylag gander in spring. This young gander lacks the white feathers that develop around the base of the bill in some older specimens. His undercarriage shows barred feathers

Fens and the Netherlands before the destruction of the marshes. Weir (1902), for example, quotes Pennant from 1776: 'This species resides in the fens the whole of the year: breeds there, and hatches about eight or nine young, which are often taken, easily made tame, and esteemed most excellent meat, superior to the domestic geese.' There were, it seems, opportunities across Europe and North Africa to catch both adult and young birds for domestication.

Egypt

As well as cranes, ducks and Egyptian geese from the papyrus marshes, there are records of the Greylag from ancient Egyptian frescoes (Schmidt, 1989). It was a sacred bird 4000 years ago, although Brown (1929) remarked, somewhat cynically but realistically, that 'Priests were always fond of good living and kept this as far as possible to themselves'.

Rome

By the fourth century BC, the Romans had developed a white goose from the Greylag.

Lucretius wrote that 'the white goose, the preserver of the citadel of Romulus, perceives at a great distance the odor of the human race'. Virgil also ascribed the preservation of the Capitol to the 'silver goose'. As well as being the sacred guard, the goose was valued by the populace for its meat and feathers. Goose liver was mentioned as a luxury of the time, and the goose was praised further:

A second commoditee that geese yield (especially those that be white) is their plume and down . . . the finest and the best is that which is brought out of Germanie. The geese there be all white and truly a pound of such feathers is 5 deniers [3 shillings and 1 penny] . . . many complaints are made of officers over companies of auxiliary soldiers . . . they license many times whole bands to straggle abroad, to hunt and chase geese for their feathers and down [the origin of the expression 'wild goose chase', Weir suggests]. And now forsooth the world is grown so delicate and dainty, that not only our fine smooth dames, but also our men, cannot take their repose and sleep without this ware, but complain of pain in their necks and heads unless they lay

8

Fig 6 Greylag goose on the nest, which is raised to make a dry site. Snow is on the ground in a cool April 1998

them upon a bolster of goose feathers and soft down.

Brown also quoted Pliny, who described the practice of 'cramming' the geese to swell the liver, and related that flocks of the birds travelled on foot from the north of France to Rome. 'Those which are tired are carried to the front; so that the rest push them on by natural crowding . . . In some places they are plucked twice a year.' Although most of Pliny's comments were about eating the geese, he also recounted, 'It is possible that they may have some discernment of wisdom. Thus one is said to have stuck perpetually to the philosopher Lacydis, never leaving him, either in public, in the baths, by night, nor by day. Our folks are wiser, who are aware of the goodness of the liver.'

Britain

In uncultured Britain, the invading Romans found that the natives appeared to treat geese as sacred. Greylags are thought to have been part of the stock at Iron Age dwelling sites, but not necessarily for eating. This situation cannot have continued, however; with domestication, the farmyard goose became part of the rural economy. The goose even became involved in paying for the tenure of the land. Harrison Weir cites a reference to William of Aylesbury, who held land under William the Conqueror; apart from straw for the bed, eels in winter and green geese in summer also had to be provided for a king's visit. Weir maintains that, until the reign of Edward III, tenure was usually paid in kind and in the list of requirements Michaelmas goose was often specified.

The Common Goose

As well as on the smallholdings and farms, geese were also produced by the cottager or commoner who had rights to graze on the moor or common. The geese could not be fed on greens and grain in a poultry yard as they would soon cost more to keep than they would fetch. So the goslings, when old enough, were trained to go out in flocks with the old goose and gander over moor, meadow and common. Where many people kept geese, and the grazing birds mingled during the day, various marks on the webs, coloured ribbon tied to the wings, or leg rings were used to distinguish ownership. But it was largely the tightly knit groups of the parent birds and their offspring that sorted themselves out in the evening. When the birds were well trained to move out to graze and return by themselves at the end of the day, the owner was spared the expense of the 'gozzard' to drive and look after them.

The London Market

In the 1700s, Pennant (quoted in Weir) related how huge flocks of geese were reared in Lincolnshire, to be eventually driven to the London market.

> A single person will keep a thousand old geese, each of which will rear seven . . . During the breeding season these birds are lodged in the same houses as the inhabitants, even in the very bed-chambers; in every apartment are three rows of coarse wicker pens, placed one above the other; each bird has its separate lodge, divided from the others, which it keeps possession of during the time of sitting. A person called the gozzard, i.e. a gooseherd attends the stock, and twice a day drives the whole to water, then brings them back to their habitations, helping those that live in the upper storeys to their nests without ever misplacing a single bird.

This system sounds very similar to that of the Aylesbury duck producers where, again, the house was the brooding area, and London the growing market for an increased scale of production. There was no sentimentality about the goose. The unfortunate birds were sometimes subjected to live plucking to obtain more than one crop of feathers from their breast and back. Their quills, four or five from each wing, were pulled out in spring to be used for writing and for arrow flights in earlier days.

Geese on the Smallholding

Geese were valued on the smallholding because they were cheap to keep. They grazed the commons and the village green. They cost nothing to feed if the land was available, yet they were probably under-valued in Britain. In 1850, Nolan wrote:

> In few countries do the value of geese appear to be fully appreciated, for, with proper management, few animals are of greater worth. If we consider that these birds, not only afford us a wholesome but a delicate food, their smaller feathers and down, contribute so largely to our nightly repose, their quills, so common in use, for transmitting our thoughts to the present and future ages – we may truly estimate their intrinsic value as little inferior to a sheep; for the feathers of the goose is equally valuable with the wool, and the flesh is eagerly sought after. Upon the whole the goose is a highly profitable animal, little inferior to that of a sheep in certain situations, and thousands are annually bred where that animal could not exist . . . In most parts of the kingdom the goose is an appendage of the farmyard; and being a hardy bird and subject to few diseases, requires no care, and is neither fed with hay nor corn, consequently her value is pure profit.

Keeping Geese Today

Towards the end of the twentieth century, the goose population has changed drastically. Geese used to be found on every small-holding, but now those smallholdings have mostly gone. Few farms keep geese, and goose enterprises rearing up to a thousand birds are a rarity in Britain.

There are various reasons for this decline in the goose population. Geese have a reputation for fouling the land for grazing cattle. General

Patten is reputed to have referred to bullets being fired 'like shit from a goose'. Maybe it was just the film script, or maybe he did say it, but the fact is that goose droppings do come out with great speed. The packets of grass look messy, yet are no worse than those of other animals, and geese on range are no problem.

Perhaps a more serious factor in the decline of the farm goose has been the recent legislation on slaughter and dressing. Farm inspections do mean that geese are more likely to be killed humanely, rather than suffer the barbaric practices common on smallholdings in my grandfather's time. However, the hygiene regulations relating to scrub-down smooth surfaces, and sinks and water supply, make poultry dressing on a small scale unfeasible for the majority.

The goose may have disappeared from the farm, but it has also defied the broiler house. The unfortunate chicken is amenable to cramming into sheds for just forty-nine days before slaughter and consumption. Goslings at seven weeks in first feathers and flights would die in such conditions. Geese need space, air, exercise and grass. There are management problems if they are reared intensively, and the larger goose units of today which produce for the larger retail outlets still use extensive methods. Successful operations, in general, began on a small scale. Mistakes can be made so easily, and this is not acceptable with livestock.

One local farmer's venture illustrates what may go wrong as a result of ignorance. Having bought one hundred goslings to rear and fatten for Christmas, he ended up with a loss. Not only was the mortality rate of the goslings high through mis-management, but the indoor fattening went disastrously wrong. The birds were given quite long hours of artificial light, to encourage them to put on weight. The ganders fretted and became fractious, and the geese even started to lay. All the birds lost weight, led by the long 'daylight' hours into thinking that it was the 'breeding season'.

Goose numbers declined as Europe became more urbanized, and the bird failed to adapt to mass production. Yet it seems that, over the last twenty-five years, the numbers of backyard geese have increased. Interest in smallholdings, organic farming, and appropriate small animals for a mixed farm economy has grown. The goose fits the bill, mixing well with sheep and providing a good income at Christmas if marketing is well organized.

Yet, for many, Christmas eating is not the main purpose of keeping geese. As with rare breeds of poultry, pigs and sheep, the birds are kept primarily out of interest. Despite Darwin's comment that 'no one makes a pet of a goose', they are now pets that mow the lawn, guard the house, go to shows and amuse visitors. They lay eggs that are superb for baking, and are extremely unlikely to suffer from salmonella due to the goose's diet and conditions. The eggs can be sold for eating, hatching or painting if they are not wanted at home. A bird costs less than a cat to keep, even when fed primarily on wheat and pellets. And, for the pure-breed enthusiast, there is the pleasure of hatching and rearing each year's new set of goslings in the hope of finding the one that will win at a show.

PART ONE: BREEDS

1 Origins ————————————————

Unlike poultry, domestic geese are recognized in only a few shapes, sizes and colours. This is surprising, in view of the goose's long history of domestication for hundreds, if not thousands, of years all over the globe. This wide distribution is reflected in their exotic names. There is the white, curly-feathered Sebastopol from Eastern Europe, the proud African from the Far East, and the Pilgrim, first standardized in the USA. Yet, despite this wide geographic distribution, domestic geese originate from just two wild species: the Greylag goose (*Anser anser*) and the Asiatic Swan goose (*Anser cygnoides*).

Ancient domesticated breeds, such as the Roman, are acknowledged to have been selected and developed from the Greylag. It was once common throughout Europe and Asia, overwintering in North Africa, Greece and Turkey, as well as India, Burma and China (Owen, 1977). There are two 'races', which are slightly different. The Western race is more orange in the bill; Eastern birds are bigger, have slightly paler plumage and an attractive pink bill. Todd (1979) attributes this colour difference to natural selection in two once-distinct populations divided by the Pleistocene ice sheet. As the ice sheet retreated, the populations merged again, so that today there are gradations of feather and bill colour across Europe.

There are other species of geese in Eurasia, such as the Barnacle, Barhead and Red-breasted, which could have become the foundation species for domestication. In Iceland, Pinkfoots were caught in 'goosefolds' during the flightless period after gosling hatching. The folds were U-shaped pens up to 38 feet long and 7 feet wide, into which the unfortunate geese were herded and slaughtered (Owen 1977). In Siberia, too, the Bean geese, Whitefronts, Barnacles and Brents were an important source of food for the Samoyeds, and Owen cites a Russian zoologist who found that the Beans sought out safe moulting sites, on areas protected by water from human and other predators.

The Greylag has several points favouring its selection by humans. As well as its extensive range, which offers numerous geographical possibilities for its domestication, it has a particularly amenable temperament. As a gosling, it readily imprints on humans and, for this reason, became the subject of extensive research of goose behaviour by Konrad Lorenz. As a child, Lorenz had been fascinated by geese, and returned to them in search of material for his studies. Those who have kept and reared wild and domestic geese will find it easy to understand why early subsistence people in Europe learned to domesticate these amenable birds, and to develop their size on the farm.

The Greylag did not always migrate; indeed, it may have derived its name from the fact that it 'lagged' behind, failing to follow the truly migratory Pinkfoots and Whitefronts north to their breeding grounds. As a result, there were many opportunities within Europe to steal the eggs or goslings from the nests of wild birds. In her book *Field with Geese*, Irvine relates how a traveller in Kashgar was presented with a flock of thirty wild goslings, which had been presented to him by the Khirgiz:

> The young birds quickly grew accustomed to me and eagerly fed from my hand, but it was difficult to keep the flock together and bring them home to roost from the grazing grounds . . . Then someone suggested that I should buy a pair of tame geese to establish discipline. It is difficult to describe the astonishment, and then the delight of this childless couple when they found a score and a half of orphans in need of their protection. They divided the flock of youngsters equally between them and then set up a regular routine . . . When they came to roost in the yard at night, the adoptive parents took up their position at the door until locked in.

In China, the wild Swan goose was the foundation stock for the eastern domesticated

Fig 7 Pink-footed goose (Anser brachyrhynchus). *This species breeds in Greenland, Iceland and Spitzbergen. They overwinter in Britain and mainland Europe. They are not as large as the Greylag, and are more wary in the wild*

breeds, which included the 'Hong Kong goose', the White Chinese and the Black-legged variety described by Nolan in 1850. The Swan goose (*Anser cygnoides*) presumably derives its common name from its outward appearance, which seems to combine both swan and goose characteristics. It is not, however, thought to be a cross between the two groups, even though it is considered to be a primitive goose. The breeding range of the wild bird was much more extensive than it is today, stretching from Japan and Korea into the interior of China, Mongolia and Russia. Todd (1979) thought that human disturbance and

loss of habitat caused the disappearance of the bird altogether in Korea, and had led to it being only a rare winter visitor in Japan, where it had formerly been common. The wide range of the bird means that it could have been domesticated almost anywhere in East Asia, but the place of origin of the Chinese and Africans is generally taken to be China.

Between the Western and the Asiatic groups are the Russian breeds. These are not well known in Western Europe, but in the Kholmogorsk and the German Steinbacher breeds there is the suggestion of a fusing of

Breeds and colours of geese officially recognized in Britain

This table is not definitive; it is the best information available at the moment

Breeds	Varieties	Admitted to Standard in Great Britain	Other early written description
Heavy weight			
Embden	white	1865	
Toulouse	grey	1865	*Nolan (1850)*
	white	1982	
	buff	1997	American Standard 1977
African	brown	1982	Hong Kong Goose *Nolan 1850*, American Standard 1874
	white	1982	American Standard 1987
	buff	1999	
American Buff	buff	1982	American Standard 1947
Medium weight			
Brecon Buff	buff	1954	*Llewellyn, 1934*
Buff Back	buff & white	1982	
Grey Back	grey & white	1982	'spotted geese', *Brown 1906*
Pomeranian	grey & white	1982	Germany 1912 (single and dual lobed); 1929 single lobed
	grey & white		only; all three colours.
West of England	sex linked	1999	the Common Goose at the first live poultry show, 1845
Light weight			
Chinese		1954	Knobbed geese 1845, American Standard 1874
Pilgrim		1982	the Common Goose in Britain, 1845; American Standard 1939
Roman		1954	American Standard Tufted Roman 1977
Sebastopol	white	1982	*Lewis Wright* 1873, American Standard 1938
	buff	1997	
Steinbacher	blue	1997	Germany 1951

Heavy geese

a   brown African, male
b   white African, male
c   Tolouse, Male
d   Embden, male
e   American Buff, male

Medium geese

f   Pomeranian grey back, female
g   Brecon Buff, female

Light geese

h   Pilgrim, female
i   Steinbacher, male
j   Roman, female
k   Sebastopol, smooth-breasted male
l   Sebastopol, frizzle female
m   white Chinese, male
n   brown Chinese, male

Fig 8 Breeds of geese

*Fig 9 Red-breasted geese. These strikingly marked small geese are a different genus (*Branta ruficollis) *from the Greylag (*Anser anser). *They breed in northern Russia and over-winter further south, in regions around the Black Sea*

Eastern and Western blood. Herein lies a problem for biologists, for distinct species are not supposed to interbreed and produce fertile offspring. However, the Chinese and European varieties certainly do produce viable cross-breeds and have long been used as commercial crosses. The Russian Kholmogorsk is a large white goose that looks like an Embden, but has an African-style knob and dewlap, which develops with age. Perhaps it, too, was developed as a utility cross-bred goose.

*Fig 10 Bar-headed geese (*Anser indicus) *breed in the Himalayas and over-winter in the Indian sub-continent*

2 Descendants of the Swan Goose

During the nineteenth century, the Victorians travelled the world for trade, and collected biological specimens for their zoos and catalogues of genera and species. From the Empire, and from trade with the East, various types of geese and ducks, such as the Indian Runner, were imported. The first Poultry Show in Britain, in 1845, had classes for 'Common Geese', 'Asiatic or Knob Geese', and 'Any Other Variety'. The 'Asiatic' geese were the Africans and the Chinese.

THE AFRICAN

The Asiatics may have first reached Europe in 1793, when the French naturalist Buffon described 'L'Oie de Guinea', a rare swan-like goose from exotic parts. According to Hoffman (1991), the illustration of this goose (which we now know as the African), complete with knob and dewlap, is evidence of its arrival in Europe even before the Chinese variety.

Sir Edward Brown (1929) quoted Willughby as saying that 'it was usual to apply the term "Guinea" to everything foreign and of uncertain origin', so it may be that Buffon did not have the Guinea coast of Africa in mind when he first described the bird. However, the name 'of Guinea' was translated as 'African', and this has stuck ever since.

Brown went on to say that 'it would appear that what we now term the African was included [as the Guinea goose], for Dixon was told by the head keeper of the London Zoological Society in 1848 that there were three varieties, namely the White and two types of Browns'.

This evidence of three kinds of goose is substantiated by Nolan (1850), who also

Fig 11 The Swan goose (Anser cygnoides), ancestor of the domestic Chinese and African. This species has a very wide range across Central and East Asia. The pure wild stock has a very long, slim bill, quite unlike the domestics. The colour pattern of the plumage is almost identical

ascribed all three of the 'knob geese' to Asia. He illustrated the 'large Chinese or Hong Kong Goose' and described it as ' . . . the largest of the tribe. As with all the Asiatic geese, they are furnished with a horny knot between the beak and forehead. Their prevailing colour is gray with a longitudinal stripe of brown, running above the back of the neck. Belly white, feet flesh colour.' He went on to describe the White Chinese and the Black-legged Chinese, a smaller bird than the Hong Kong, but similarly marked.

Despite Nolan's illustration, and written evidence, several waterfowl authors in the UK and in the USA persisted with the idea that the 'African' (Nolan's Hong Kong goose) was produced by cross-breeding the smaller Chinese goose, for its colour, with the larger Toulouse, for its dewlap. This kind of cross was certainly made in the USA, for Grow (1972) deplored the use of such cross-breeds as authentic Africans, and credited certain breeders with maintaining pure blood lines, free from Greylag influence. Cross-breeds failed in body shape, tending to have a keel and over-heavy paunch, and too much fat on the carcass, instead of the leanness of the African. As Grow points out, there is no need to invoke the Toulouse to produce the African, since African specimens with good dewlap development pre-dated the evolution of the decided dewlap on the Toulouse by about fifty years.

The Tse Tay

It seems obvious from the colour of the birds that the African is a relative of the Chinese. Both are coloured like the Wild Swan goose, and the Chinese behave and call in a similar manner. Certainly, they did not look very different from each other in Britain in the 1930s (although the British specimens were then probably rather poor compared with those in the USA).

An examination of the chromosomes of the birds was one obvious way to prove that the African actually originated in China. Hoffman (1991) found that this had already been done, to prove that the Chinese is a domesticated Swan goose, and that other researchers have indirectly confirmed that the African is also its relative. The evidence was a chromosome characteristic unique to the Asiatics, and not carried by the Greylags of Western Europe.

Hoffman visited South China and found the geese in the rural villages of Swatow. In this part of China, it is relatively warm in winter, and there is surplus food to grow the geese and overwinter the stock. The birds are big, weighing up to 26lb (12kg), and look exactly like the American Africans in size, colour and posture. Small flocks of birds graze the road-side pastures and Hoffman estimated that as many as a million goslings each year are sent north to Shanghai and Peking for rearing. Hoffman's photograph confirmed it: the Tse Tay or 'Lion Head' is the 'outrageously

Fig 12 Nolan's Hong Kong goose (1850) 'Is perhaps the largest of the tribe, and has been but recently known here. They were first introduced by the Ornithological Society of London, from China . . .'

Fig 13 An African for comparison with the Hong Kong goose. The similarity of the head shape is striking: the birds have changed little in 150 years

misnamed African'. He also found an 1852 reference confirming that such geese had been exported to America from the province just north of Swatow.

Although early twentieth-century American literature frequently mentions the African, the breed seems to have virtually disappeared from Europe at that time; indeed, there was no British standard until 1982, when the American standard was adopted. The birds have very much grown in popularity, with four imports in the last two decades, some of which have been mingled with the stock of earlier breeders such as Reginald Appleyard's.

Quality Africans are big and outreach the top of 36-in show pens. They are coloured like the brown Chinese, but are much larger. The standard 1997 weights – 18–24lb (8–11kg) in females and 22–28lb (10–13kg) in males – match the weights recorded by Hoffman in China, and current exhibition specimens in Europe. Previous standard weights were 20lb (9kg) and 18lb (8kg) for male and female.

Description

Head: Large with a stout bill. A broad, forwardly inclined knob protrudes from the front of the skull. Eyes large and bright. A large dewlap, crescentic in shape, hangs from the lower jaw and upper neck.

Neck: Long, massive, nearly the same thickness along its length. Slight arch.

Body: Large, long and nearly the same thickness from back to front. Breast full and round. Breast and underline free from keel. Paunch clean or dual-lobed. Stern round and full. Tail held high, especially in ganders.

Legs: Thighs short and stout, shanks medium length, stout.

Plumage: Tight and sleek, except on the neck where it is like velvet.

Carriage: Upright, especially when active; 30–40 degrees above the horizontal.

Colour of the brown (or grey): Dark brown stripe running from the crown of the head down the length of the neck contrasts with the cream throat and dewlap. Outline of off-white feathers around the bill in mature specimens. Darker brown smudge along the jaw line. Pinkish-buff blush on the breast fades to pale buff then white on the paunch and stern. Sides of the body and thigh coverts ash brown, each feather laced with lighter shade. Back, wing bow and coverts similarly marked; primaries and secondaries brownish-grey.

Bill and knob: Black.

Eyes: Dark brown.

Legs and feet: Dark or brownish-orange.

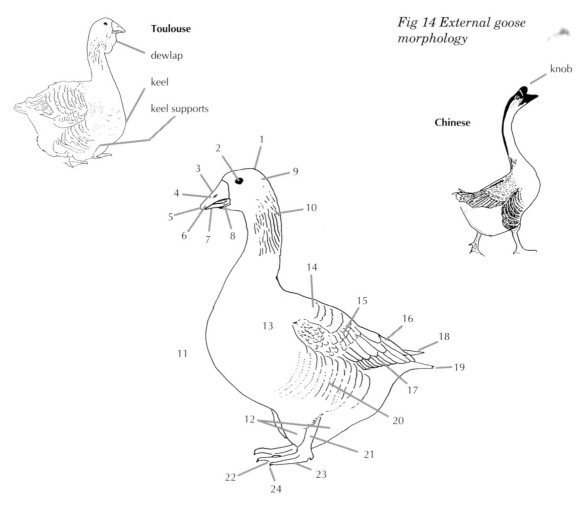

Fig 14 External goose morphology

External goose morphology

1	crown	9	ear	17	secondaries
2	eye	10	greylag neck-feather partings	18	primaries
3	culmen	11	breast	19	tail feathers
4	nostril	12	paunch or abdomen	20	thigh coverts
5	bean (or nail)	13	wing butts or fronts	21	shanks
6	upper mandible	14	scapular feathers	22	webs
7	lower mandible	15	coverts	23	toes
8	serrations	16	tertiaries	24	claw

In addition to the brown (grey) African, there are also the much less common white and buff varieties. The white is scarcely obtainable in Britain, but has been developed in the USA. It is a large white bird, very similar in appearance to the white, knobbed Kholmogorsk, but more upright. It may be possible to make a white African by crossing a heavy Embden with a brown African, but this would take several generations of selective breeding, to stabilize the colour and type. Buffs have been developed in America by Dave Holderread, and recently imported by Christopher Marler.

Breeding Stock

Quality Africans must be tall and massive, so birds that are very squat and round should be avoided. Avoid thin-necked birds; height is needed, but not if this goes with a fine neck indicative of the Chinese type. Choose birds with a tight breast and underline, as a keel is not wanted. Even though the original standard demanded little development of the paunch, most birds in Britain and the USA have this feature. However, make sure that the paunch is dual-lobed. This is more likely in ganders than in geese, and in specimens that are not too fat. The birds should have a knob and dewlap; remember that these features do develop with age. If you are buying young birds, look at the parents.

Colour is an important consideration, too. Crossing with white Africans in the past has spoiled some lines, so a bird of standard colour should be preferred to one with an obvious white blaze on the breast, or white flights. Similarly, in brown Africans, avoid birds with orange in the bill, orange around the eye and matching bright orange feet, as these colour points show a white ancestor. Orange in the knob can come with age, or with frost-bite. American breeders need to protect their Africans and Chinese in severely cold weather, but the temperature in Britain rarely persists below minus five degrees, which is the damage point. British birds are extremely unlikely to have suffered from frost-bite, even in the severest winters, despite having lived most of their life outside.

Eggs and Goslings

As with all geese, Africans vary in their laying capabilities. American birds have been reputed to be rather poor layers, but imported American stock has produced birds that have

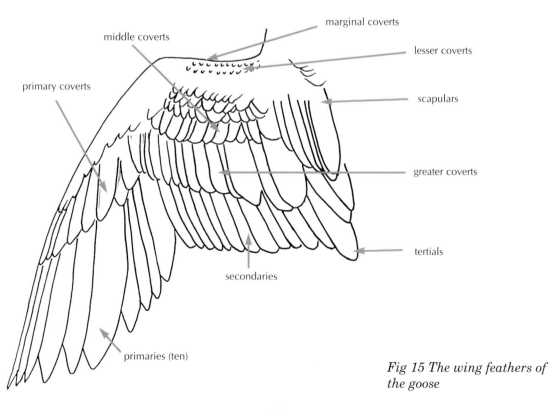

Fig 15 The wing feathers of the goose

Fig 16 A group of 16-month-old African geese bred by the author. These birds will put on more weight up to 3 years old as they mature. They are bold, vocal birds but can also be very tame

laid over thirty eggs. Hatchability of both African and Chinese eggs in incubators is good, compared with those of Pilgrims and Brecons. The goslings should be quickly on their feet, and should grow strongly and rapidly. The parent goose can be a good sitter, but should not be allowed to hatch the goslings, for fear of trampling. Hand-reared, the African may be one of the tamest and mild-mannered of geese, especially if the heavier exhibition strains are used.

Parasites

Adult Africans seem to suffer more than most geese from throat worms, which impede their breathing. This may be because of the birds'

habits; like the Chinese, they tend to pull at roots in the soil and may get infected this way. If a bird is holding its neck at an awkward angle, or making noises in its throat, then worming is in order.

THE CHINESE

Origins and Colouring

Chinas come in two colours – white, and brown, also called grey or even fawn – and two 'types': the 'American' and the traditional 'English'. The breed in both colours was introduced early to the Western world, and 'China' is said to have been an early preferred name. The brown variety is a direct descendant of the Swan goose, which has identical colouring and feather texture. The Asiatics lack the Greylag feather partings on the neck, the plumage instead looking like velvet. The beak in the Swan goose is black, as in the brown Chinas, but does not exhibit the raised knob. This feature seems to have developed after the domestication of the bird. Contrary to expectations, the knob, covered in soft skin, is warm to the touch.

Despite the type's origin from the Swan goose, and its attractive wild brown colouring, the Chinas first imported to the West seem to have been white. White birds occasionally arise as a colour variant in different birds, such as pheasant and mallard, and one presumes that early selection of such birds in the Chinas resulted in this colour variety. The knob, beak, feet and legs of these birds are a strong, clear orange, contrasting well with the white feathers.

Chinese geese probably reached America before Britain, as Robinson (1924) states:

> The earliest record of Chinese geese in America is in the correspondence of George Washington, and was first published in Haworth's *George Washington – Farmer* in 1915. It dis-

22

Fig 17 African geese out-reach the top of show pens. This bird was Champion Gander and Champion Waterfowl at a British Waterfowl Association Championship Show. Africans are heavy birds to take to a show, and need a large box. At a show they behave perfectly, enjoying the attention

closes that in 1788 he received from Governor Morris two Chinese pigs and with them 'a pair of white Chinese geese, which are really the foolishest geese I ever beheld; for they choose all times for setting but in the Spring and one of them is even now (November) actually engaged in that business'.

Robinson surmised that these geese were probably white, as geese of that colour were well known in Virginia early in the nineteenth century.

Chinas must have been in Britain prior to 1845, because of the inclusion of the 'Knobbed or Asiatic' geese in the first Poultry Show. However, the first poultry breeder's reference to them seems to have been as late as 1848, when Dixon stated that 'Mr Alfred Whittaker of Beckington, Somerset, owned a flock of white Chinese which were from imported parents, and were hatched on board ship from China'.

Whittaker described the white China goose as follows:

[It] is of a spotless, pure white – more Swan like than the brown variety, with a bright orange-coloured bill, and a large orange-coloured knob at its base. It is a particularly beautiful bird either in or

Fig 18 An African gander imported by Christopher Marler from American breeder Dave Holderread. Imported lines are important for healthy breeding stock, introducing new genetic material

23

Fig 19 A pair of white Chinese geese. These graceful birds are excellent layers, and are easier to breed than heavy geese, Brecons and Pilgrims

out of water, its neck being long, slender and gracefully arched when swimming. It breeds three or four times a season, but I was not successful with them, owing, as I fancied, to my having no water for them except a rapid running stream. A quiet lake, I believe to be more to their taste and more conducive to the fecundity of their eggs. I believe my birds are still in the neighbourhood, as I lent them to a farmer to try his luck with them. The egg is quite small for the size of the bird, being not more than half the size of the common goose . . . You will see both varieties of brown and white China geese on the water in St. James's Park (Browne, 1853).

Nolan (1850) also recorded the white China. 'It is a beautiful variety, next in size to the above [the African] and approaches nearest to the swan of any other goose. It is snow white, knobbed on the beak with orange legs, and truly ornamental on a sheet of water.' He was more dismissive of the Black-legged Chinese goose, which was smaller than the white, but marked like the Hong Kong (African). He also noted a Pigmy Chinese goose that was about the size of a Rouen duck and a complete miniature of the Black-legged. This seems to have disappeared into obscurity.

Popularity in Britain

Chinese geese may not have been very popular in Britain from the 1850s to the 1920s, with other breeders, besides Whittaker, complaining that they scarcely bred. Interest grew in alternatives, and the Embden was developed at the time, followed by the Toulouse, the Sebastopol and eventually the Roman. Chinese only merited a couple of sentences under 'Other Breeds' in the 1926 Poultry Club Standards. (Incidentally, the brown variety was recorded as having black legs, although the Americans had already plumped for 'dark or dusky orange' by 1905.) There seems to have been little interest in showing them – only Embdens were recorded in the *Feathered World* 'Palace Show Number' in 1925, and Embden and Toulouse at the Dairy Show in 1931. There must, however, have been some commercial flocks of Chinese, because one of these was featured in the same magazine in 1930, the article highlighting the exceptional egg production and, thus, the productivity of the bird as a commercial cross.

Appleyard, writing in the 1930s, kept the birds as a good utility line. His geese often laid 50–60 eggs a year, and instances of 100 lays were not unknown. He stated that the Chinese was occasionally shown, but that he knew of no written standard of perfection in Britain. By 1954, a standard had been established, and the birds were popularized in the 1950s by Colonel Johnson. His birds, which won the top awards at the time, were of a large, dual-purpose breed, long in the body and without a very pronounced knob. They are well illustrated in his book on Chinese geese. They had the reputation of being prolific layers, the white variety often seeming to have the edge over the brown in egg production.

We have kept white Chinas that have started laying in early January and have continued without many breaks until June; unfortunately, I do not know exactly if any of them outdid a brown China we had who totalled 74. Figures of 100 have been achieved from white Chinas, but only from young geese. Old stagers settle down to a much more reasonable 30 eggs or so, and the American show strains are unlikely to be prolific, even when young.

The preferred type for exhibition now is the American strain, which is smaller but much more attractive than the English. The ganders weigh 10–12lb (4.5–5.5kg), and the females 8–10lb (3.5–4.5kg). The Americans had selected a light-boned, short-bodied bird, with a view to producing a small but economic goose for the table. It seems likely that their show specimens went the same way, and this refined goose, with its elegant carriage and refined head, came to Britain in the late 1970s. Christopher Marler first imported these birds when pure breeds of waterfowl were difficult to obtain. They are beautiful to watch in action, being graceful on

Fig 20 Chinese geese love swimming water. Brown and white Chinas share this pool with three Snow geese at Blackbrook, Staffordshire (a British Waterfowl Association information centre)

land and water, and usually have a better temperament than the English types.

Description

Head: Medium in size. Bill stout at base. Large rounded knob. Eyes alert and prominent.
Neck: Long, carried upright, with graceful arch. Slender.
Body: Compact and plump. Back sloping to give characteristic upright carriage. Well-rounded, plump breast. No keel or dual lobes; single central fold in laying geese. Wings large, strong and carried high. Stern well-rounded. Tail carried high in American exhibition strain birds where the wing tips cross over in front of the tail.
Legs: Medium length.
Plumage: Sleek, tight and firm, except at the neck, where it is soft and without furrows.
Colour: As in the brown African and white African.

Breeding Stock

The right type of stock will depend on its purpose. The heavier English types are better layers, while the lighter American types are the show birds, and have a better temperament. In America, exhibition birds average one or two pounds less than commercials, and are not penalized for this lack of size in the show pen, with shape being more important. In Britain, there has been a tendency to maintain size by introducing 'English' blood, but this should not be at the expense of the bird's carriage.

It is impossible to choose the best exhibition bird or breeder from a flock of youngsters. It takes up to two years to develop the perfect head shape, which should have a well-rounded, but forwardly inclined knob, shown in the specimen in the 1982 Standards book. It is, therefore, important to see the stock birds if you are buying youngsters.

Fig 21 Flock of brown Chinas. In a gaggle they can be extremely noisy, because they tend to bicker. They are wonderful 'watchdogs'

Ideally, birds of 2–4 years would be bought, but youngsters are, of course, more generally available.

Show birds will gain many points in the show pen for a lively, elegant carriage. The best exhibition birds will have an upright stance and hold their heads high when excited. This posture will exaggerate their reach. A gracefully curved neck should be combined with a short, deep body, but finding these two features together in the same bird is difficult. Shorter-necked birds often have a better body, and vice versa.

Regarding colour, follow the advice as for the Africans. White Chinas are crossed with brown Chinas, but this spoils the colour characteristics of both. Browns acquire white

Fig 22 Head study of a female China. The 'knob' has developed upon domestication of the Swan goose

under the chin, and even a blaze of white across the breast. Whites may have a dull orange bill instead of a bright orange one. They usually come out self-coloured nevertheless, the Chinas not appearing to carry the 'pied' gene, unlike European breeds.

Broodiness

Chinas sometimes go broody, but this generally happens at the end of the season, when it is too late to bother with eggs that are not likely to produce excellent specimens. This is a breed produced for laying, so they need not be expected to go broody, especially if you do not encourage them with the right conditions. Should the goose go broody, she is less likely to crush the eggs than the larger breeds. The

ganders are excellent fathers and love to guard the goslings. In the absence of goslings, ganders sometimes adopt ducklings in the breeding and rearing season.

Rearing and Temperament

China goslings are great fun to hand-rear. They are light and strong, and quick on their feet. They are great talkers if kept in the kitchen for a week or so, and benefit from being handled. They become extremely tame, especially the ganders, and are likely to remain so as adults, especially if they are an American strain, where it is rare to get peevish birds. The heavier English type can be good-tempered too, but they do have the potential to be implacably nasty. It is important to rear goslings as a group, so that they imprint on each other as well as on their owner, otherwise the gander will trail around after its owner in the breeding season.

Uses

Chinas are useful geese. They have a well-deserved reputation of being marvellous watchdogs. They are sensitive to the slightest noise and, once spoken to, cannot resist shouting back. If you have immediate neighbours, this watchfulness might be a nuisance, especially if they are out in a fox-proof pen. In a flock, ganders tend to get involved in minor scraps, and the others are likely to egg them on. They are better shut up at night, to keep them quiet.

White Chinas were once employed as guard-geese at a distillery in Scotland, where they patrolled the fox-proof grounds at night. They were supposed to alert the watchman if there were any intruders. The irony is, so I am told, that the geese themselves were stolen.

Chinas can also be a big advantage in the garden. They were used as weeder geese for crops such as mint and cotton in the USA, and are excellent for this purpose in a garden or tree nursery. They are not nearly as destructive as Brecons and Embdens. Unlike the Greylag derivatives, they tend not to chew twigs and saplings. They will keep the grass down and leave the shrubs, but not the vegetable garden, alone. They may not eat many weeds if there is good grass around, and they have to be trained from young to eat large quantities of chick weed and other annuals. However, dandelions and buttercups will not last long on patches of grass grazed by any geese, and especially by Chinas. Chinas can produce the perfect turf, but they do like to pull up lower creeping stems of grass and buttercups, and dunk a mouthful of grass and mud in a bucket, which can be messy.

Remember that birds fed on weeds are not on a nutritious diet; they will need supplementary evening feeding if they are working for their living.

Ease of Sexing

A final advantage of keeping this breed is that, without vent sexing, you can be reasonably sure of being able to distinguish the geese from the ganders by sixteen weeks old. The ganders are invariably taller, have a fuller developed knob (although this takes two years to reach its full size), and a different voice from the geese, which give a very distinctive 'oink'.

3 Developments from the Greylag: The Older European Breeds ———

THE ROMAN

A Small White Goose

Some of the oldest written records of European domesticated geese come from the Italian peninsula. The Romans are said to have selected white 'sports' from the Greylag stock for their breeding, 'so that in the course of time a white and tamer species was produced, which differed considerably from the grey wild-goose and its descendants' (Hehn 1885, cited in Brown, 1929).

This goose is famous for its part in saving the Capitol at Rome during the siege by the Gauls in the fourth century BC. During the night, the assailants climbed to the summit, hoping to take it by surprise. The dogs slept on, but, as Livy observed, 'They were not unperceived by some geese which, being sacred to Juno, the people had spared even in the present great scarcity of food, a circumstance to which they owed their preservation, for by the cackling of these creatures and the clapping of their wings Marcus Manlius was roused from his sleep.' Thus, the Capitol was saved.

Livy, Lucretius and other ancient writers mention both white and coloured geese, and Brown (1929) still distinguished between two varieties. The Roman and Padovarna, he said, were evidently of one race, not distinct breeds, differing only in feather colour. The Roman was pure white, but in the Padovarna the head, back of neck, wings, and sometimes the back, were grey. Brown concluded that this white domestic goose could have been disseminated throughout Europe by the Roman Army, and via commercial dealings between the conquered lands and Rome. He felt that the small white goose that he found on his travels throughout South Germany, Austria, Hungary and the Balkan States was probably descended from the Roman, the oldest breed of all.

In contrast, Soames argues that the Central European small white geese originated from the plains of the Danube, where farming and metallurgy were advanced prior to 1000 BC. Invaders from Hungary and Romania took their technology and livestock with them as they settled in the valley of the River Po and, later, in peninsular Italy. It is likely, of course, that domestication took place at several points across Europe. For example, when Caesar invaded Britain, in 55 BC, the Romans found that the Britons already kept sacred geese.

Whatever the origin of this small white bird, it certainly seems to have appeared first in writing in Italy.

Italian Geese

According to British Poultry Club Standards, Romans were introduced into Britain in about 1903, around the time when there was considerable interest in importing geese. An early reference to white 'Italian geese' appeared in the magazine *Fowls for Pleasure and Profit* (1888). A pair of geese belonging to Victoria Poultry Yards of Dorking were exhibited at the Dairy Show in 1887 but, owing to some error, were not actually judged. The author of the article considered this to be unfortunate, because it delayed recognition of this breed.

Although the birds did not compare favourably with Embdens for size, they were said to have no equal as layers. These fast-maturing birds made 9–10lb (4–4.5kg) weight at three months and, of the white and grey varieties available, the white was said to be the superior. These birds, too large to be the typical Romans, grew on to up to 16lb (7kg), but Wright (1902) also wrote of 'a variety . . . highly recommended about ten years ago under the name of Italian geese. It has been stated to be unusually prolific, laying 50 to 60 eggs in one laying and sometimes a second. Mr Tegetmeir describes them as mainly white, with a blue-grey head, a grey roundish spot between the shoulders, and grey thighs. But a great many we have heard of have not come up to that standard, and have been decidedly small.' Were these small geese, in fact, the Romans?

A British Standard for the Roman

Brown (1906) described the Roman as follows:

The body is long and broad with a well-developed sternum; breast broad yet not very prominent, thus resembling the Embden; back broad; neck long, fine and arched; head fine, in some specimens with a small crest at the back of the head; eye blue, surrounded with bare skin of pale yellow; beak very thin and short, nearly rose in colour, with a tip of ivory white; wings large, not carried far back; legs strong, reddish grey in colour, with white toe nails; the general appearance is a well developed goose, not so upright or large as the Toulouse or the Embden. Weight: males 10 to 14 pounds; females 8–12 pounds.

In the USA, the weights of the birds were quoted at 12lb and 10lb (5.5 and 4.5kg) for the gander and the goose respectively. Emphasis

was put on the fine bone and plumpness of the birds, this shape being complemented by the straight, short neck (under medium length). This remains the current standard for the bird both in Britain and in the USA, so that the accepted Roman today no longer resembles an Embden in general shape and stance.

Romans also come in a crested variety. This is unusual in geese, although a crest can appear in Pilgrims, Sebastopols and otherwise unremarkable white geese. The crest is not as in crested ducks, but is merely a slight raising of the feathers, rather like a close-fitting helmet instead of a bobble. Crested Romans can be found in Britain, but are more popular in the USA.

Description

Carriage: Almost horizontal.
Head: Neat, well-rounded. Bill short.
Neck: Upright, medium length, not thin.
Body: Compact and plump. Back wide and flat. Breast full and rounded, not carried high. Paunch dual-lobed, not too heavy. Wings long, strong. Tail carried horizontally.
Legs: Short, light-boned, set well apart.
Plumage: Sleek, tight and glossy.
Colour: Glossy white plumage. Bill orange-pink, eyes light blue. Legs and webs orange-pink.
Weight: 12–14lb (5.5–6kg) male, 10–12lb (4.5–5.5kg) female.

Breeding Stock

Embdens and Romans are both white geese, but not all white birds belong to these breeds. There are many commercial white crosses made between the two breeds, and white Chinese and Danish commercial geese. These cross-matings are made in order to maximize the benefits of the prolific egg layers, and to add weight. The resultant cross-breed is also an easy hatcher and an easy-to-

Fig 23 A crested Roman goose, which is now also mentioned in the British Waterfowl Standards. The crested types seem more popular in America, but can occasionally be found in Britain. The crest is not an exaggerated feature, merely a slight raising of the feathers on the crown

rear youngster. Many people have bought commercial white geese in the belief that they are Embdens, just as others have bought 'Romans' that are double their ideal size. It is, therefore, essential before buying either Romans or Embdens to get to know these breeds at first hand, by visiting the larger waterfowl shows and reputable breeders.

Birds for breeding stock should conform to the standard in size and shape, and preferably be free from grey feathers. This used to be a problem with Romans when they were first imported but, according to breeders, this is no longer the case.

Temperament is important when choosing this breed. The 1982 Standard described the breed as 'active, alert, docile rather than defiant'. This comment on their demeanour

Fig 24 Roman geese – chubby, white birds – with Pomeranians, for size comparison

applies to some strains, but not to others. We have had some very fractious Romans, which were fierce to handle. However, breeders who have stuck with these little geese for years have generally found them charming. Find out how the geese behave with their owners if you want them in close contact with you.

Eggs

Romans have been reputed to be marvellous egg-layers, managing between 45 to 65 eggs in a season, according to Appleyard. (He found them to be the ideal small goose. His Romans slept in the open, and, even when given a shelter, preferred to live out in the snow, quite happy and contented.) Because they are small and active birds, one Roman gander can be kept with up to five females and fertile eggs may still be expected. This is unusual for geese, which frequently pair or trio, making them a rather uneconomic proposition, with a high proportion of males to females being required for breeding.

Remember that figures in an old book often bear no relation to a particular bird's breeding record. The number of eggs produced, the fertility of the eggs and the viability of the goslings will depend on the breeding vigour of a particular strain. Inbreeding in order to retain outward physical characteristics, particularly smallness, can reduce reproductive capacity, so do not expect exhibition Romans always to produce a text-book performance. It may be necessary to try crossing different strains if you want volume production. Avoid under-sized birds in this breed, as they are less likely to reproduce than a bird of average size.

THE SEBASTOPOL

Origins and Development

Like the Roman, the Sebastopol originated in Central Europe. The original birds were white, very small (9–12lb/4–5.5kg), weighed about the same as Romans, were sometimes crested like the Romans, and had a similar head shape in some strains. The Eastern birds were also pink-beaked.

Brown reported that the first Sebastopols arrived in Britain in 1859, but whether the birds came from the port of Sebastopol, as the name implies, is not actually known. However, Brown did say that the birds were widely distributed in the countries

Fig 25 A Roman gander. These small, white birds have a neat head and striking blue eyes.

Fig 26 Frizzle Sebastopol geese have curled feathers on the body, and trailing flight and back feathers. Their feathers look best in the late summer and early autumn, when they are new and spotlessly clean

surrounding the Black Sea and, on his visits to Hungary and the Balkans, he saw numerous birds with loose feathers in the lower regions of the Danube. Indeed, 'Danubian' was the bird's preferred name in nineteenth-century Britain; the breed was also referred to as 'Danubio' in Spanish and Italian, but in France it became 'oie frisse', and in Germany 'Lodengans' or 'Struppegoose' ('unkempt goose').

Brown thought that the breed had been developed from the ordinary white goose (the Roman type), with curled feathers having arisen as a mutation, since feather and down were an important part of production in Eastern Europe at that time. Since these early imports, the West European and American birds have developed along slightly different lines. Standard weights have increased to 12–16lb (5.5–7kg) and 10–14lb (4.5–6kg) in the gander and goose respectively, and the preferred bill and leg colour is orange.

Colour and Feathers

Most Sebastopols are white, but many have pale grey juvenile feathers on the rump around the preen gland. The females are greyer than the males (a useful autosexing characteristic in white geese, as long as the strain is known, because it is not infallible). The pale grey in juvenile feathers does not usually matter, because it will moult out by about sixteen weeks. Solid grey that remains is a fault, however; this has become rather prevalent, possibly because buff geese have been crossed with white Sebastopols to produce the buff Sebastopol. The first cross of buff and white can produce an all-grey or a saddleback, so such colour crosses will spoil the next generation of whites, frequently with grey feathers.

Sebastopols come in two feather types, the frizzle and the smooth-breasted. Frizzles, as the name implies, have curly feathers all over the body except for the head and neck, whereas the smooth-breasted types have long, curled feathers only on the back (falling from the scapulars and sometimes the wing coverts) and thigh coverts. In good specimens, the scapular feathers lift from the back and cascade to the ground.

Description of the Frizzle

Carriage: Horizontal.
Head: Neat, bill of medium length. Eyes large and prominent.
Neck: Medium length and carried upright.

Body: Appears round because of the full, loose feather.
Legs: Fairly short and stout.
Plumage: Only feathers of head and upper neck smooth. Remainder profusely curled. Feathers of wings and back should be long and broad, not wispy.
Colour: Pure white preferred; traces of grey in young females allowed. Bill orange, eyes blue. Legs and webs orange.
Weight: 12–16lb (5.5–7kg) male, 10–14lb (4.5–6kg) female.

Breeding Sebastopols

If you prefer the smooth-breasted type, look for birds that have a profusion of feathers and a fork or gap in the tail feathers. These will breed the best birds and, possibly, frizzles. In frizzles, avoid birds which have Silkie-type feathering on the back – wisps, rather than broad feathers. Also, choose birds with long wing feathers that trail softly to the ground. The shafts of the flights should not be stiff. If frizzles are always mated to frizzles, there may be a progressive deterioration in feather quality; it pays to pair up one of each feather type.

Eggs and Goslings

Despite their 'pantomime goose' appearance, Sebastopols have much to recommend them as a utility breed. They can be good sitters and, being light in weight, are not inclined to smash the eggs if they have a good nest. They are capable of laying up to 35 eggs. As in all white breeds, the eggs are very hatchable in incubators and often beat the larger breeds' bigger eggs by 'pipping' a day earlier, usually on day 28. As with Embdens, the goslings are autosexing. In some strains, the ganders are lemon yellow and the geese grey saddleback in the fluff. In other matings, the ganders are pale grey saddleback, and the females have a grey haze over all the fluff. As well as being easy hatchers, the goslings are fast growers.

Rearing

Sebastopols can suffer more than most birds from a condition known as 'oar wing'. This condition can be inherited, but most commonly arises from rapid growth caused by over-feeding. It is prevalent in Sebastopols because the frizzle type lacks thigh coverts to hold the wing feathers in as they grow. Also, the primaries can become extremely long and heavy, and their sheer weight can pull the bone joint out of place.

Check the birds for this condition as they grow, by picking them up and feeling the wing bones and joints. See the section on rearing goslings for managing this condition.

Management

Although Sebastopols are a good utility bird, most people prefer to keep them as ornamentals. They are relatively easy to keep clean. If the turf is unbroken, they will just need a bucket of water for washing. If the ground is muddy, they will need clean water for washing their underparts; this is particularly important in the breeding season, when a gander with dirty feet can make a sorry muddy sight of a goose if there is no bathing water for the mating birds. If the birds are going to be shown, it is essential to keep them in good condition all the time. Dirty Sebastopols cannot be cleaned up, as the mud becomes thoroughly ingrained in their feathers.

SEX-LINKED COLOUR: PILGRIM, WEST OF ENGLAND AND SHETLAND GEESE

It is not known when sex-linked colour arose in geese domesticated from the Greylag stock, but it is certain that it pre-dated the development of the Victorian exhibitions and shows. In the excitement of standardizing the Embden, Toulouse, Roman and Sebastopol, the Common goose was ignored. There was a class for it in 1845, along with the Asiatic or Knob Geese, and 'Any Other Variety', into which Toulouse and Embden then fell, but after that point it seems that the farmyard goose of Britain did not find favour at the shows.

There were certainly white geese in Britain in the 1800s, for it is known that they were used to improve the Embden. In an even earlier reference, in 1615, it was said that geese for breeding should be 'white or grey, all of one pair, for pyde [pied] are not so profitable and blacks are worse'. But the text is enigmatic. Should the geese both be white, or both be grey, or should they be one of each colour?

Following the piecing together of various bits of evidence, it is now generally accepted that geese with sex-linked colour were the Common geese before their place was usurped in the nineteenth century by the Embdens and Toulouse and their commercial cross-breeds. The small useful goose, which could fend for itself on the farm, was gradually pushed out and left only in the rural back-waters of Britain, France, the USA and Australia, far-flung birds that had arisen from a common European stock. They variously became known as the Pilgrim (USA), the Settler (Australia), the West of England and the Shetland.

Autosexing Geese in the USA: the Pilgrim

The Common goose was rediscovered in America by waterfowl breeder and geneticist Oscar Grow. He coined the name 'Pilgrim' for the small farmyard geese that he developed as a breed in Iowa, after the family's 'pilgrimage' from Missouri during the depression of the 1930s. Ives, who later became Editor of the magazine *Cackle and Crow*, became interested in the birds after an article

about them appeared in the magazine in 1934:

Immediately I wrote to Mr Grow for more information; but except that tradition said they were very common in New England in early days, that he had taken the ancestors of his flock from Vermont 40 years before (circa 1895), that they were said to have been a part of the Pilgrim Fathers' farm stock when they first reached Cape Cod and that there were very few in the country today, he had little or no information.

Grow was a geneticist and felt that, without a knowledge of this field of science, it would have been impossible to understand the inherited colour of the geese. According to him, even if there had been 'some accidental instance of colour dimorphism in earlier times, the genetic significance of such a phenomenon could not have been understood and therefore would have soon been dissipated through aimless selection'.

Despite Grow's contention that the breed is of comparatively recent origin, evidence has accumulated to indicate that they were the common farmyard goose both of America, and of their point of origin, Europe. Hawes (1996) has determined that geese were probably not aboard the *Mayflower*. The first mention of any poultry dates from 1623 when, in the description of a village, only 'divers hens' were mentioned; this stock presumably arrived with the *Mayflower*. The second ship, the *Fortune*, was criticized for bringing no provisions. However, the geese must have come on later boats. As well as Grow's foundation stock, Ives also found a small autosexing flock in Connecticut, where they had been kept as a closed flock for 35 years; Hawes also cites a reference to such a flock of geese, in Alabama.

Ives finally concluded that 'from all the evidence I can find in a fairly complete reference library of old poultry literature which I have had fun in collecting for more than forty years, I have come to the rather fixed opinion that the ancestor of the Pilgrim was nothing more or less than the common or farmyard goose of early Britain'.

Ives goes on to cite several nineteenth-century references from America, England and France, which said that, in the farmyard birds, the gander was white. In some cases, the goose was said to be grey, or this was implied in the text. Added to this is evidence of the autosexing, which still remains in those white domestics, the Embdens and Sebastopols. Female goslings are greyer than the males, so these breeds retain in the juvenile stage this basic European goose characteristic.

Normandy

Since Ives's detective work on the Pilgrim goose, other references have substantiated his conclusion. Even in 1924, Robinson had listed the 'Normandy goose' amongst French breeds and stated that 'the Normandy geese resemble the common goose of England and America before the introduction of the Embden and Toulouse. The females are grey and white; males mostly white.' These geese

were therefore autosexing and looked rather like the Pilgrim, or perhaps the West of England, if they had rather more white than grey. It may be that both types are found there, but in *The Magazine of Ducks and Geese* of winter 1959, Normandy Pilgrims were illustrated. The females appear all grey on the main feathers, having no white flights. They have the typical 'spectacle' pattern on the face. One gander may be all white; the other is a typical specimen with pearl grey on the flanks and some on his wings.

Australia

The Common goose also reached Australia. Andreas Stoll (1984) encountered autosexing geese on numerous farms in isolated parts of the continent, and could trace one of these flocks back to an import from London in 1836. The birds varied, from the typical Pilgrim to the heavier West of England. This importation also suggests that this type was the common farmyard goose at the time when the Embden was beginning to make its mark. As the white geese multiplied in both Britain and Australia, the obvious sex-linked colour was lost, except in the outback (and in the

Fig 27 A group of grey Pilgrim females with their white gander. The breed's colour is sex-linked but the reliability of the sex-linkage to colour depends on the strain

west of Britain), where innovations are fewer on the remoter farms.

Britain

It has been said that Pilgrim geese were imported, but there is no anecdotal evidence from older goose breeders to suggest that this is the case. It is generally accepted that there would have been no point, since this is a farmyard goose, not an exhibition goose. Interest in the Pilgrim has recently grown, however, and they were imported from Canada in 1997.

During the 1980s, all the Pilgrim geese that were publicly on show at the major events were owned by Ashton, Murton and the Domestic Fowl Trust. The birds originated, in part, from a pair discovered on the Fylde coast of Lancashire by Malcolm Stephenson in 1972. He recognized the breed and distributed the stock fairly widely. With the growing interest in waterfowl, more birds were discovered. There had always been autosexing West of Englands in Devon and Somerset, and all-grey females doubtless turned up here too. Charles Martell of Gloucestershire, who has a herd of the ancient breed of Gloucester cattle, has also developed a flock of silver Pilgrim geese. These came from local flocks, and look exactly like the silver (light grey, laced with white) Pilgrim shown in Delacour. The stock from which they were derived also bred all-grey females. Another flock, in Herefordshire, had perfect grey females, but rather grey ganders. The origin of the birds was unknown.

The conclusion is inescapable, as Ives found; the birds have been on the farm for centuries, but nobody in Britain put in writing exactly what they were like. To Appleyard, they were the common geese, and unremarkable. He was probably familiar with Harrison Weir's (1902) experience that 'the ganders are invariably white, and that even if the geese are grey. But this may be and is perhaps attributable to centuries of selection as to colour . . .' Credit is due to Oscar Grow for publicizing this ancient breed, which might have disappeared without written recognition and breed status.

Description

Carriage: Just above the horizontal.
Head: Medium in size, oval. Bill medium in length, straight.
Neck: Medium length, upright, slightly arched.
Body: Well-fed adults plump and meaty. Dual-lobed. Young birds and stock on grazing only quite light and racy.
Legs. Shanks moderately short and stout.
Plumage: Tight.
Colour of the male: White desirable for exhibition birds; out of a hatch, many ganders show pearly grey on the thigh coverts, rump and wings. This grey denotes a gander carrying the sex-linked colour gene. Solid grey feathers should be avoided.
Colour of the female: Head light grey, front part white; the white extends around the eyes as a typical 'spectacle' pattern. White area grows with age up to about four years but should not cover all of the head. Neck light grey, upper portion mixed with white in mature specimens. Back and sides of body light ashy grey, laced with white. Breast lighter grey, becoming paler then white on the stern. Flights grey. Tail grey and white. Bill, legs and feet preferably orange (rather than pink). Eye blue in gander, brown in goose.
Weight: Originally low, 9–10lb (4–4.5kg) given by C. D. Gordon (1938), probably from under-fed farm geese. Dressed weights of 9–10lb (4–4.5kg) given for the Normandy geese, approximating to live weight of about 14–15lb (6–6.5kg). American Standard weights: 14lb (6kg) male, 13lb (5.75kg) female. British Standard weights 1997: 14–18lb (6–8kg) male, 12–16lb (5.5–7kg) female. Higher weights given are due to better feeding and condition.

Breeding Stock

Autosexing geese immediately appeal to those who have heard of the difficulty of sexing geese. Pilgrims seem to provide the instant solution to the problem. A reliable pair of breeding birds will undoubtedly obviate the difficulty, but totally reliable breeders are very difficult to come by in British Pilgrims. Indeed, they seem to be the most difficult goose to get to breed true. There are two reasons for this. Firstly, they have not been bred as exhibition geese until fairly recently. Secondly, there is the colour dimorphism. How to be absolutely sure that a newly purchased white gander is a Pilgrim? The truth is that it is impossible, until he has been bred with a guaranteed Pilgrim female, and all of the progeny have turned out correctly, or almost. The same is true of a grey female. Although Pilgrim females are quite distinctive in shape and colour, the males they produce can vary quite a lot.

Even if all the male goslings in a hatch turn out white, some will almost certainly carry varying degrees of colour in the plumage. This is usually most evident in the secondary wing feathers, in the thigh coverts, and on the rump. In some strains, this grey will moult out during the second year. In others, as noted by Grow, the grey will intensify.

The female offspring should also be closely examined for colour. Quite frequently, what seems to be a flock of uniformly grey females shows, on closer examination, a great deal of colour faults. The British stock always seems to be striving to become West of England, the females often having a number of white flight feathers. As these increase in number, so a white blaze of feathers develops on the breast, and the goose begins to become more like a saddleback. It is rare for a pair of Pilgrims to produce many perfect females that are all grey, apart from the distinctive markings on the face. Even if you are lucky to find a pair of apparently perfect birds, you will still need to be careful when selecting the offspring for future use.

Photographic records of American and French Pilgrims show few females with white flights. The ganders vary a little in whiteness, several of them showing pearly grey on the thighs and wings. However, it is fair to assume that these photographs show selected breeding stock, whose less than perfect siblings may have been culled. An indication of this is given by Gordon (1938) who, in describing sex-linked colour in geese, said that the 'females are mostly grey or parti-coloured with white areas on the head, *breast* [a fault] and the ventral regions'. Gordon was apparently unaware of Grow's new breed. The geese he was describing were in Alabama, and Hawes (1996) surmised that they could have been derived from Normandy geese brought to Louisiana by French settlers.

Pilgrim Goslings

Because the Pilgrim is a sex-linked colour breed, it might be reasonable to expect the goslings to be autosexing too. However, if the goslings are newly hatched, this is not always easy, as they tend to look very similar to each other. The difference in colour between male and female goslings seems to vary with the strain. In the USA, breeders are advised not to continue with a line where the goslings show little difference in colour. However, if the adults are good birds, you do not need to be too fussy about this. Pilgrims are a very difficult breed, so the colour of the day-old goslings is the last thing to worry about if they are right at two weeks old.

If the individuals in a batch do appear to be similar they may, of course, all be the same sex. However, you should also look for colour differences in the beak. Newly hatched females have a solid dark grey bill, whereas the males have a lighter colour. The males should be paler but are often quite grey, but not as dark as the females. Occasionally, there is a paler gosling with a grey bill. This will turn out to be a white female that does not carry the sex-linked colour.

Fig 29 Pilgrim gosling: this grey female also has a dark bill, the most reliable autosexing characteristic. She has a slight colour fault on one wing; the pale fluff will develop into white primaries

As the goslings grow, new fluff will begin to replace the first fluff after about ten days, and the males will whiten. By four weeks, scapular feathers will begin to cover the wings, and the white or grey will be obvious.

Sex-Linked Colour

Research on colour in hybrid geese (*Magazine of Ducks and Geese*, 1956) has suggested that it is controlled by a colour inhibitor. Toulouse x Roman (in other words, grey x white geese) may result in hybrid geese, in which the females are light grey and the ganders almost white, the sex-linked inhibitor diluting the Toulouse colour to a light grey in the female, and almost to white in the male. In the same research, a Greyback gander mated to a white Roman female resulted in a Greyback female with less colour than the parent gander, and an almost white male. The sex-linked colour inhibitor in the Roman goose impeded the feather colour of the Greyback.

The feather pigment intensity (dilution) gene is carried on the sex chromosome, thus 'males carry two doses of dilution (two sex chromosomes) while females carry only one dose (one sex chromosome). The two dilution genes in males are able to prevent colour formation and the white plumage results,

Fig 30 Pilgrim gosling: this lighter yellow-grey male has a paler bill. He also has a white tip on the fluff on his wing. His feathers will become all white, but the white fluff at this stage suggests that he may breed white-flighted females

Fig 31 A large West of England female at a show. Like this specimen (probably bred in Cornwall), West of Englands should be large, practical farmyard geese

geese, and therefore why white domestic geese became so common, it does not explain why the Pilgrim expression of colour is carried only by these birds. Something must give these geese their distinctive looks or 'type', as well as the special face markings in the female. They may be subject to a factor that inhibits the Greyback gene, so that the females are a diluted grey all over instead.

The West of England

Whilst some farmyard geese in Britain were the pale grey Pilgrim type, others were only partly grey in the females. 'In breeding the common domestic goose, some think the mixing of colours best, such as a white gander with dark grey geese, or at least grey and white, or what is termed saddleback' (Weir 1902). The saddlebacks can still be found on farms in Devon and are kept by a very few goose breeders, who often start off with stock obtained direct from a farm. There is now (1999) a written Standard for the breed, as the goose is exhibited in a class for 'West of England' at the major shows. It is generally accepted as being larger than the Pilgrim. The gander is white; the goose has grey feathers in a saddleback pattern, and some grey on the head and neck.

while in the female one dilution gene cannot completely over-ride all pigment formation, resulting in the soft grey colour.' (Hawes, using the work of Jerome 1953, 1954, 1959, 1970.)

Whilst this reasoning explains why white is dominant over colour in ordinary domestic

The Shetland

These are like West of England geese, perhaps made smaller by their tough existence on these northern isles. The geese are described in detail in Bowie (1989), where they are seen to differ little from small West of Englands.

4 Later Developments: The Heavyweights

THE EMBDEN

Origins

Whilst the mid- and south Europeans kept their small white geese, and the 'Pilgrim' seems to have become the norm in northern France and Britain, the Germans went for size. Jurgen Parr (1996) claims that selective breeding of these white birds, which we know today as Embdens, started as early as the thirteenth century in the area of North Germany known as Ostfriesland. They seem to have been named at the time when the English for the German port of Emden included the extra letter 'b', in the first half of the nineteenth century.

The breed was recorded in Britain in 1815, when Moubray said that 'Embden geese are held in the highest esteem. They are all white, male and female, and of a superior, indeed very uncommon size.' The Embdens also caused a stir in America. First imported in 1820 (and initially named 'Bremens', after their port of departure), their owner James Sisson reported that these perfectly white geese 'lay in February and set and hatch with more certainty than the common barn-yard goose, will weigh nearly, and in some cases, quite twice the weight, have double the quantity of feathers, never fly, and are all of a beautiful snowy whiteness'. Note that both writers stressed that the Embden goose **was** white, in contrast to the farmyard grey goose with which they were familiar.

The Americans were content with weights of 20lb (9kg) and 18lb (8kg) for the Embden gander and goose. In Britain, the desire for the heaviest birds at the Victorian shows resulted in weights of 30lb (13.5kg) for ganders and 22lb (10kg) for geese being quoted in Wright (1902), and up to 34lb (15.5kg) for males in Brown (1906). Wiscombe's naïve-style painting 'The Easter Goose' depicted a bird claimed to weigh 42lb (19kg); such weights had regularly been reported at the Dairy Show in white birds showing an obvious Toulouse influence.

The fact that this size was achieved by crossing Embdens with Toulouse was indicated by a quote by the Amhursts in Wright (1902). This cross affected the shape of the birds, and also resulted in an increase in egg production, from 15 to 30 eggs per year. The English Embden acquired its deep beak and strong head set on a long but fairly thick neck. In contrast, the German birds were finer, but showed less propensity for a keel and dewlap, and this can still be a recurrent problem in the bigger English Embdens bred today.

Embdens in Britain

True Embden stock has become extremely difficult to obtain, because few people really understand what an Embden is. It is not just a white goose; it has to have the correct shape and stance, and be massive. Well-fed, young Christmas birds can dress at 22lb (10kg) in weight, and older live birds reach 34lb (15.5kg). Such birds are not produced by commercial goose-rearers, as they come from large parents, of whom the gander may not be particularly fertile, and the goose may lay fewer than 30 eggs.

Exhibition Embdens are at present produced by very few breeders. There are probably two reasons for this. Firstly, the demand for the breed has never been particularly high, except for use as a commercial cross, so breeders have not been encouraged to produce many of the birds; even top-quality birds do not command a particularly high price compared to the amount of work involved. Secondly, the English exhibition birds have become increasingly inbred. Generally, the goslings are very difficult to rear. The eggs may be fertile, and hatch well, but the largest goslings are often distinctly unhealthy and fail to thrive. The smaller ones, which obviously inherit different genetic material, are fine, but they do not grow into exhibition birds.

The Embden has also had its setbacks in other countries. Parr related that, even in the mid-nineteenth century, there were few Embdens. The 1863 flood seems to have caused the virtual extinction of the geese, although some must have remained for further exports to America in 1862 and 1882. These direct exports probably explain why the American Embden is lighter than the English type. It looks much more like the taller, swan-necked German stock, which has a different standard from the English and weighs 24–26lb (11–12kg).

Fig 32 Embdens at Tom Bartlett's – a tall German gander with a traditional English goose. Good Embdens became extremely difficult to breed in the late 1980s, and almost unobtainable. To revive the breed, Tom imported stock from Germany, which was very different from the traditional English type

German Embdens

Some texts say that, as well as Embdens being exported to Britain, the breed was re-exported to Germany. Brown, in the early twentieth century, thought that the present-day Embden was the result of crossing the German white and English white geese. He noted that many English Embdens were exported back to Germany, so that the stock on both sides of the North Sea became closely allied. Parr considers that this was a retrograde step, the English type spoiling the elegance of the original. According to him, German breeders complained about the large head, thick neck and Toulouse characteristics, such as the dewlap and breast keel. During the First and Second World Wars, little attention was paid to the breeding of the birds in Germany, and it was not until 1960 that the typical look was regained. A big show line-up in Germany now is likely include up to fifty of these birds, compared with just a few at a British show.

Tom Bartlett, of Gloucestershire, appreciating the paucity of English stock, has recently imported these tall German birds, which reach nearly one metre in height. They have a long body, as well as a long neck, a trim dual-lobed paunch and no suggestion of a keel. Perhaps significantly, Parr demands that the German Embdens should show no trace of 'a hump between the bill and the forehead', which would indicate the presence of Chinese blood. The lack of feather partings on the birds' necks does suggest that Chinese may have been used at some point in the past, in order to regain the German Embden look. The head of the German bird is also different from the English Embden. It is rather slim and, when viewed from the side, gives the impression, together with the beak, of being oval. The bill itself has a straight culmen. At present, these imports are being crossed with the English line; it will be up to breeders to decide the future of the Embden, although the genetics and health of the birds may well make the decision for them.

Description of the Traditional English Embden

Carriage: Upright and confident.
Head: Large and bold; bill deep at the base. Eyes blue.
Neck: Neck long, fairly thick, without a gullet. In proportion to the massive body.

Body: Broad, well-rounded breast. Dual-lobed paunch. Straight, broad back. Large, strong wings.
Legs: Strong, thick shanks and toes.
Plumage: Hard and tight.
Colour: Pure white. Legs and webs orange.
Bill: Orange.
Weight: Males 28–34lb (13–15.5kg), females 24–28lb (11–13kg).

Breeding Stock

The first obvious requirement is a good size, but there are also other points to look for and avoid. Overweight birds may develop a slight dewlap under the bill or keel on the breast; Embdens should not have these features, so reject any lightweight birds that have them. Ganders should be white, but young females may show a certain amount of grey on the rump as a sex-linked feature. This usually moults out when the birds are in their second feathers, by 16–18 weeks. The preferred colour of the bill and feet is orange in Britain, but some birds show pinkish extremities, a characteristic of East European geese. Although this is not desirable, this is a minor point, especially if the pink is not dominant. Although Embdens are supposed to be large,

Fig 33 Close-up of the two contrasting birds – the traditional English Embden and the German type. The goose on the left has a much stronger, deeper head. The bill is short and powerful

43

the birds should be able to walk about comfortably. They should stand upright and alert when approached, and not dip at the breast. Always move the birds around carefully to make sure they do not limp. If they are overweight, they should be slimmed down a bit before the breeding season, particularly the gander.

Breeding Embdens

Obtaining Embden stock may be difficult, unless you are content with an average white goose. It is essential to understand something of the breed by visiting breeders and shows before you buy, otherwise you are likely to end up with just a white goose. You may be lucky to come across a flock of Embdens which have originated from a pure line, but considerable expertise is needed to grow these birds up to exhibition size, and size is soon lost over a couple of generations without good management.

Typical Embdens should lay in mid-February; they seem never to wait until March. The Embdens that we owned laid up to 30 eggs in the season, usually with a rest in the middle. The largest geese had a tendency to lay some double-yolked eggs, which was a waste for breeding, but fertility was not a problem using young ganders weighing about 26lb (12kg). The females, unlike the Toulouse, were quite keen on going broody and would undoubtedly have sat had we let them. However, knowing the propensity of geese to trample their goslings, we discouraged sitting.

The Embdens need a very large nest with easy access if they are to hatch their own eggs successfully. The eggs tend to be more hatchable than most in incubators, the embryo growing well, and the air sac achieving the correct size for hatching, when the Brecon and Pilgrim eggs may fail due to insufficient water loss. Sisson's comment about the Embdens hatching with more certainty than the 'common barnyard goose' seems to be accurate.

Rearing

On hatching, Embden goslings need more care than most. They are large, much bigger than the Toulouse, and the largest goslings always need the most care. It is essential to place the goslings on a rough surface, where they can get a good grip with their feet, otherwise spraddled legs will result. It is probably a good idea not to get them eating too quickly. The aim is to get them on their feet first, and this is best achieved if they use their reservoir of food in their resorbed yolk. It is important, however, that they do not get dehydrated under a heat lamp.

When you get to know your strain you will find that Embdens, as well as white Sebastopols, are autosexing with about 80 per

Fig 34 An Embden imported from Germany in 1997. This bird is not the typical German type. It is more like the heavier English Embden than the typical Swan-like exhibition Embden in Germany today

cent reliability. Males and females typically have saddleback markings and a coloured head in grey fluff, the males being paler in these areas compared with the females, which are quite dark grey there.

In strains produced from large parents, the goslings are the fastest growers I have ever seen. For this reason, they cannot be kept in a mixed bunch with Chinese, for example, after about a week old, otherwise the smaller goslings may get crushed (*see* the chapter on rearing). By three or four weeks they will seem to have enormous feet and thick legs, but these are necessary to support their weight. It is important not to let them get too obese. They readily develop rolls of fat on the breast at this stage, so it is probably better to cut their food back a bit, particularly the protein. However, they will not grow if they are not well fed; there is a fine line between over-feeding and ruining their legs, and under-feeding, so that they do not grow enough.

Embdens do better if they get exercise and grass, rather than sitting down to a bowl of pellets all day. Apparently, in Yorkshire there was a tradition of 'walking the geese', the job of the children when they came home from school, and this undoubtedly served to strengthen the birds. A supplement of brewers' yeast in the diet may also help.

THE TOULOUSE

Origins and Development

The other traditional European heavyweight breed is the Toulouse. Developed in Haute Garonne (France), where Toulouse is the regional centre, the breed was first imported into Britain in the 1840s by the Earl of Derby. These grey geese, which went to his menagerie at Knowsley, were also called the Mediterranean or Pyrenean, before the term Toulouse was finally favoured.

Nolan illustrated the breed in his book (1850) using a print of the bird he had successfully shown, taken from an 1845 edition of the *Illustrated London News*. He had obtained specimens from Lord Derby and was successful in breeding from them, distributing them to other breeders, and winning first prize with them at the London Zoological Society's Show in 1845.

The Toulouse birds of 1850 were nothing like the exhibition bird of today. Nolan's bird, illustrated here, scarcely had a keel or dewlap, at the time when the Hong Kong goose showed the latter feature. Nolan described the Toulouse as follows:

With the exception of their great size, they resemble our common domestic goose, but of a much more mild and easy disposition; and what is most important to the farmer, they never pull the stacks

Fig 35 Nolan's Toulouse. 'The annexed print has been copied from the Illustrated London News of 21st June, 1845, drawn for that publication, from my birds; it makes a record of their having twice taken the prize in London, in competition with all England Scotland and Ireland.' In the mid-nineteenth century, the breed lacked the dewlap and was not as heavy as modern British exhibition specimens

Fig 36 Head study of Toulouse, showing the typical dewlap of exhibition birds today

in a haggard. Their prevailing colour is blue-grey, marked with brown bars; the head, neck (as far as the beginning of the shoulders), and the back of the neck, as far as the shoulders, of a dark-brown; the breast is slaty blue; the belly is white, as also the undersurface of the tail; the bill is orange-red and the feet flesh coloured. The London Zoological Society have pronounced them to be unmixed descendants of the grey-lag.

Subsequent authors have expressed doubt about the Greylag ancestry, but it is difficult to see any other. It is well known that any breed of geese will develop a dewlap and keel if stock birds are well fed and constantly selected for size for breeding. These features, which are not desirable in utility birds, were developed after 1850 for exhibition purposes.

The original French Toulouse birds were used to make the controversial product *pâté de foie gras*; the rather ordinary grey goose of 1850 was perfectly adequate for that purpose. Postcards and cookery-book pictures of Toulouse geese from France still show an average grey bird, with slight development of keel and dewlap.

Credit was given to English breeders in developing the exhibition bird, and a very complete account was given by a Miss Campain in Wright, 1901 edition. She described the best birds as 'very wide and deep, and not showing the least tinge of brown in the plumage, but of a beautiful silver grey'. Her birds originated from the Fowler family, probably of Aylesbury duck repute. This family's heaviest Toulouse weighed 38lb (17kg), but there were suspicions about this bird carrying 'white blood'. By 1875, when the

Fig 37 Both the Pilgrim goose and the Toulouse are originally from the Greylag stock, despite the difference in size and shape. This Pilgrim goose was a favourite of this Toulouse gander

the USA, where the Toulouse eventually became the most popular breed.

The Toulouse in America

First imported into the USA in the early 1850s, Toulouse birds were exhibited at the Albany County, New York Fair in 1856. The breed was not particularly popular at first, but Robinson (1924) considered it to be the most numerous of the standard breeds. It was most popular in the Centre West, where there were large flocks of average quality, but the best specimens, he said, were concentrated in the hands of breeders. Ives (1947) showed illustrations of the birds at the Government experimental farm in Canada, which had tremendous length in the body, and also those of Oscar Grow from 1945. These specimens already showed what is now required of the American Exhibition Toulouse, and Grow defined exactly what he wanted of the best.

Not only were size, length and a well-developed dewlap essential. The birds also had to display a well-developed keel on the breast (the 'bow', in the rather nautical terminology once applied in the Standards), which bifurcated as it approached the legs. From the front, this sort of keel gives the appearance of being very broad, and when a bird stretches and flaps its wings, two broad supports are seen to run outwards on either side of the central keel, to join the two lobes of the paunch. These structures fill in the hollow area seen in front of the legs of rather more ordinary utility types.

extreme fattening for weight was going out of fashion, the heaviest Birmingham Show greys were 51lb 9oz (23.5kg) for a pair, and subsequent to that show, weights were even less.

Photographs of Toulouse in several texts in the first half of the twentieth century show birds with features that are now considered to be faults in the British and American show pen. The usual bird, such as those shown by Appleyard in the 1940s, had a dewlap and keel, but with hollows either side of the keel in front of the legs. The broad keel favoured by the American breeders has now become a feature of the exhibition Toulouse. The assumption is that this was first developed in

Description of Exhibition Grey Toulouse

Carriage: Almost horizontal. Birds move carefully to manage their weight distribution.
Head: Massive; effect exaggerated by loose cheek folds around the bill. Bill relatively short, deep. Slightly convex top line.
Neck: Quite long; thick. A well-developed

Fig 38 Toulouse goslings are plain grey to start with. As they grow, they develop a dual-lobed paunch, and look as if they are wearing baggy pants. The photograph was taken at two and half weeks old

Fig 39 Toulouse geese, the author's exhibition gander on the right of the pair. This bird was unbeaten in Toulouse classes, and won Show Champion on several occasions – a 'once in a lifetime bird', as someone remarked. Breeding a top-quality bird is partly a result of luck, and partly down to breeding and management expertise, and knowledge and experience of the breed

dewlap extends in folds from the lower mandible down the neck.

Body: Long, broad and deep. Keel on breast is balanced by supports either side, which diverge along the lower ribs, in front of the paunch. This gives fullness to the breast and keel when the bird is viewed from the front. Wings large and strong, smoothly folded against the sides. Tail slightly elevated.

Legs: Quite short, stout. Hidden by thigh coverts.

Plumage: Soft and full.

Colour: Neck blue-grey, darker at the back; back and thighs darker, each feather laced with white. Primaries and secondaries dark grey. Breast light grey, becoming paler under the body and finally white on the paunch and stern. Tail grey and white. Eyes brown, bill orange or orange-red, legs and webs orange.

Weight: Males 26–30lb (12–13.5kg), females 20–24lb (9–11kg).

In addition to the grey Toulouse, there are also a few white Toulouse (colour character-

Fig 40 That champion's sister is also an exceptional exhibition bird. Females tend to be less noticed in show pens than males, simply because they are smaller. It takes a good judge to 'put up' quality females

istics corresponding to the Embden) and buff Toulouse (colour corresponding to the American Buff).

Breeding Stock

The problem with breeding Toulouse is that there is a huge variety in size and type of grey geese. A bird advertised as 'Toulouse' is not necessarily a genuine Toulouse. There is a wide range in quality, from the 'Giant Dewlap' exhibition birds to a very ordinary grey goose, with little embellishment to the average goose shape. If you are looking for exhibition stock, you must familiarize yourself with the genuine bird before you buy. There is little point in breeding for exhibition purposes from anything other than the very best you can acquire, because even exhibition parents can produce quite mediocre offspring.

Birds related to American imported stock are usually far better growers than average stock, and will continue to increase in size well into their second year. They peak in size, shape and carriage at about three years old, but for breeding it is better to use a young, fit gander. Assess a gander's potential by seeing the parent birds, as Toulouse take a long time to develop.

Fig 41 Parent goose of the exhibition birds. The parent was bred by John Hall, who has produced top quality Toulouse geese for years

Fig 42 Buff Toulouse, bred from the greys, are almost as good in shape. The buff colour may have come from American Buff/Toulouse crosses bred in Britain some years ago, but is more likely to have come from American Toulouse. Good Toulouse stock has been exported to America, as well as being imported into Britain on several occasions. Top-quality Toulouse are in demand and it is worth paying the transport, blood testing and quarantine fees. Importing from Europe is easier

When selecting from a flock of youngsters, choose big birds with a good development, for their age, of dewlap and keel. The keel should be straight and symmetrical, preferably broad at its base when the bird is viewed from the front. Youngsters are unlikely to be as big or as well-developed as their parents. Also look for a large, strong head. The bill shape is important; it should have a straight or slightly convex topline, and not look slightly dished, or long and 'snipey'.

Breeding Toulouse

Toulouse geese have a reputation for being difficult to breed and, in general, they are. Fertility in the gander depends on how fit and healthy he is; we have been able to breed from ganders which reached 30lb (13.5kg) in weight in the show season, but which lost weight to 26–28lb (12–13kg) in the breeding season. The birds should be given plenty of space and exercise to keep fit and, although water can be made available for mating, it does not seem to be essential for fertility. Healthy, alert ganders are more likely to

be successful breeders; such birds cannot be run with another gander in the group in the breeding season because of serious fighting. Toulouse that are very placid and take a back seat will probably not be good breeders.

A great deal has been written about special diets for breeder geese. Our Toulouse are fed the same as all the others, except in the amount of breeder pellets, for which they have a bigger appetite than the others. This suggests that they have a higher protein requirement. They also have constant access to wheat and short grass, which they like to graze as much as the other geese. Spring grass seems to provide essential vitamins that may be lacking in pellets. Nothing is certain in goose breeding, however. The odd early 'green' year, with grass growth in a warm winter, has provided one of the worst breeding seasons ever. Geese are a law unto themselves when it comes to breeding and this applies especially to the Toulouse.

For the best chance of success, have young, fit ganders, and give the pair peace and quiet, so that other birds do not interfere with them. However, a little confrontation through a

Fig 43 A utility Toulouse for comparison with the exhibition birds. This bird lacks dewlap development and has a round breast, which may not develop a proper keel when he is much older. These birds are easier to breed than the exhibition strains

eggs per year, at between two and six years old. Another strain laid only six to ten eggs and, consequently, gave far fewer opportunities for goslings. The goose is not likely to go broody; if she does, do not encourage sitting. The eggs and goslings do far better under a goose or hen of lighter weight. The eggs, if fertile, are no more difficult to hatch than those of most other breeds. Getting fertility is the more likely problem in breeding.

Rearing

The goslings are rather small, and slower on their feet than Africans and Chinese. They grow at a rapid rate, but do not overtake the Embdens. It is worth looking after them very carefully, in order to maximize their growth. As with the Embdens, brewers' yeast should be added to the diet. High-protein pellets, always preferred by the Toulouse, will be needed for a much longer growth period than for geese of medium or light weight.

Toulouse are quite shy goslings in most strains; if you want them as pets, they should be handled and talked to regularly, and encouraged to take bread and greens from the hand. If they are brought up in a gaggle of mixed breeds, the Toulouse tend to take a back seat when they are young. If they are kept with tame geese, they will become much more confident by about one year old, and then suddenly become very tame indeed.

Although the birds are big, they are quite nimble for their size and should be encouraged to walk and flap about with the other geese. However, by the time they are two years old, the exhibition birds will be too heavy for this and need a quiet life on a piece of flat ground by the house. If you watch their weight, they will continue to breed. The heavier birds have a more limited life span, of up to ten years, compared with twenty years or more for an average goose.

fence, in a low-risk situation, can do wonders for the gander's ego. You also need a pair that suit each other and are not too inbred; this is very difficult to assess if the breeding history of stock is not known. Pairs are much more successful than trios, especially if the gander is two or more years old. Young ganders are not so choosy, and will mate successfully with other breeds in a flock.

Toulouse are quite good layers. We have had large American exhibition geese, as well as smaller nondescript strains, laying over 30

5 Relative Newcomers ——

With the exception of the Common goose, the breeds described above have been produced by careful selection of size, shape and colour, over a long period of time. These breeds, apart from the Pilgrim, have often been regarded as the elite by waterfowl breeders, their characteristics having been arrived at by systematic development from a basic parent stock. The Common geese are different; they seem to have been through a process of traditional selection over a long period of time, even though the Pilgrim was only standardized in the twentieth century.

In contrast to these older breeds, most of those developed since around 1900 have either arisen as deliberate cross-breeds, or from the 'geese of the land', as the Germans put it, in other words, from unselected farmyard stock. This is true for the Steinbacher and Buff breeds, but possibly not of the Pomeranians.

THE POMERANIAN

There is often a basic misunderstanding in Britain about the term 'Pomeranian'. This has arisen because the first imports of these birds under this name, in the early 1980s, were Greyback in colour. 'Greyback' and 'Buff Back' are terms used to describe geese that have a heart-shaped mantle of coloured feathers on the back, and coloured thigh coverts and head, which contrast with the main white body feathers. This colour arrangement has also been described as 'saddleback', 'pied' and 'spotted'.

The Pomeranian is a particular breed of goose which comes in white, grey, and saddleback, and is identified by its single lobed paunch. In the USA, the term 'Pomeranian' has become almost synonymous with the saddleback in grey, and even buff. In the USA, saddlebacks are said to be Pomeranian, while British saddlebacks result from crossing grey (or buff) with white geese and resemble the Embden in type.

History

In Germany, the 'Pommern gans' is a specific breed, which, according to German authors, has a long history. Geese had been kept for centuries in the marshy lowlands of Germany. Schmidt (1989) found in a work called *Pommerania* (1550) that the geese of Rugen Island, just offshore in the Baltic (annexed to Pommerania in 1335), were driven to market on a regular basis. Geese were an important product of the region and large numbers were bred for the delicacies of smoked goose breast, salted goose, and 'goose lard'. These products were sold in the entire kingdom and the neighbouring countries, earning the goose the title of 'breadwinner of the farm'.

It is not known if the 'Rugenshe ganse' of the sixteenth century looked the same as the Pomeranian geese of today, because there are few records. There has been the suggestion that Pomeranians were developed from an Embden/Toulouse cross. Brown (1929) quotes Moubray as saying, in his section on Pomeranian geese, that the saddleback geese 'are the production of white (or Embden) with the grey (or Toulouse)'. However, Schmidt

Fig 44 Pomeranian Greyback geese (with smaller white Romans) bred by Steph Mansell. Pomeranians can be active, assertive geese and are great characters. They are very eye-catching in contrasting grey and white, but getting the perfect markings is a difficult task. This is easier in some strains than others

denies that the development of the Pomeranian had anything to do with such a cross. The type of the birds is completely different, the rather portly appearance of the Pomeranian having been arrived at by careful selection, in order to build up meat and fat.

The 'Pommern gans' was officially recognized as an independent breed in 1912 and in the following years two different but officially recognized types existed: the single-lobed or the dual-lobed (referring to the under-carriage). In 1929, the single central lobe became an obligatory criterion for the breed, making the Pomeranian unique in this respect among the European Greylag descendants. The oldest written description of the breed was attributed to Baldamus in 1897 by Schmidt. In this he stressed that the frame was longer and higher than that of the other German geese, distinguishing it from the Embden and Toulouse crosses.

Fig 45 A Pomeranian gander at Malvern's Champion Waterfowl Exhibition with his Best of Breed rosette

53

Description

Carriage: Nearly horizontal.
Head: Fairly broad, slightly flattened crown; stout beak; large prominent eyes.
Neck: Medium length, stout, carried upright. Same thickness along its length.
Body: Plump, with prominent, round breast; single-lobed paunch, lobe centrally placed.
Plumage: Head and upper neck grey, lower neck white. Body mainly white; grey feathers of the thigh coverts and saddleback marking laced with white. Wings white.
Weight: Males 18–24lb (8–11kg), females 16–20lb (7–9kg).

Schmidt also says that the breast and shoulders should be full, so that the bird is 'egg-shaped' in long profile, emphasizing the breast. Between the legs, the central lobe must be straight and not misplaced to one side. The wings fit snugly to the body and the long back is slightly arched. Most important in the appearance of the gander is the neck; this must be strong, straight and of medium length, and of equal width along its length.

The head shape is also distinctive. The beak, viewed from the side, is deep. The culmen is straight and the crown of the head slightly flattened. The colour of the bill should indicate a typical east European origin in its red-pink, also the colour of the feet. In its general demeanour, the bird should look confident and arrogant, this being emphasized by the slightly flattened head and the prominent chest.

The distinctive head shape of the Pomeranian gives the bird a rather arrogant look, which seems to be a common characteristic of the German breeds. The Steinbacher and German Embden also have this slightly convex topline, given by the outline of the crown and bill.

Colour

Pomeranians exist in three colours. In 1906, Durigen (cited in Schmidt) said that the colour of the feathers did not play a major part in the breeding process, but white was preferred. The grey type was grey all over, except for lacing on the body feathers and the underparts, which fade on the stern to white. These birds have brown eyes, unlike the white birds, which are blue-eyed.

On the saddlebacks, the grey on the head should extend one-quarter to one-half of the way down the neck, ending in a neat, symmetrical ring all the way round. Both this, and the heart-shaped saddle of feathers on the back, are difficult to obtain. Schmidt says that

Fig 46 The author's Pomeranian geese. These beautiful geese unfortunately passed on a leg-joint problem to some of their offspring. This is a penalty of too much inbreeding, probably before we got the birds, which were of German origin. The line was not used for pure breeds again

breeders of the Greyback Pomeranians need to produce quite a number of the birds every year, in order to obtain just a few with perfect colour markings. Some birds are over-marked and acquire the incorrect brown eye. Others are under-marked and the grey markings fail to close under the chin.

Breeding Stock

It will be difficult to keep Pomeranians true to type in Britain because there have been few imports of the breed. Apart from one in grey, the rest are in greyback. The birds tend to have rather orange feet and bill, rather than the red-pink that is required. Also, much of the stock, whilst having a good head type, with deep bill and flat crown, is dual-lobed. Such birds should be disqualified as Pomeranians. This type of undercarriage is an inherited feature and can arise from parents that are both single-lobed, their type obscuring their genetic inheritance (genotype).

In practice, these dual-lobed saddleback birds are being shown as Greybacks, and the strong contrast between the white and grey on them is very eye-catching.

Temperament

Temperament varies from strain to strain, but the Pomeranians are generally not recommended for families with children. The females have a wonderful temperament. Those that we have hand-reared have been some of the most confident geese we have seen. They have fed from the hand, allowed nests to be searched while sitting, and enjoyed shows. Some of the ganders, however, have a temperament that matches their arrogant demeanour. They are alert and watchful at the gate, make a lot of noise, and put on a display of interest in visitors. When people have backed away from them, or showed other signs of nervousness, these ganders have become a family nuisance; fortunately, they may be re-trained when moved to a different owner. Geese, and especially this breed, are very quick to pick up on human body language.

Eggs

German specifications are very thorough and give the weight of a Pomeranian egg as 170–180 grams (6½–7/oz). The breed is designed as a utility goose, but egg production does vary greatly, from very few in some individuals to an exceptional number in others. Our Pomeranians have been the first to start laying and have produced the earliest, easy-hatching goslings. They have also been the last to finish laying, sometimes having produced over 40 eggs each.

Unfortunately, this interesting strain carried an inherited leg weakness, so we no longer breed them. A restricted gene pool can be a problem where there have been few imports, although it seems that other strains of imported Pomeranians in Britain do not have the weakness.

THE BUFF BACK AND THE GREYBACK

History

The terms 'Buff Back' and 'Greyback' have been used to describe pied geese, with white and coloured markings, which have probably been familiar for centuries. Gervasse Markham referred to 'pyde' geese in 1615 (quoted by Brown in 1929), and the pattern seems to have been popular around the Baltic. Not only are there the Greyback Pomeranians, but small Greyback geese are also found on Oland, an island in the Baltic off Sweden (*Avicultura,* 1995). The 'Skanegas' (Scanian goose) is shown as a 'spotted' or Greyback goose in a short article on colour in

The Magazine of Ducks and Geese (USA 1956). In America, the term 'Pomeranian' has even become synonymous with saddleback in both Buff Back and Greyback varieties. In short, the 'type' and size of a saddleback goose varies, depending on the location in which it is found.

In Britain, the saddleback goose is quite a large, practical farm goose. Standard weights are similar to those for the Pomeranian, but a well-fed saddleback adult female produced for the Christmas market, particularly if she has an Embden in her ancestry, can reach over 22lb (10kg).

Colour

Saddleback birds can be made from self-coloured birds. A white goose such as an Embden can be crossed with a buff goose, for example. This cross can either produce a self-coloured grey, or a white goose flecked with grey. If this cross is then mated with another white bird that shows some evidence of carrying colour, 25 per cent of the offspring can turn out buff back.

In the experience of one breeder who tried this, the buff back colour was also sex-linked, all the pied geese being female. This colour control recalls the research cited on dilution, in which females show more colour than males (*Magazine of Ducks and Geese*, 1956). Jerome (1970) found that his Embden/Buff crosses resulted in solid-pattern dilute grey males, but undiluted buff females. This showed 'that the genes for buff and grey behaved in a sex-linked manner and therefore were located on the sex chromosomes'.

A similar phenomenon was recorded when

Fig 47 Pair of English Buff Backs with a Greyback for comparison. 'Harold' the Buff Back gander is showing his age and developing a dewlap – a fault in this breed

Fig 48 Steinbacher – head study showing dark serrations along the line of the bill (like lipstick), and dark bean. These markings are characteristic of the breed and birds look somewhat 'under-dressed' without them

buff Toulouse were produced in Britain. The first-generation Buffs we produced from John Hall's American stock carrying buff were all female, but the next generation that we bred from those daughters and grey sons (which carried buff) produced some buff males as well. Jerome also found this when he used the first-generation colour crosses as breeders. They reproduced buff males in the ratio of roughly one male to three females.

Description of the British Buff Back

The British Standard (1982) for the Buff Back breed was derived from the Pomeranian Standard, with the exception of the shape of the paunch, which, in the Buff Back, is dual-lobed. In practice, a Buff Back is like a small Embden, with markings similar in distribution to the saddleback Pomeranian.

Weight: Gander 17lb (7.5kg), goose 15lb (6.5kg) (as Pomeranian) in 1982; weights increased in 1997 to gander 18–22lb (8–10kg), goose 16–20lb (7–9kg) (as Pomeranian 1997).

These weights show that the British Buff Back should be a medium-weight goose, slightly larger than the Brecon Buff.

Description of the Greyback

This is simply a colour variant and is similar in type to the British Buff Back.

THE STEINBACHER

The Steinbacher fighting breed was standardized in the twentieth century and, like the Pomeranian, began its development around 1900. It is different from the other breeds recognized at British shows. It is not only a colour cross, but also a Eurasian cross.

Many types of geese have originated between Poland and China as crosses between the 'geese of the land' (farmyard geese of Greylag origin) and the Asiatic knob geese. These crosses, according to Durigen, produced the fighting geese of Russia – the Tula and the Arsamas. The only difference between the two was the larger size of the Arsamas. The most noticeable feature was the short bill, with no indentation where it was set in the forehead, its shape reminiscent of the Cereopsis goose.

The Steinbacher was produced as a cross-breed in this same way as these fighting geese, either as a direct Asiatic/farmyard goose cross, or through a cross with the Tula (de Bruin, 1995). This may have been surmised from the fact that trainloads of geese were brought from Russia to Thuringia before the Second World War. Ehrlein, a Steinbacher breeder from the former East Germany, also reported that, even now, crosses between knobbed geese and Pomeranians, Diepholz or Czech geese will produce first-generation progeny strongly reminiscent of the Steinbacher.

The fighting goose had already been established as a distinctive type in the Steinbach-Hallenburg area, and it was first properly classified in the Thuringer 'Gerflugelzuchter' in 1925. The breed was recognized and standardized in 1932 in its original grey colour, then in the popular blue in 1951.

Description

Carriage: Slightly upright, proud stature.
Head: Neat; no knob or dewlap. Straight beak.
Neck: Medium length, upright, straight.
Body: Stocky, with wide, full breast. Back slightly sloping. Underline clean. Wings long, carried close to the body. Tail short, carried level.
Legs: Thighs and shanks strong.
Colour: Plumage light blue-grey; larger feathers show a distinct white lace. Beak bright orange with black bean and black serrations (a feature of the breed). Legs and webs bright orange. As well as the blue and grey, there is also a pale buff variety.
Weight: Ganders 13–15lb (6–6.5kg), geese 11–13lb (5–6kg).

Breeding Stock in Britain

This breed, introduced into Britain in the late 1980s, gained immediate popularity. It has a distinctive type and temperament, and it is the only blue goose in which the colour is stable. Although it can occur in grey and light buff, the blue is preferred. De Bruin recommends that the silver progeny, which can come from the blue, should not be used for breeding, as the distinctive dark bill markings will be lost.

The breed was first imported by the Shintons in 1988, and subsequently by Tom Bartlett, among others. The birds have proved somewhat erratic in their breeding record, some individuals failing to breed at all, and others mostly reproducing only in small numbers. This has meant that there are still comparatively few in Britain.

The geese have come in two slightly different types, the stockier, shorter birds being a better blue than the more upright,

Fig 49 A pair of Steinbachers. They have pale lavender-blue plumage laced with off-white. This is the only blue standardized breed of goose. The blue colour is difficult to 'fix', and may only have been achieved in the Steinbacher because of the Chinese in the breeding

slimmer individuals. None are particularly good layers; 12–15 eggs seems about normal. De Bruin remarks, however, that the greater the number of eggs, the greater the chances of infertility. Maybe the Steinbacher is destined to remain a comparatively rare breed.

Fixing the Colour

Blue is an unusual colour in poultry and waterfowl. The colour is not usually attributed to one gene; it results from a cross and therefore cannot be typical of all the progeny from a pair. Blue geese are known in flocks of cross-breeds, and were referred to in an HMSO publication on geese. We have known blues result from crossing white geese with buffs, but further breeding from the blues always resulted in a variety of markings, including flecked and saddleback, as well as self-coloured white, buff or grey.

The Steinbacher blue must be different, as blues breed blues. The secret ingredient is probably from the Chinese. The Asiatic geese do not appear to carry the European saddleback gene, so, if this is eliminated from the gene pool, self-colour in the blue can result. Chinas were crossed in Britain with buff geese and Greylags by Frank Mosford of Clwyd, and attractive blue and buff 'Chinese' were produced as a result. If the Steinbachers were to become too inbred, a selective breeding programme, from a coloured Chinese cross showing little knob development (in other words, going back to basics), could eventually improve their fortunes.

Temperament

Although supposedly bred as a fighting goose, the Steinbacher has a wonderful, calm temperament as a pet. Geese that are self-confident and aggressive with their own rivals are often confident with people too. This confidence means that they are not frightened and therefore do not feel the need to be aggressive with humans, who are not competitors.

With other geese, it may be a different matter. As long as the Steinbacher gander is recognized as the boss, there should be no problem. In the breeding season, however, this may be problematic. Large Africans, which may have backed off earlier in the year, will no longer do so, and a determined fight will ensue if the birds are not properly penned. Pig netting, generally satisfactory for separating pens of geese, is inadequate, because the ganders can get their necks through and fight. With most breeds, this is usually a brief confrontation that ends in a quick separation, but the Steinbacher will hang on, and live up to its name as a fighting goose. Bloodied backs can result. The situation will be especially serious if the opponent is an African or Chinese, which, when roused, will indicate by its tenacity where the Steinbacher has inherited its temperament.

BUFF GEESE

Buff is not a popular colour in the wild. From the Pacific to the Atlantic, wild species of geese exist in shades of dark and silver grey, sometimes mingled with white. There is the occasional unusual marking of the Bar-heads and the odd splash of colour in the Red-breasted, but goose plumage is generally conservative. Judging by the domestics, there is a good reason for this. Buff feathers simply do not stand up to the rigours of a harsh climate, unlike grey, or even white. Buff feathers lose their sheen and fade badly by spring, and in a hot, sunny summer they can be damaged even as they grow. This weakens the feather and spoils its water-proofing qualities, and this would prove to be too great a disadvantage in the wild, and select buff birds out of a wild population.

Buff is very much a domesticated colour. It probably arose naturally as a mutation from grey and white farmyard crosses. Like the white before it, the buff probably caught the eye of breeders for both aesthetic and practical purposes, but this seems to have been mentioned only fairly recently in the nineteenth century by Weir. It did not emerge as a breed colour until the 1930s. Buff is recessive to grey and it may be that a knowledge of genetics was needed before appropriate stock could be selected, in order to maintain this recessive colour gene.

As well as having the appeal of a new colour, buff has other advantages. The American Buff was developed as a commercial goose and, although this was not specified, it may well have been because of the feather quality that the buff was favoured. The feathers of buff geese pluck much more easily than whites, greys, or brown Chinese, since they are less strongly rooted. The down is extremely pale and any 'pens' left behind on the carcass do not detract from marketing as much as on a grey bird.

Despite the obvious advantages of the buff, commercial growers still seem to stick with the white Embden and Danish crosses. Hatchability and fecundity are presumably more important, especially since plucking machines are so efficient. It is now left to the fanciers and the owners of small farm flocks to persist with the more unusual strains.

The Brecon Buff

Origins and Development

The Brecon was the first standardized buff goose. Although farmyard flocks had probably had buff 'sports' for decades before, Rhys Llewellyn of Swansea was the first to use these in order to standardize the Brecon. He published how he did this in *Feathered World* in 1934:

> In 1929, while motoring over the Brecon Beacons in Wales, I noticed a buff-coloured goose among a large flock of white and grey geese. This buff 'sport'

interested me greatly and I purchased her there and then, with the definite intention of producing a breed of this attractive colour.

Unable to find a buff gander, he used a white, medium-sized Embden-type male. All of the goslings from this first cross turned out grey, and he kept a gander from these. He then acquired two other buff females from different hill farms and, using the young gander, produced several buff goslings. Keeping the best buff gander, he then had an all-buff breeding pen; he was able to avoid inbreeding too closely, because his original three females were unrelated. During the 1933 breeding season, the geese bred 70 per cent true to colour and type, and in 1934 he achieved 100 per cent true colour birds.

Llewellyn's birds were deliberately reared in rather harsh conditions as they were meant to be self-sufficient hill-farm geese. They had free range over a large area of good pasture land and were kept in open grass runs at night. The eggs were hatched by the geese themselves; under these natural conditions, results were good throughout the breeding programme, even though the geese did not have access to swimming water. The birds were, not surprisingly, only fair layers, but their owner was pleased with their table qualities and appearance, as they plucked out a good colour. As market requirements changed in favour of a smaller goose, he set out to produce a medium goose weighing on average 14lb (6kg) live. His standard allowed ganders up to 18lb (8kg) and females up to16lb (7kg).

The Brecon Buff was first on show at the Crystal Palace Show in 1933, where it caused a stir beside the standard white Embden and grey Toulouse. Llewellyn described the breed as not unlike the Embden in shape, but of a lighter build, and more active. The buff colour was marked as in the Toulouse – well laced on the larger body feathers, which have a pale fringe. The underparts faded to white behind the shanks and under the tail. He liked a

Fig 50 The Brecon Buff. A mature goose with some white feathers around the base of the bill. Some strains do not develop this feature. Pronounced feather partings on the neck are characteristic of European geese derived from the Greylag

deep shade of buff throughout and noted that the ganders were usually a shade lighter than the geese. Although birds with a 'flat' unlaced buff did occur (Appleyard, 1933), and can still be found today, the laced sort is preferred.

The actual shade of buff can vary according to exposure to sunlight but, even so, some individuals hold their colour better than others. As a general requirement today, a pinkish-brown is preferred to a tobacco colour – in other words, almost a hint of blue, rather than orange. Llewellyn standardized a pink bill, and pink or orange feet. In practice, the pink bills and feet go together, and pink is now the standard colour today.

Description of the Brecon Buff
Carriage: Slightly upright, active.
Head: Neat; bill medium length, fairly deep at the base.
Neck: Medium length, no gullet.
Body: Plump. Breast full and round. Dual-lobed paunch. Strong wings. Medium length tail.
Legs: Fairly short. Shanks strong.
Colour: Plumage a deep shade of buff throughout with markings similar to the Toulouse. Bill, legs and webs pink. Eyes brown.

Weight: Ganders16–20lb (7–9kg), geese 14–18lb (6–8kg).

Breeding Stock
Pink-billed Brecons are not easy to breed. Stock that conformed to Llewellyn's standard was virtually unobtainable when we first wanted exhibition stock, in 1982. Few geese were then on show, and even those breeders who showed geese were not particularly interested in the Brecon. Most birds advertised as 'Brecons' were quite orange in both bill and foot. The pink colour of the bill and feet is recessive to orange, and even perfect parents can produce offspring with a great deal of colour variation, ranging from pale rose-pink to salmon. Without much selection to maintain the breed's colour points, prior to the import of the American Buff, few good individuals were available.

The difficulties of getting reliable stock were compounded by the effect of nutrition and geology on bill colour. Free-draining soils derived from red sandstones, such as in Cheshire or Brecon, produce the best pink bills. An ideal stock bird bought in such an area, and then grazed for two weeks on grass grown on solid clay, could soon change. The desirable pink bill colour can rapidly become

Fig 51 Brecon gander – flecked feathers of the undercarriage are correct

an undesirable bright orange. The same effect occurs when birds are fed only on wheat and pellets, or kept indoors. The orange drains away because of the lack of pigment provided by the grass.

Whilst the birds may look good for exhibition, their quality as breeders is unknown until they are grazed outdoors. Fortunately, the recent increasing popularity of Brecons has meant that the colour of the birds is now much more uniform than it was, and quality breeding stock is easier to obtain.

The feather quality of a bird is much easier to assess. Obvious colour faults are white flights in the wing feathers, and even a white blaze on the breast. As with the bill colour, continued selection has reduced the incidence of these faults, although they will probably never be completely eliminated due to the breed's origin from greys and whites. A patch of white feathers on the 'chin' below the lower mandible is the first sign of this problem, so it

Fig 52 Brecon goslings are an attractive light toffee colour. The bill is almost dark purple at first, in pink-billed strains

is probably better to leave such a bird out of the breeding pen, unless it has other particularly desirable qualities.

While breeders have sought the ideal pink bill, and the legs and feet are now standardized as pink only, the buff feathers have tended to lighten a little in some strains. Care needs to be taken that the buff colour is maintained and does not fade to white too rapidly on the undercarriage. Incorrect colour tends to go with an eye that is pale instead of a good deep brown.

Llewellyn described his birds as having a rather long, thin neck, but this is not accepted as typical today. The birds illustrated in October 1934 were quite lean – it seems likely that they were young stock, which do not have the weight of well-fed adults or exhibition birds. Grass-fed young birds are quite small and racy, and will only reach the 14lb (6kg) average desired by Llewellyn.

The Brecon is accepted as a table bird, and is ideally plump, with a round, full breast and dual-lobed paunch. Although the frame of the bird is not particularly large, so that they look smaller than Pomeranians, they carry a lot of weight. Grass-fed adult birds look just as round as breeders' birds fed on wheat and pellets, but there is a difference when they are picked up. Birds fed from bags are much more solid and are deceptively heavy, often weighing up to 20lb (9kg), even though they look the same as their farmyard cousins. For this reason, the weight standards of the Brecon (in common with other geese) have been given a range of values, because the management regime plays a large part in the condition and weight of the birds.

With all breeds, I prefer to use two-year-olds rather than yearling geese as breeders. Young birds lay small eggs, which produce small goslings, and so on. Brecons and Pilgrims are particularly prone to loss of size in the progeny if poor breeding and rearing practices are followed. All too often, Brecons end up as bantams, weighing in at about 10lb (4.5kg).

Temperament

Brecons have the reputation of being calm, friendly geese. This was particularly true of the first good original stock birds that we obtained from Lancashire and the Dolgellau area (from British Waterfowl Association members). Hand-reared, the adults are usually trustworthy with children, as long as they are treated well.

Eggs and Broodiness

The Brecon is also a good sitter. Grass-reared Brecons, fed as geese were intended, usually lay 12–18 eggs and then go broody. This was ideal for the farm without an electric incubator, where the goose did the job of rearing half a dozen goslings for extra Christmas income.

In certain seasons, however, the geese will lay up to 40 eggs and show little sign of going broody. As German Steinbacher breeders have pointed out, this is not always good news. There have been seasons with huge amounts of eggs, the majority of which are infertile.

Hatchability

Brecon and Pilgrim eggs are particularly difficult to hatch in still-air incubators. This is because of insufficient water loss, particularly early in the season, when humidity is too high and/or eggshells are not very porous. Poor hatchability could be due to shell structure being different in these coloured breeds, compared to white geese and Asiatic geese. To get good hatches of Brecons, it is necessary to regulate the humidity of the incubator very carefully and, if it is impossible to get the humidity low enough, the goose or broody hens are essential. In very wet seasons, even eggs under the goose will fail.

The American Buff

Origins and Development

Buff birds were produced independently in the USA and named 'American Buff', to distinguish them from the Brecon. Although Schmidt (1989) does not mention buff Pomeranians in his detailed history of the breed in Germany, American authors consider that these birds were common in the USA in the first part of the twentieth century. Ives says that the American Buff was developed, through forty years of selective breeding in the USA, from the general farm goose found among the flocks of the peasant farmers of Pomerania. Unfortunately, the development of the self-coloured American, from the pied or saddleback buff, was not documented. Even American writers, including Sheraw, who have easier access to their own country's journals, have been unable to find much information.

The American Buff breeders, who developed and standardized the breed prior to its official recognition in the *American Standard of Perfection* in 1947, were primarily interested in it as a commercial goose They did nothing to document its origins, or to advise others on breeding it for exhibition. It is possible therefore to surmise that breeders would have used over-marked saddlebacks, which can show a great deal of variation in colour, eventually to produce the buff goose. The fact that American Buffs originated from the buff Pomeranians is indicated by the wholly buff birds occasionally producing buff back geese. Ives (1947) says that the pied buff goose or the saddleback is a sub-variety of the American Buff. Also, according to John Hall, the American Buffs first imported into Britain in the late 1970s bred buff backs, although the stock does not seem to do this now.

Another throwback to Pomeranian ancestry is the tendency for some American Buffs to have rather pink beaks and feet, which tell of an East European origin. This is

Fig 53 American Buffs are bigger and 'rangier' than Brecons. Some strains tend to have rather long, flattened heads, whilst other more attractive birds are proportioned more like the average goose

considered to be a fault in the Americans. Somewhere along the way in the breeding programme in America it must have been decided to select for orange feet and bill, and a dual-lobed paunch. These were moves away from the Pomeranian characteristics, and perhaps quite deliberate, intended to make the new breed distinctive.

Distinguishing Americans from Brecons

In the early 1980s, soon after the American Buffs had been imported, there was some misunderstanding over what constituted good Brecons and Americans, probably because there were very few good specimens on show at the time. Brecon classes frequently contained orange-beaked, medium-weight birds, which had not been bred from the imported buff line. It was simply that, until the American Buff arrived, people had thought that any buff bird was a Brecon. After the import of the American strain, there was a need to distinguish between the two. Probably due to an error, the top standard weight of the Brecon had been given as a pound greater (at 19lb/8.5kg) than the American (at 18lb/8kg), proving a further confusing factor.

There were some good specimens, however. Fran Alsagoff's top-quality American Buff goose, photographed in 1984 at the Federation Show at Stafford, clearly showed the superior size of her breed, compared with our pair of Brecons illustrated in the same book (Roberts, 1986). Our Brecons at the time were only grass-fed, and so were attributed a 'keel' rather than the dual-lobed paunch they now have. Americans from that strain and Brecons from that pair have gone on to provide the basic stock for many breeders in both the 1980s and '90s. 'George' from Lancashire (hatched 1978) and 'Berry' from near Dolgellau (hatched 1980) still bred successfully in 1995. When well fed, they weighed in at about 19lb (8.5kg) and 16–18lb (7–8kg) respectively, depending on the season. Berry's older sister (1978), still laying in 1998, reached 22lb (10kg) one year,

showing how deceptive the weight of Brecons can be, in comparison with the larger-framed American Buffs.

Description of the American Buff

Carriage: Rather upright.
Head: Broad, oval. Stout bill of medium length. Any tendency for long, flat heads should be avoided.
Neck: Fairly upright and strong.
Body: Plump. Back medium length. Broad, deep, full breast. Dual-lobed paunch, which should follow through as symmetrical lobes at the rear.
Legs: Shanks stout, moderately long.
Colour: Feathers a rich shade of orange-buff, with markings similar to the Toulouse – laced on buff feathers; white fluff at the stern. Bill and legs orange; eyes brown.
Weight: Ganders 22–28lb (10–13kg); geese 20–26lb (9–12kg). They should look significantly larger than Brecons, as the first imports did in the late 1970s.

Selecting Breeding Stock

It is now recognized that American Buffs are larger than Brecons. Americans weighing up to 28lb (13kg) have been exhibited in the USA (*Fancy Fowl*), and birds bred by John Hall in Britain regularly reach 26lb (12kg). The birds are 'rangier' (taller and longer-necked) than the Brecons, and standard weights are now higher, to allow for the difference in size between the two breeds. Recently, smaller but well-coloured American Buffs have been shown, but it would be a retrograde step if these smaller weights became the norm.

The American head tends to be a bit longer and flatter-crowned (rather like the Pomeranian) than the Brecon, but an excessively long head and 'snipey' bill should be guarded against when selecting breeders. The birds should be full in the body, and dual-lobed in the paunch, with this feature also symmetrical at the rear. Feather faults are the same as in Brecons with respect to white in the coloured plumage.

Fig 54
When the rain raineth,
And the goose winketh
Little wots the gosling
What the goose thinketh

Skelton,
The Garlande of Laurell, *1523*

PART TWO: SETTING UP

6 Why Keep Geese? —————

People keep geese for a variety of reasons. Some want them simply as lawnmowers and for a few eggs in spring, in which case there is perhaps no point in choosing a particular breed. However, many people are now interested in the pure breeds that have been selected, not only to fulfil a particular economic purpose, but also to look good.

Different breeds behave differently, although a generalization about a breed's behaviour may not apply to a particular individual. Some breeds also have a certain reputation, which has 'stuck', even though it may generally have become untrue. Despite these reservations, before making a choice, do try to find out about a breed's usual behaviour, size and nutritional requirements,

whether you want a pet, exhibition birds or geese for the table.

GEESE IN THE GARDEN

All geese graze copious amounts of grass, and the most voracious grazers are goslings. Pilgrims seem to be the best of all; they do not seem to have forgotten that they are farmyard geese, whereas Toulouse geese still like their 'rations' ad lib. Goslings eat such huge amounts of grass, in order to feed their rapid growth rate, that their sheds need cleaning out regularly if they are not to become a slimy mess. Geese, and especially goslings, cannot be expected to eat long grass, only to maintain a turf, but they will reduce the need to mow considerably, depending on the rate of stocking.

Grass regularly grazed by geese improves in quality, while the probing beaks of ducks leave bare earth that encourages the growth of weeds. Geese will seek out dandelions and eventually dispatch buttercups. If there is a large infestation of these weeds, you can use any breed of young goslings to eradicate the dandelion, and Chinas especially to deal with the buttercup. Dense stocking of the birds for a short time is most effective. Chinas have slightly different habits from the Greylag-derived geese, and they particularly like to root up creeping stems. Turf well grazed by geese will eventually become very short and fine.

There are some weeds that geese will not touch. Nettles and plantain will remain, but these are easy to remove with a selective weedkiller. On the other hand, docks and knotweed are very resistant to weedkiller, and will need to be controlled by hand weeding and cutting. The birds will not touch thistles, but if the young plants are broken at the base, the geese will eat down into the root and kill them.

Beware! As well as keeping down your lawn, geese will also 'weed' your best flowers, vegetables and saplings, and they can be quite destructive. Brecons and Embdens, in partic-ular, will chew twigs and saplings, and ring-bark them. Protect these plants with a tube of netting or plastic wrapped around the trunk. Greens such as lettuces and brassicas will also be snapped up. We had one bird that even, most unusually, went for our leeks. If your vegetable garden is important, keep the geese out of there until after the crop. At that point, they will be useful in keeping the growth down and will manure the garden.

As pets, which will add interest to the garden and weed the crazy paving, Chinas are probably the best choice. They do not chew bushes, but they may dig up small patches on the lawn in order to dunk mud and roots into the bucket. Chinas were commonly employed as weeder geese in America in cotton fields, and in crops such as mint. They might work for weeding strawberries too, early in the season, and after the crop has been harvested.

If you are gardening with geese, bear in mind that certain plants are toxic for them. Foxgloves are poisonous, and are best cut down. Daffodils are reputed to be dangerous too, but our geese never seem to touch them. They simply tread them into the ground.

EGGS

For Eating

If large quantities of eggs are required, the best breed is definitely a utility strain of Chinese, although these eggs are small. All birds will produce more eggs if they are given supplementary wheat and pellets.

Pellet quality has improved since 1996 legislation banned mammal remains from processed animal foods. Higher protein levels in such foods are now typically achieved by adding fishmeal to starter crumbs, and soya and oilseed residues to maintenance pellets. Pelleted foods will contain additives, including vitamins and trace elements such as copper and selenium, which are desirable, but also antioxidants as a preservative. A standard poultry layer's ration may also contain an agent, to enhance the yellow of the egg yolk. This agent is not added to mainte-nance and breeder pellets produced by some companies for waterfowl and pure breeds of poultry.

Visit your local feed mill and find out what they produce and what is in the food by reading the labels carefully. The egg yolks from geese that graze are always rich in colour, and it is quite unnecessary to have a colour enhancer in the diet of the birds if you want to sell their eggs for eating.

The quality of the contents of a goose egg is usually very good. Waterfowl eggs contain less water than chicken eggs, and the protein content is higher. When the egg is cracked on to a plate, or into a frying pan, the yolk sits up high and the albumen forms a neat disc, instead of running away. It is this property of the goose egg that makes it so suitable for baking. It also makes a good omelette, but chicken eggs are better for making meringue.

For Painting and Decoration

For eggs that are large enough for painting, you will have to keep the larger breeds. Toulouse geese generally do not lay a massive egg, but Embdens, or birds bred from their crosses, such as large Buff Backs, are better. Egg size is frequently 6–8oz (175–225 grams). Double-yolked eggs can reach 12oz (350 grams), but they are not very good for 'blowing'. The shell is often thin and breaks into radial cracks when it is punctured.

Eggs for painting first have to be blown of their contents. This is done by piercing a larger hole in one end, and a smaller one at the pointed end. The contents are broken and mixed up with a knitting needle and then blown out. You can do this orally but a small pump may also be used. Once the contents have been removed, the eggs should be thoroughly washed out with bleach, and then dried. The holes made at the ends of the egg are blocked by ornaments or concealed with materials that mimic the eggshell.

If eggs are required for both hatching and painting, 'incubator clears' can be used. After 5–7 days in the incubator, and with the use of a good candling lamp, you can be certain of distinguishing the fertiles from the infertiles. The useless eggs will not be smelly; and will look little different in content from an egg that has not been incubated. Apparently, in the past the cake industry would use infertile hen

Fig 55 A decorated egg, delicately sawn in half and made into a hinged, satin-lined container

Fig 56 Painted and decorated eggs in competition at a show. There are also classes for waterfowl eggs, for the whole egg itself, as well as for contents. Generally, duck eggs are shown, as they are available for a longer season. Eggs need to be fresh for the 'contents' to look good

and duck eggs candled at 2–3 days in baking, but the practice was stopped well before the salmonella scare. It may be possible to use such eggs (cooked) for dog food, but you might prefer not to.

The market for goose eggs for painting is limited, but it is also difficult to find a supply. A local college may provide an outlet.

For Exhibition

There is often an egg section at bird shows, and the most popular competition is among the painted or decorated eggs, entered by adults and by children. Decorated eggs differ from painted eggs in having various embellishments stuck to them.

The laying season of the goose is quite short, compared with that of the duck or hen, so it is often not possible to show goose eggs in any other section because of the timing. If the show does coincide with the laying season, waterfowl eggs often do well where the egg is judged for content, because the yolk looks so rich and the albumen holds together so well. There are written standards for eggs in *British Poultry Standards,* and Poultry Club egg judges should be able to provide more information.

7 Exhibiting ————————————

Initially, we intended to keep geese just for the table, but we changed our minds after rearing the two cross-bred goslings given to my daughter as a birthday present (to be eaten at Christmas). They both turned out to be female and died of natural causes years later. Although we did breed a few birds from these for table purposes, we resolved that any further geese should be pure breeds, so there was a purpose other than eating them. Quality geese of a good size, and Brecon Buffs in particular, could be sold as stock birds; in our area of the Welsh Borders there was quite a high demand for these from farmers. However, the main fun of rearing pure breeds turned out to be in exhibiting them.

THE HISTORY OF EXHIBITIONS

According to Ambrose (1981), the idea of the exhibition began in the early nineteenth century, when village poultry shows were popular. The first National Poultry Show was held at the Zoological Gardens in London in 1845. It had goose classes for 'Common Geese', 'Asiatic or Knobbed Geese' and 'Any Other Variety'. The inclusion of poultry in the Great Exhibition of 1851, and Queen Victoria's personal interest in exhibition poultry, helped to increase the status of this section. Further impetus was given when the two most prominent agricultural societies in England – the Royal Agricultural Society and the Bath and West of England Society – began to include poultry sections in their annual shows in 1853. This encouraged poultry shows to be held all over England, and led to such events becoming a familiar part of agricultural life.

Before the show in the gardens of the Zoological Society in 1845, no geese had been exhibited alive in competition for prizes (Weir 1902). All ducks, chickens and geese were shown dressed for the table and, even as late as 1954, a description of dressed poultry was included in the Standards. However, the Victorian view of the exhibit had to change; exotic poultry, which were valuable breeding stock, imported at great expense, were a more interesting spectacle alive than dead.

NEW BREEDS

As long as contact between the different regions of the world was limited by slow transport and long distances, exotic specimens were a rarity, and usually arrived back in Britain skinned, stuffed or preserved. However, the Victorian transport revolution made it more likely that livestock would survive long journeys back from the Far East. The expansion of the British Empire, together with faster transport, led to the export of British species to Australia and North America, and the importing of plant and animal specimens to Kew Gardens and London Zoo.

The nineteenth century must have been an exciting time for bird fanciers. Having been limited to the English white Aylesbury duck and the Common goose, traders now began to introduce the Embden from the continent from 1815 (or even earlier), as well as the Toulouse and Sebastopol, and the Chinas and

Africans from the Far East. A tremendous interest developed in these newly imported breeds. They were painted, exhibited and written about in journals. As they began to be judged alive, there was a need to establish a standard, describing the bird's feathers and its size and shape.

STANDARDS

The first *Standard of Excellence in Exhibition Poultry* was published in 1865 and, in waterfowl, included the Aylesbury, Rouen, Black East Indian and Decoy (Call) duck, together with the Embden and Toulouse geese. The birds were judged on a fifteen-point scale. The Poultry Club Standard of 1886 adopted a hundred-point scale, and this has been retained ever since. Over the years, more breeds have been added, as they have been imported or have become more numerous. For example, the Roman was first standardized in 1954, the Brecon Buff in 1934 and the American standard for the African adopted in 1982.

Until 1982, the indigenous geese of Britain (the Common goose of 1845) were neglected in favour of the imported breeds and, even in 1982, the American standard for the Pilgrim was used. It had been given recognition as a breed in the USA, while it was ignored in Europe. The 1999 British Waterfowl Association standards at last give recognition to our farmyard breeds, as well as to the original farmyard breeds of the rest of the world.

The *Standard* is a very useful guide to knowing what each breed should look like and the Poultry Club 1997 edition has excellent colour photographs. Before buying or exhibiting geese, it is essential to be familiar with the standard bird.

THE SHOW

If you want to exhibit your geese, there is no need to jump in at the deep end. Go to a couple

---

Part of the schedule for a major show, indicating the breeds and colours officially recognized. This is a complete schedule, but also allows for newly imported breeds to be shown in the 'Any Other Variety' class. Experimental colours and breeds can also be shown in this class

Heavy Geese

1	African	m
2	African	f
3	Toulouse	m
4	Toulouse	f
5	Embden	m
6	Embden	f
7	American Buff	m
8	American Buff	f

Medium Geese

9	Brecon Buff	m
10	Brecon Buff	f
11	Buff Back	m
12	Buff back	f
13	Grey Back	m
14	Grey Back	f
15	West of England	m
16	West of England	f
17	Pomeranian	m
18	Pomeranian	f

Light Geese

19	Chinese White	m
20	Chinese White	f
21	Chinese Grey	m
22	Chinese Grey	f
23	Pilgrim	m
24	Pilgrim	f
25	Roman	m
26	Roman	f
27	Sebastopol smooth-breasted	m
28	Sebastopol smooth-breasted	f
29	Sebastopol frizzle	m
30	Sebastopol frizzle	f
31	Steinbacher	m
32	Steinbacher	f
33	AOV Non-standardized colour/breed goose	

of big shows first to eye up the competition, and assess how your geese match up to those on show. To get a good selection of geese, it is best to go to one of the larger British Waterfowl Association shows. The dates for these can be obtained from the BWA secretary, who can also give you the address of show secretaries. On request, they will supply a schedule of the breed classes offered at each event. Information is also available at the BWA Centre at Blackbrook World of Birds, at Winkhill in North Staffordshire.

The larger shows have a class for each breed and also a male and female class, so that the sexes are judged separately. At smaller shows this is less likely and, unless the judge is very experienced, the larger males tend to beat the females. There may be only one or two classes, such as Any Variety Goose or Gander. Sometimes, the classes are split into 'heavy' and 'light'. This means that Toulouse, Embdens, Africans and American Buffs go in the heavy section, and all the rest in the light. If a medium-weight class is offered as well, this will include Brecons, Buff Backs, Grey Backs, Pomeranians and West of England, with the remainder in the light class.

Shows require a good deal of planning, and you will need to fill in an entry form to book pens for the birds, and pay for these in advance. The show will produce a penning slip with your pen numbers, and this will either be posted in advance or given to you on the day. Shows always have a set of rules; these should be read carefully, as there is a certain etiquette to be observed. The larger shows also provide a catalogue and have good catering facilities and trade stands of interest to livestock owners. Some, including the East of England Autumn Exhibition, also have exhibits of other small animals and are a very good family day out.

Getting to the Show

Some exhibitors travel miles to get to the big events, and this requires a good deal of forward planning, even for just one or two geese.

The birds have to be clean for the show. Geese are naturally clean creatures, always preening and oiling their feathers, and, generally, if your birds are in good condition, they will be in show condition. All you will need to do to make them ready for a show is wash their bill, legs and feet with warm, soapy water. This is a lot less trouble than shampooing and blow-drying white Silkie hens, for example; you will already have put in the effort in the preceding weeks, by providing clean water and clean ground. This is vital, particularly for Sebastopols, which cannot be cleaned up specially for a show, and have to be kept in show condition all the time.

After you have cleaned the birds the day before the show they should be shut up for the night on absorbent bedding, such as sawdust or shavings, in their usual shed, otherwise they will shout all night and keep you awake. It is useful if they have been fed on wheat and pellets beforehand rather than grass, especially if they are white. Stains from grass droppings are difficult to remove. To avoid soiling the birds' feathers with droppings, always box the birds just before you leave so that as much food as possible has passed through the gut.

You will need to get up early in the morning to box the birds. The best bedding material for the boxes is a layer of paper (from a bag of pellets), followed by a layer of chopped straw, then whitewood shavings. The paper contains the bedding, the straw gives the bird a good grip with its feet, and the shavings are the best for mopping up any mess. The box itself should be well ventilated and large enough for the bird to stand up. Wire crates can be made from weldmesh, but the harsh wire can scrape the skin on the bird's beak. Some plastic poultry crates are good for small breeds, but you may have to make your own boxes, if you want permanent ones, out of wood and wire. Birds should not travel loose in a vehicle. Finally, make sure that the box is placed in a well-ventilated part of the vehicle. A sealed boot will not do. If the show is in summer, follow the recommendations for boxing on page 89, and think very carefully about going to the show at all if the conditions are extreme.

At this time, you will appreciate tame birds that are quiet when they are handled and talked to. Your voice should reassure your birds, and such birds will quickly adapt to show conditions, especially if they hand-feed.

Catching and Carrying Birds

Never run geese around or use nets when you want to catch them. Nets have to be used at large establishments, but there is no easier way of making birds nervous and suspicious. If the birds are tame, simply pick them up. Otherwise, drive them to their usual shed and pick them up in a confined space.

Some people handle chickens suspended by the legs, but geese (and ducks) should never be carried in this way. Waterfowl legs are not as strong, and you could injure the bird. It is also against Ministry regulations.

It may be necessary to catch hold of the bird by the wings or neck but, when you are carrying the bird, its weight should always be supported by your hand and arm. If you are right-handed, hold the bird with its body on your right arm, so that its neck is under your arm and its head is looking behind you.

Fig 57 The correct way to carry a bird: tuck the goose under your arm, so that you support its body and also control the wings. Hold the legs together if the bird is small and slim

Fig 58 Tame geese can be carried facing you. They feel more secure this way. They will not bite your face . . . really

Fig 59 Awkward customers should be carried under your arm. As well as holding the legs together with your right hand, hold the flights in the other hand, so that the bird cannot flap. A few birds are real biters: wear a thick jacket, so it does not matter what happens behind you

Your right hand should hold its legs together, and your left arm can be placed across its back, or even hold the flights of both wings together if the bird tries to flap.

Years ago, birds were sent off to shows by rail in poultry hampers, and regularly carried by the wings by show officials; this resulted in heavy birds returning home with dropped wings. Carrying the bird in one hand suspended by the wings strains the joints badly.

At the Show

Always make sure that you have placed your bird in the correct pen at a show, and remove any identifying material such as a leg ring. (Unlike dogs at dog shows, your birds are supposed to be anonymous.) Closed rings that will not come off, since they have been placed on the bird as a gosling, are allowed. Correct pen numbers are essential, both for judging and bird identification.

Geese generally behave well in a show pen. Chinas and Africans, especially, will deliberately show off and display themselves. Very tame geese can either be watchful and amenable, or spend most of their time trying to get out of the pen. After one or two shows, however, all geese generally settle well and become quite used to the situation.

Fig 60 'Little and Large' – a Champion Brecon Buff goose next to the Champion Drake (a Call, the smallest breed), at Malvern's Champion Waterfowl Exhibition, 1997

Fig 61 Christopher Marler's Champion African gander has his photograph taken. The 'Best of Breed' winners and Show Champions are often photographed for reports in journals such as Fancy Fowl

Fig 62 The author's waterfowl awards in the 1997 season. These were mostly won by the Africans and Toulouse, but the Runners and Calls also scored

Fig 63 Special trophies for a special event at Malvern's Three Counties Showground in November 1987 – The BWA Celebration Show, marking 'One Hundred Years of Waterfowl' for the association

The birds are best fed and watered after judging, so that they do not get wet, and so that the drinking utensils do not identify your birds. If you are early penning, give the birds a quick drink and feed before the judging, but remove the bucket. If you know the judges, do not try to engage them in a conversation before the show; make yourself scarce and allow them to get on with their job unhindered.

Judging and the Results

If you have bought quality stock, you might be very lucky as a beginner, but you cannot expect to win prize cards on your first outing. If you do get a red card, remember that it may be because the quality of the opposition is not very high. You need to visit several shows before you really size up how good or bad your birds are.

In a class of mixed breeds, it may be difficult to understand the judge's placings. There is much to learn about each breed, and a judge at a smaller show may be expected to be familiar with all 37 breeds of waterfowl. Not surprisingly, he or she may not be an expert in all of them. If the result is puzzling, ask for the judge's opinion, and also ask around the other exhibitors. Waterfowl standards are, after all, arrived at by a consensus of opinion and are largely based on aesthetics. Judging should be according to the *Standard*, but this gives a very brief description and can never account for each judge's personal preference, and knowledge (or lack of it) of the finer points.

8 Table Birds

Keeping geese can produce organic food economically, which can be marketed for what seems to be a very high price at Christmas. Commonly quoted prices for dressed birds in the early 1990s were £2.80 a pound, very expensive compared with broiler chicken. This disparity in price can be accounted for by the costs of production, and the limited extent of the supply.

FEEDING

To rear geese well on a small scale, the birds should have extensive range on pasture that is well grazed by cattle and sheep. To keep costs down, a large part of their diet, at least in the middle stages of production, should come from grass. Geese cannot be expected to survive on restricted, dirty grazing. They can suffer from diseases such as coccidiosis and leg infections, and there will be a build-up of parasites, such as gizzard worm. Breeders who stock intensively avoid these problems by feeding the birds almost all of their diet from pellets and wheat, which is part of the reason why pure breeds from breeders are much more expensive than table geese from farms. Intensive feeding is uneconomic for Christmas production for the table because the birds are up to 8 months old when ready for slaughter, considerably older than broiler chickens, which are 6–7 weeks old.

Birds fed entirely on grass do not grow in size as well as those that are fed supplements. There will be a progressive deterioration in size over the generations, and this is probably why farmers often need to go regularly to breeders for new stock. In our area of Wales, for example, the cross-bred farm geese tend to lack size, so Embdens are sought after to improve the birds. If the goslings do not grow in stature to equal the parents it does not matter, if they are intended for slaughter. The object is to keep costs down and the birds are kept in store condition on grass feed between, for example, four weeks old and mid-autumn.

If larger, quality birds are required for the market, supplementary feed will be needed, not only in the first few weeks, but also throughout the period to slaughter. Our farm-reared Buff Backs weighed (bought per lb in the feathers) 25–27lb (11.5–12.25kg) in October. The farmer who had reared them understood well that good feeding puts on bone and muscle. The birds were given a ration of barley and pellets throughout their life, and were not confined (except at night) up to slaughter. Incidentally, this farm does not buy in geese for re-sale, because the product is likely to be a disappointment to their regular customers.

The flavour of goose is also improved by feeding cereals. Geese fed exclusively on grass may be plump enough, but they can taste 'fishy'. Apparently, geese were once reared along the banks of the River Severn by an old lady, the geese swimming the waters and getting the grazing for free. When buyers came to the Christmas auction at the Shrewsbury market, those in the know avoided these birds because of their dreadful taste.

SLAUGHTER AND PREPARATION

If your home-reared geese are entirely for your own consumption, you may wish to kill the birds much earlier as plump, mainly grass-fed, tender summer geese. The traditional time for slaughter used to be at Michaelmas (29 September). If the birds are for personal use, you are not bound by regulations relating to carcass preparation, but you are obliged to slaughter them in an accepted way.

If the dressed birds are to be sold, you will need to check with the Ministry of Agriculture about the regulations for the facilities required in the preparation area. There have been frequent changes in legislation over the past few years.

The birds should not be fed prior to killing, so that the gut may be clear of food. This makes preparation easier, and also more hygienic, as the gut is less likely to burst. The old-fashioned method of bleeding birds to death is illegal. The birds should be stunned by an electrical stunner, and then bled while suspended. You must read the ministry regulations on this. Care should be taken with the wings, which flap quite strongly after death.

Other approved methods of slaughter are by decapitation, or neck dislocation. Dislocation is done by hand with smaller birds, but the length of the neck and body of the goose makes this impractical; the following method can be used instead. Hold the bird by the legs, its breast away from you, and its head and neck laid out across the ground facing towards you. Place a pole, such as a broom handle, across the back of the neck. First, applying only restraining pressure, elongate the bird's neck, legs and body until they are tight, while you are standing with bent legs and straight arms. When you are ready, stand with your full weight on the pole, with one foot on either side of the bird's neck. The dislocation will occur as you straighten your legs; thigh muscles are much

stronger than arm or back muscles.

The distance you need to pull is very small. The vertebrae are quickly and easily dislocated, and you need not fear pulling the head off. Pulling at 90 degrees to the line of the head clicks open the vertebrae and severs the spinal cord. Sometimes the blood vessels will rupture, so that blood spills out of the bird's mouth, but the bird is already dead at this stage.

I should emphasize that, if you are unfamiliar with the method, you should be shown by an expert how to do it. It is not something you would want to practise unsuccessfully.

I have also seen this method illustrated the other way around, with the goose breast facing towards you, and the bird's head facing away.

A similar result can be obtained by using the humane dispatcher, which can be obtained in different sizes for dealing with different species of birds. This is frequently advertised in magazines aimed at smallholders.

Birds should always be handled quietly prior to slaughter. If several are to be done, they should be herded into their shed as normal, and handled in small batches, so that they do not panic.

Plucking

Plucking and dressing the birds is no small task. Dry plucking is necessary if you want to save the goose down because, unlike chickens, you need to pluck the bird twice. First, remove the large outer feathers, then remove the down. This should be done after the carcass has cooled, as warm skin tends to tear easily. If quality down is required, with no soft, fleshy pen feathers, the birds must be in full feather and at least 16 weeks old. Alternatively, they can be killed when they have completed their first set of feathers, at 7–8 weeks. Appleyard recommended this for his Roman geese for economical table production. Avoid killing birds when they are moulting their first set of juvenile feathers, at 12–16 weeks old.

Plucking machines can be used with geese, but many small-scale producers use wet-plucking methods. A small, open-topped boiler is used to heat the water to about 65 degrees centigrade (149 degrees Fahrenheit). Then the bird is hung by a piece of string tied to the legs, and held in the water for 1½–2 minutes. To ensure that the water penetrates the feathers, they should be ruffled up under-water with a stick. Try this, then test the feathers to see if the time is correct. The feathers and the down should easily roll off, leaving a clean carcass. The advantage of using water at this temperature rather than boiling is that it is safer for you, and there is more leeway over the timing. The ADAS leaflet of 1981, for example, recommended up to 3 minutes. If you have no boiler, pouring boiling water into a metal container can also produce good results.

Gutting

The plucked bird should be hung in a cool, airy place, and will keep for several days like this if it has been dry-plucked. Hanging will improve the flavour and tenderness. Evisceration should take place in a clean area. If you put the carcass on to newspapers, the eviscerated contents can be rolled up inside, leaving no mess.

BREEDS FOR THE TABLE

Quantity production of goslings will only come from breeds that are prolific layers; those who wish to rear a flock of a hundred often buy their goslings at a day old or a week old from commercial producers. Commercial birds are often crosses rather than pure breeds. A good cross for the table, recommended in the USA, is a white China crossed with an average-size white Embden gander

(Acheson, 1954). The egg-laying capacity and hatchability comes from the China, and the slightly larger size from the Embden. Remember that the first cross will be the best, and that subsequent ones will give a great deal of variability in the offspring.

White Chinas make a good meal; their flavour is preferable to that of the brown China, and their carcass looks better too. However, the ganders need to be killed before maturity, preferably before 16 weeks old, otherwise they develop a stronger flavour. Browns are particularly difficult to feather, and a lot of dark fluff and pens are left behind.

When Roman geese were first introduced into Britain as small table birds they were ideal – they would lay 50–100 eggs a year, and their plump, round bodies were perfect for small ovens. However, today's exhibition Romans may not produce this kind of laying performance, which depends more upon the strain than the breed.

The Brecon Buff is the ideal small-scale production goose. It was originally produced as a hardy, economical farm goose. Larger than the Roman, it carries a relatively large amount of muscle for its size compared with other breeds, and can be fattened up easily after grass-rearing. The soft buff feathers pluck out more easily than white feathers, without tearing the skin, and leave a clean-looking carcass. They dress at 7–12lb (3–5.5kg) in weight, depending on the strain.

For large table birds you will have to opt for the larger breeds, which need more feeding. Pure-bred Embdens and Toulouse are un-suitable, because pure breeds are more difficult to hatch, and these large birds do need special care (see the chapter on rearing goslings). Also, in the Toulouse, the gullet and keel is wasted weight, while the Embden has a large frame with plenty of bone. Commercial Toulouse in France are a lighter-weight version of the English exhibition birds.

Commercial heavyweights are often Embden-Toulouse crosses; this produces an attractive, light grey bird, whose feathers shade to white on the neck. They are fast growers and outgrow their parents. Do not be tempted to use these first crosses as breeding stock for the next year's stock birds. It is the pure-bred parents that produce the first cross vigour, so the same parents should be kept. If, however, the parents were poor layers, it would be worthwhile seeing if the offspring are better. The Toulouse-Embden crosses in Victorian Britain increased the egg-laying capacity of English Embdens to 35, bettering by far the German strain's total of 15 (Parr, –1996).

The disadvantage of opting for a larger table breed is that you may have to keep a higher ratio of ganders for fertility, and replace the ganders more often than you would with light breeds. Older overweight birds become infertile; seven to nine years is the recommended breeding span for commercial ganders. If several geese are to be kept in a group for flock mating (as opposed to breeding pens), a ratio of one to five is possible with young light breeds, but even in flocks the birds will tend to settle eventually in pairs and trios as they get older.

EATING GEESE

Over-fattened geese, force-fed in confinement, are obviously much greasier than birds that have been out on range. Grass-fed birds that have been able to exercise are leaner; the fold of their intestines is separated by less fat, and the gut itself is different in quality, being much greater in diameter than that of the corn-fed bird. However, the older grass-fed birds tend to be a bit tougher, and less tasty. You will have to decide for yourself on the quality of the product. The quality of the feed will also determine whether you can market the bird as 'organic' or not.

Goose meat was originally alleged to be full of cholesterol, but, during the 1990s, this opinion seems to have changed. It has been observed that the rural French eat duck and goose quite frequently, and that they seem to suffer relatively few problems. However, there are few uses today for the goose fat; even Granny's Goose Grease Treacle Toffee recipe required only a spoonful, and using goose grease on a bad chest has certainly become a less popular practice in recent years!

Because of its high fat content, goose meat is very rich and filling. Servings can be quite small, therefore, and this is fortunate, since goose is so expensive per pound. A good deal of the weight is bone. A small goose weighing 10lb (4.5kg) should make a good Christmas meal for six, but the amount of meat will depend upon the breed and how well the bird has been reared. For example, a small white China goose should provide enough meat for six, as long as it was well fed.

9 Acquiring Stock

GETTING TO KNOW THE BREEDS

Once you have decided to buy a particular breed, because of its utility qualities, looks or behaviour, you will need to familiarize yourself with its characteristics, to make sure that you are acquiring genuine birds. When you respond to an advertisement offering 'Brecon Buffs', do not expect always to find Brecon Buffs. In general, breeds of geese (and ducks and poultry) are not widely known and, unless you happen upon someone who bought reliable stock from a breeder, or upon a breeder who exhibits his or her birds, there is no guarantee that the stock will be pure, or will even *look* like the breed it claims to be. Often, you will see 'Embdens' the size of middle-weight geese, and 'Chinese' which might have only a great-uncle of that type in their family tree. There are several ways of finding out what the breeds should be like *before* you start looking.

Shows for Poultry and Waterfowl

Since the 1970s, the number of poultry and waterfowl shows has increased dramatically. Summer county shows often have a small livestock tent, but these are frequently not well attended. Summer is the wrong time for showing waterfowl. It is often too hot to travel, the birds are in moult, and breeders are too busy rearing young stock. The main waterfowl shows are between September and March, when the birds are in full feather and the birds travel in better conditions in the lower temperatures.

To look at a specific breed, visit one of the largest shows, where there is a class for every breed. At the smaller shows, the only class might be 'Any Variety Goose or Gander'. Specialist goose breeders are not likely to bother entering such a class, so it is quite common to see geese of no particular breed exhibited. Compared with ducks, geese are not easy to show, so a good range of breeds can only be expected at the larger, more prestigious shows.

If you visit one of the larger shows, you may see several examples of the breeds that interest you, and you can look for the good and bad points of the birds, according to the judges. The advantage of visiting is that you will be able to see at first hand what constitutes a good bird, and also talk to their owners. Bear in mind that some people who show are not breeding the birds, whilst others may show once in a while, but are doing most of the breeding.

Visiting a Breeder

Having got to know your breeds at first hand and decided which one fits you and your purpose, visit a breeder with stock for sale. Some breeders are open to the public, so there is no problem in going to see the stock. Most breeders are not, but are quite willing to show anyone with a genuine interest in the birds around the stock. Make an appointment first.

Fig 64 A row of goose pens at Malvern, where 120–150 geese are on show, plus 800 or more ducks. (This show now takes place at Solihull Riding Club)

OTHER CONSIDERATIONS

Apart from your basic reasons for deciding to keep geese – as pets, for the eggs, for exhibition, or for the table – there are other factors that will influence your choice of breeds. Availability, price and ease of management will need to be taken into consideration before making any final decision. Remember that geese have a long life and, like any livestock, you have a commitment to looking after them, or to finding them another home if you can no longer keep them.

On the whole, geese are more expensive to buy than chickens and ducks, although this does not apply to rescue birds. Just as cats and dogs are abandoned by their owners, and end up with the RSPCA, unfortunately, waterfowl are abandoned too. If you want cheap birds as grazers, look no further than the local paper. Pure breeds, on the other hand, have had time and care lavished upon them by committed breeders for generations. They do not reproduce in large numbers, and some of the rarer breeds have only recently been imported. With a small supply, and a relatively high demand, the price will be high, and this has always been the case with good-quality Africans and Toulouse.

If you are just starting with geese, think about whether you want to begin with an expensive pair of birds, which may be very difficult to breed, or whether you should start with a breed with an easier reputation for management. In general, the heavy breeds such as the Africans, Toulouse and Embdens, are not for beginners. There can be problems with fertility and managing the birds because of their size. It is often better to start with something attractive of an average or lighter weight, which is in reasonable supply. The Brecon Buff and Chinas would come into this category, but not the Steinbacher, because of its relative scarcity. The Pilgrim is a very difficult breed in which to obtain quality, because of its specific colour requirements, but it is an easy bird to manage.

OBTAINING STOCK

Eggs

In the USA, it is common for goose establishments to sell eggs and goslings of the pure breeds, but these are probably not from the top exhibition lines. In Britain, breeders with quality stock rarely sell eggs. If, for example, a breeder has just imported birds from the USA, he or she is unlikely to be interested in this after the considerable expenses of importation. Importation from Europe is less expensive, but breeders still need to sell quality adult stock in order to cover their costs. In addition, since neither the fertility nor hatchability of goose eggs can be guaranteed, it would be difficult to arrive at a price that was fair for both vendor and buyer.

The only way to obtain eggs from quality birds in Britain is probably from a friend who has bought a good pair of geese and who does not want the eggs. Eggs advertised in the paper or on sale at markets are generally a waste of time, even if they are advertised as fertile pure breeds. The vendors may or may not know the breeds, but you will certainly not know how old the eggs are, how they have been stored, or even if they have already been incubated and are 'incubator clears' (infertiles).

Goslings

Pure-breed goslings are rarely sold by breeders, unless they are of a breed where the faults can be identified early, such as Buff Backs and Pilgrims. A pair of geese typically produces about eight goslings, and breeders aim to grow these birds to see which are the best. They will want birds for showing (since the breeding stock are not necessarily the show birds), as well as replacement stock for themselves, or stock to place with other reliable breeders, so that a line is not lost. Only this kind of co-operation allows good lines of birds to be kept going over a long period of time.

It is impossible to tell at first which of the goslings will make the best birds. Out of the same hatch there can be two superb exhibition birds, some good-quality breeders, and birds that are not considered good enough to breed from. The birds will vary in quality and, therefore, in price. Before thinking that

you may be buying 'breeder's rejects', remember that the average bird from a top-quality breeding pair is better than most of the birds you can buy elsewhere. We have bought such birds from breeders and done very well from them at shows. Equally, the birds we have kept for showing have been beaten by others we have sold; geese take a long time to develop.

Adult Birds

Adult birds are those which are in their second feathers and are at least 16 weeks old. Even after that age, the birds will continue to grow, especially the larger breeds.

Quality birds are unlikely to be sold before August, when some from the earlier hatches are 16 weeks old, but it can be much later for the heavy breeds, which take longer to mature. The better the quality of the birds you want, the longer you may have to wait. It is a good idea to go and see what is available, and place an order when you are clear about what you require. If you change your mind you should, of course, let the breeder know.

Older Birds

You do not want to buy aged birds past their prime, but if you are able to buy two- or three-year-old birds, particularly females, so much the better. However, guard against buying a female with a broken-down, distended abdomen; such birds often lay double-yolked eggs, and are also prone to infertility. Wild geese do not lay and breed until at least two to three years old. Domestic geese lay in their first year but, depending on the breed and strain, eggs from a yearling goose are not generally successful. She needs another year to mature before she will lay eggs of the full size.

Small eggs from a yearling goose may well hatch; they can even hatch more easily than larger eggs from a mature goose, but the goslings are usually smaller and weaker. These are fine for table birds, but they will not produce exhibition birds or breeders. This is particularly true of the medium-weight birds that are closer to the Greylag than to the Embdens and Toulouse. Brecons and Pilgrims, in particular, lose size in this way, whereas eggs from an American-strain yearling Toulouse can develop quite well.

Buying a two- or three-year-old gander can also be advantageous. Sometimes a late-hatched male can fail to breed in the following spring. On the other hand, I prefer young ganders in the heavier breeds. At one year old they have not reached their full weight and size and are much more agile for breeding. Toulouse in particular need to be fit, not fat, in the spring, and young ganders are generally more successful. Heavy-breed males often have to be pensioned off by the time they are 9 years old (or less), whereas ganders of a lighter-weight breed can still breed at 20 years old.

Unrelated Stock

Some specialist breeders will keep more than one breeding set of geese, and can sell pairs that are not closely related. If the birds' breeding background is unknown, try to acquire those that you think are unrelated. It is desirable not to use siblings, or a mother/son or father/daughter relationship, unless you know how long the geese have been inbred, or whether there have been any problems in the goslings. Breeders can only carry out this selective inbreeding if they know the stock's breeding record in detail, and know how the geese are performing.

Whilst selective inbreeding is successful in the hands of experienced breeders, it also results in recessive traits coming to the fore. The offspring may be small and have physical defects. More commonly, even if fertilization of the egg does take place, the germ will die early and a pair may seem to be infertile. New blood or out-crossing has the opposite effect, of introducing hybrid vigour. This is why commercial strains are so successful in comparison with pure breeds.

The rarity of some breeds is a result of the fact that they come from a very few imported individuals. There have been very few imports of Africans, for example, and it is unrealistic to think that you will get completely unrelated top-quality show birds; a certain amount of inbreeding will have to have taken place, in order to retain the breed's characteristics. This is, after all, how pure breeds are made.

The Right Sex

Most breeders are sufficiently experienced to know the sex of birds by their behaviour, but this is not a fool-proof method. This is particularly the case with Toulouse, especially if hatches from different parents are run together in a flock, and birds of the same sex turn out to be of different sizes. Vent-sexing is the only certain method. This is much easier to do in goslings at about 3–5 weeks old (see page 180) and in adults (see page 120). Errors are most likely to be made with juvenile birds at 8–16 weeks.

It is impossible to sex Toulouse reliably at this stage; if the record of the goslings has been lost, you will have to wait, to study the bird's behaviour. Vent-sexing juveniles is particularly difficult in this breed, and upsets these birds.

Prices and Availability

Some larger breeders have a price list, which they will send on receipt of a stamped, self-addressed envelope. However, it is much easier to give a list price for most poultry and ducks than for geese. Geese do not lay many eggs, are not nearly so numerous as ducks, and their breeding is much more erratic, even in the hands of experienced breeders. For this reason, they will be more expensive than most domestic ducks and their price may be available only 'on application'.

Not only are geese less reliable to breed, but breeders also tend to limit the numbers they breed to what they can reasonably rear in good conditions, even if there is a particularly good year for fertile eggs and hatchability.

Buying Stock from Sales

If you feel you are getting to know the breed you want by having studied good specimens at the shows and reading about it, you might like to start by buying birds at auction. Beware – you are buying the birds 'as seen', and you have no guarantee of the age of the birds, or even of their sex. I have known a 'trio' of geese (which means two females and one gander) turn out to be three males. This may have been a genuine error, as not every goose producer is proficient at sexing the birds.

Entering into any dispute over a vendor's description of birds could be quite time-consuming, and the vendor might not have the correct birds needed to rectify the situation. In contrast, if you buy direct from breeders, they will usually guarantee you the sex and the breed of the bird or birds that you buy.

Choosing Quality Birds

Shape

Assuming the birds you are going to buy are more than 16 weeks old, they will be in their adult feathers. By this age, the shape of the birds will be well developed, but it may still not be possible, especially in the heavier breeds, to determine how well the birds will turn out. The keel of the Toulouse, and the dual-lobed undercarriage and full weight of the Embden, do not fully develop until the birds are over two years old, so young birds

will have to be assessed in other ways for their potential.

Size, Colour and Carriage

Looking at parent birds will give you a good idea of their offspring's potential. In some breeds, such as the Toulouse and Embden, size is of great importance, and it is as well to choose big birds from the outset. In others, such as the Buff Back and the Brecon, colour and markings are more important, while in the Chinese the carriage and shape of the bird count for a lot. Read the standard descriptions of the birds carefully, and compare them and the photograph with the individuals that you intend to buy. In the coloured breeds, look for specific colour faults – such as white in the plumage of Brecon Buffs on the flights and under the beak – and avoid them.

General Faults

Apart from specific breed faults, there are general faults to look for and avoid when choosing stock. Never accept a bird already parcelled up in a box. A bird should always be picked up, and its weight checked. If it is too heavy, that can be rectified. A lack of weight could be related to underfeeding or worms, but the bird could also be ill. While you are holding the bird, check its eyes. Are they the right colour for the breed, and do they look healthy? Birds can have poor eyesight from an opaque growth over the pupil, and this will affect their behaviour. Also check the bird's feet and legs. The hocks and ankle should not be hot or swollen. The toes should be straight and the undersides of the webs should not be thickened or calloused in a young bird. (In older heavy birds and frizzle Sebastopols this will happen with age, and is unavoidable unless your ground and water are particularly good.)

Make sure you see the bird standing and moving. It should move easily and not limp. Any defect of the spine, such as a wry tail or problems with the neck, will become apparent. The way the bird stands is especially important in the Chinese, which should be showy and alert.

Fig 65 Birds that come to their owner will give far more
pleasure than those that run away. The Africans are usually
more confident than the Chinese

Fig 66 Train birds to like
tit-bits such as bread and
cauliflower trimmings.
Bread is an acquired taste;
goslings tend to learn the
habit from the adults, or
humans

Fig 67 Birds that have been handled quietly seldom become seriously aggressive. This Pilgrim gander is hissing because his goose has been picked up

Behaviour

Finally, the behaviour of the bird is important. Do the birds come to their owner, or run away? When they are moved they will undoubtedly be a bit nervous, but tame birds should soon adapt, whereas initially nervous ones rarely do. The behaviour of the birds is determined by both nature and nurture.

We have had breeder birds, bought as adults, which were a real problem to handle, because they meant serious business with their beaks and wings. Yet the offspring of these same birds were some of the gentlest, calmest birds we have bred, and were kept as companions to calm the more nervous Toulouse. In other breeds, even the most careful handling can result in birds that run away nervously as youngsters.

To a certain extent, temperament goes with a breed. Africans are usually the calmest and tamest of all, but can be intimidating because of their size and voice. Brecons should also have a calm disposition, but I have bought one that disproved the rule. His owner was quite keen on selling him, and I did wonder why, as he seemed quite a good bird and not too expensive. The gander was in front of the farm with the goose, and I agreed to buy him, because I liked the look of him. His owner made a fuss of driving him into a shed to pick him up and box him.

When the bird arrived at his new home, the first thing he did was to see off the resident stock gander. Having got into middle of the fight, I tried to drive the new gander back. The usual outstretched arms had no effect. The bird sidled up to me meaningfully, neck arched, and a glint in his eye. I now knew why his owner had wanted to drive him into the shed. I picked up a stick, the ultimate deterrent for driving geese. (Geese usually unfailingly behave well for a stick; little goose girls in Victorian pictures are able to drive great flocks of Embdens, as long as they are wielding one.) This Brecon Buff now turned his gaze on the stick. He obviously had no intention of backing off. He raised his wings, and began to beat at and bite the stick. I threw it down, and he attacked it even more. He must have spent a good five minutes trampling it, chewing it and talking about it, before he decided to give it a rest and wander off. Remember, not all individual birds will live up to the reputation, good or bad, of their breed, and each bird must be assessed on its own merits.

PART THREE: MANAGEMENT OF ADULT STOCK

10 New Birds ─────────────

TRANSPORT AND ARRIVAL

Before going to collect new birds, think about containers for carriage. A large, strong cardboard box, perhaps of the kind used to pack a television, with several holes (3 x 2in/8 x 4cm) cut out for ventilation, may seem ideal. However, you will need to bear in mind the time of year and use your common sense. Many waterfowl are bought in the summer, as the goslings come up to adult feathers, but this is the worst time of year for transport, because of the heat. Imagine what it would be like sitting in a well-insulated cardboard box, under a goose-down duvet. Geese over-heat rapidly in these conditions and can die even after a journey of one hour.

If it is hot, birds must be boxed individually. In a pair or trio, they will suffer from the accumulation of body heat. They should be transported in a crate made out of wooden slats, weldmesh, or in a perforated plastic poultry crate of a design that allows free air circulation. Unfortunately, most poultry crates are not big enough for a goose, and you may have to resort to a box. Cut off the flaps and tie (with string or plastic electrical ties) a piece of chicken wire across the top as a lid. The birds must be securely restrained for transport.

A sealed boot is not suitable for the birds. They must have a good air supply into the car to keep them cool. Always park the car in shade, so that the vehicle is cool, keep the boxes in the shade before packing, and do not

Fig 68 *When birds are moved, small breeds (which might be able to fly) should be clipped. Only clip the primary feathers up to the flight coverts*

Fig 69 *Clip about six feathers on one wing only. If it attempts to fly, the bird is unbalanced, so it gives up*

put the birds into the vehicle until you are ready to go. If birds are distressed by heat on the journey back, put them straight out on to water to cool them, and to allow them to drink.

In many ways, new geese are easier to manage than new chickens or ducks, but more difficult in other ways. They are more intelligent and need sympathetic handling if you are to get the best out of them. A tame pair of geese will be no problem for their new owner. Put straight into their new shed, they can be let out after ten minutes. Most birds, except for flighty Chinese, will not run off (as upset ducks sometimes do), and they will remember the shed when driven back to it later in the

evening. After a couple of nights of being driven into the shed this becomes a simple routine.

CLIPPING

If the new birds seen nervous and you are worried about them flying off, clip five flight feathers off just one wing. Using a pair of scissors or sharp secateurs, snip each flight where it meets the coverts. This means you clip the flight about half-way along its length. If the birds do try to fly, the unbalanced wings will put them off.

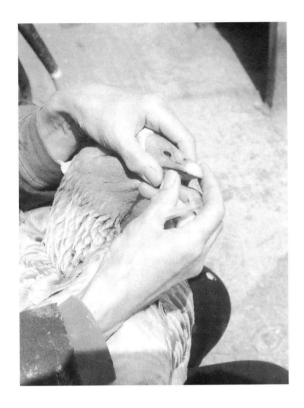

Fig 70 Worming a goose: hold the crown of the head in the left hand and open the beak

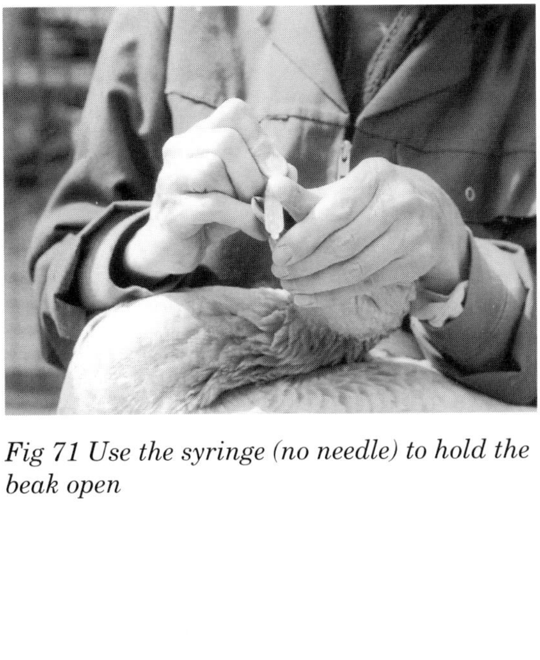

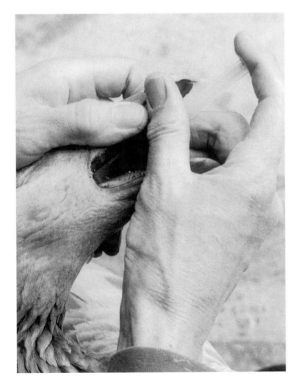

Fig 71 Use the syringe (no needle) to hold the beak open

Fig 72 Squirt the liquid wormer down the throat

Geese that are accustomed to flying around can manage to fly away quite easily, especially if they forage on range, and are light. However, most domestics will not bother, unless they are frightened. They may try to escape if certain conditions prevail, for example, if they live on a hill with a good lift into a head wind. The only goose we ever (almost) lost was one who was light after sitting; having had a mad rush around the pool, she took off in the excitement of the freedom. She disappeared down the valley, but the following morning she responded to our calls from just the next field, and we managed to retrieve her.

WORMING ON TRANSFER

Geese can carry a number of parasites, the most harmful of which is the gizzard worm. All geese should be wormed on transfer from one place to another; if this were routinely done, it would lower the incidence of this pest. Always ask if and when the birds have been wormed, and do the worming yourself if necessary. For dosage and medication, *see* the section on diseases. The parasite proliferates by eggs being passed out with the droppings and being picked up from the pasture. This is why litter from the sheds should be used elsewhere, and why geese raised entirely on grass need extensive, clean grazing.

11 Giving the Birds What They Need

HOUSING

Security from Predators

Before obtaining new stock, you will need to plan fencing and housing because the birds must be kept either in a fox-proof pen, or they must be shut up at night. If you have a farm or smallholding, there is no problem. There is often a suitable outhouse, and the geese can graze out with sheep during the day. Sheds need to be secure against polecats, mink, foxes and badgers. Vermin can squeeze through very small holes when hungry, and badgers are known to pull wooden sheds and wire mesh apart. In a badger-free area, wooden sheds are fine, but a brick shed with a solid door is safer if there are badger setts about.

If you intend to rear goslings with the geese, the accommodation will also have to be rat-proof. This generally means a concrete floor or a new wooden shed, as rats will soon work their way through old, rotting materials.

Sheds

A pair or trio of geese can be housed quite happily in a shed four feet square (not a kennel). This floor size allows 5–8 square feet per bird. The shed will need to have a large door, so that you can clean it out easily. Geese do not require expensive nesting boxes or perching bars, and a plain floor of exterior grade plywood or tongue and groove boarding is fine.

Most new wooden sheds will have been treated with a preservative, and you should allow a reasonable time to elapse after treatment for the fumes to escape. If you want to treat an existing shed with creosote, the stock will have to be re-housed elsewhere for at least a couple of weeks to allow the smell to subside. The fumes are an irritant to the throat and eyes, and the stock should not be subjected to this. For this reason, only the exterior of the shed should be treated after purchase.

Wire mesh for ventilation is essential. This can be in a window in the door, but it is better at a higher level; use weldmesh if there are determined foxes in the area. The opening should face away from the prevailing wind and rain, so an entrance facing north-east is usually best in Britain. A roll-down flap tacked over the mesh will keep the shed warmer and drier when necessary, offering protection from north-east winds and snow.

Many garden centres stock sheds designed for general garden use, and these are often ideal for geese, sometimes with slight adaptations, such as mesh instead of glass in the door. The *Yellow Pages* will give you plenty of information, and there are often sheds for sale in newspapers' classified advertisements. If you buy second-hand, bear in mind that the shed may be infested with red mite if it has been used for poultry; avoid any shed that may be thus infested.

Shutting Up

If you have tried to drive chickens, you will know how difficult this task is; these birds seem to have no logic. Geese are different.

Fig 73 Suitable housing for a pair of geese – a 4 × 4ft dog house (with sleeping ducks). Geese do not need complicated poultry houses with perches and nesting boxes. A secure, well-ventilated box with a flat floor is sufficient

Fig 74 A 6 × 4ft 'Wendy House' with a weldmesh window, suitable for this trio of Brecon geese. Look in garden centres for various designs

Once they have been put in their new shed, they will usually remember what it is for and where they are supposed to go. You may drive them easily by using outstretched arms to guide them, and if they have been accustomed to being in a shed (rather than a fox-proof pen), they should drive easily. Always move slowly, talk to the birds and use hand signals as well. Geese understand pointing, especially at food!

Birds that are unused to living inside at night may need to be encouraged in the right direction by a stick, but be careful not to cause panic. Geese seem to have an instinctive sense of danger from long, tubular objects that look like snakes, such as sticks, and hosepipes lying on the ground.

Bedding and Cleaning

Grass-fed geese produce copious droppings, while those on concentrated food produce less mess. The bedding is basically to mop up the mess and absorb moisture, so that the birds' feathers stay clean and waterproof. The bedding also keeps the birds warm in winter and is more comfortable for their legs. Birds kept in dirty conditions often have their legs encrusted with muck and develop a flat, calloused area behind the hock. In really cold weather the birds will tuck their feet up into their flank feathers to keep warm, so that only their breast rests on the ground. This is why it is important to provide clean bedding, to keep their under-body feathers in good condition in winter.

The litter available will depend on the area in which you live. I have seen peat and chopped bracken recommended, but the most commonly available materials are wood shavings (sold in bales, untreated with preservative) and straw. Chopped straw is easier to handle than long pieces when cleaning the shed, and can be topped up more easily with small amounts of straw or wood shavings over the week. Bales of dust-extracted chopped straw may be available at your local agricultural store, but this material is still not as good as white wood shavings which generate less ammonia than straw bedding.

If rough sawdust from a timber yard (not fine sawdust from a carpenter) is available, this is a good bedding material, especially in summer. It must be preservative-free. The sawdust will last for about a week, with topping up, before it should be discarded. After a week, maggots from manure flies will be growing, and the sawdust is, therefore, best removed.

In cold winter weather, if the bedding is still dry, it should be left to accumulate. One method to reduce work and keep the geese comfortable is to have a shed without a wooden base, which rests directly on the earth. Litter placed on the earth will biodegrade, and excess moisture will drain away. In theory, you can just keep adding litter in small amounts to the top; this will probably work well on a free-draining soil, but not so well on clay. The shed is also not rat-proof and needs a weldmesh base, which protrudes about 12in (30cm) beyond the edge of the house, to stop foxes or badgers digging in.

Discarded material, composted in a heap for some time, seems to make a good fertilizer on pasture. Human urine will rot straw quickly and effectively. I tend not to put discarded muck back on to the goose area, as this might cause a build-up of parasites.

Fig 75 A 2-gallon bucket of water is sufficient for a trio of geese if it is re-filled twice a day in hot weather. The bucket also contains wheat; wild birds will not be able to eat it, so there is less wastage this way. These two mature Pilgrim females show characteristic white face markings, or 'spectacles', which are the trademark of the breed

Fig 76 A shallow concrete pool on an incline. This is a bit shallow for geese (these Call ducks are tiny), but shows how land on a slope can be used to advantage to flush out and re-fill pools

Fig 77 This pool on a natural stream has been built with concrete shuttering. The floodgate allows for occasional heavy discharge into the fox-proof pen

WATER

Drinking Water

Geese must have water available for them to wash and clean their nostrils and eyes. The minimum for a pair of geese is a 2-gallon bucket of water per day in winter; this will need to be replenished frequently on a hot day in summer. The advantage of buckets is that the water is from a clean source daily and can also be used for feeding (*see* below). If it is topped up regularly, the geese will also be able to dip and throw water over themselves, to help oil their feathers. In this way, they can keep themselves in good condition without swimming water, although show-condition birds do need to bathe.

Small geese can up-end and drown in a bucket, stuck head downwards, so choose a bucket of an appropriate size. Birds that consistently knock buckets over, by jumping on top of them to get a better wash in the breeding season, and trying to mate in the bucket, need a bigger bath or a bucket inside a rubber tyre, so they cannot knock it over.

Buff Back Pair. Buff Backs are 'pied' or saddleback geese, produced from crossing buff geese with white geese (though not as a first cross)

Old Grey Chinese goose. Grey (also called Brown or Fawn) Chinese are almost identical in colour to the Asiatic wild Swan Goose. The domestic birds have a shorter, deeper body and a pronounced knob on the head, which has developed since domestication

Buff Back goose. This strain is a large, practical farmyard goose weighing well over the standard weight of 16–20lb.

White Chinas

Steinbacher pair

*Steinbacher goose,
the head showing
dark serrations
and bean on the bill*

Buff Toulouse goose

A pair of frizzle Sebastopols at Folly Farm

Embden goose, a traditional English type.
She has a deep, short bill and pronounced
feather partings on the neck

Embden gander, imported German type. His
head is shallower and the bill
proportionately longer than the English
birds. The German Embdens have a more
trim body than the heavier English types

Brown Chinese Gander typical of the style of
Chinese favoured in the show pen in Britain
today. He shows a short, wedge-shaped body
and arched neck in contrast to the coarser
utility Chinese

Brown Chinese goose. The knob is smaller in
the goose than the gander. She has the
characteristic white feathers around the base
of the bill

Exhibition pair of Toulouse

Smooth-breasted Sebastopol preening. The trailing feathers fall mainly from the thigh coverts and the scapular feathers

Brecon Buff goose showing the typical pink bill which, together with her smaller size, distinguishes her from the American Buff

Buff Toulouse are, as yet, unusual in Britain

Head study of Grey Toulouse pair

Pilgrim geese

Keeping in step. These eight-week-old Chinese are already showing which are female and which are male by the difference in their height. The African gander is the same age, but almost twice their weight

African goose. The cream dewlap and throat contrasts well with the brown stripe of the neck, the same colour pattern as the Swan goose

Pair of Buff Africans at Blackbrook. This new colour was imported in 1995 by Christopher Marler

Pair of Brown Africans. These Heavy Geese, hand reared, are very tame and can be taken anywhere. They show off well at exhibitions

American Buff geese with Toulouse

Roman geese are small and neat

Grey Back geese. These striking birds are from German Pomeranian stock, but are dual-lobed (incorrect for the standard Pomeranian)

Bar-headed geese with single Swan goose. Wild Bar-heads have an extensive range in Central Asia but are unlikely candidates for domestication because of their small size. They migrate at over 29,000ft, passing over the Himalayas to over-winter in India

Red-breasted geese breed in northern Russia and over-winter further south in regions around the Black Sea. These brightly coloured birds are the smallest wild goose and so were not a good species for domestication

Pilgrim female showing characteristic face marking

Wary Swan geese, ancestor of the domestic Chinese and African

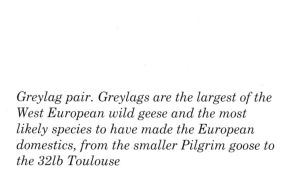

Greylag pair. Greylags are the largest of the West European wild geese and the most likely species to have made the European domestics, from the smaller Pilgrim goose to the 32lb Toulouse

Fig 78 Swimming water is always appreciated and keeps birds in show condition. Activity on the pool keeps it free of fine sediment. The Call ducks and Appleyards also help

Fig 79 Pools are especially appreciated on hot days, when wing-beating on the water creates a shower

Swimming Water

Swimming water is more important for some breeds of goose than for others. If the pasture is good and there is little mud, the birds will stay clean without washing water. On muddy ground, bathing is essential for Toulouse geese, which otherwise become caked underneath with mud. Sebastopols also need to wash their underparts. Female Sebastopols are a sorry sight in the breeding season when they have been 'trodden' by (mated with) a muddy gander. Since the birds prefer to mate on the water, the females stay a lot cleaner if the gander's feet are clean. Water is preferred for mating, but it is only essential for large, heavy birds.

The birds do enjoy water, so you may want to build a pool for their water supply, but it will quickly become fouled up with droppings and, in a hot summer, it will become smelly and a possible source of disease. I have seen a pool constructed quickly in the form of a hole in the ground lined with heavy-duty polythene, but the claws of the birds tend to rip the liner, and the water becomes a cesspit very rapidly. Children's fibreglass paddling pools have been used successfully for geese, but it does need to be located where it can be emptied into a drain. The best type of pool for geese is a concrete one, in which you can pull out a plug to allow the waste water to drain into a culvert or ditch.

A pool does not need to be deep to keep the geese happy – 6in is plenty for washing and mating. The sides should be of a roughened material and inclined, so that goslings do not drown. The edges of the pool tend to become fouled up with droppings and rather muddy, but rounded gravel can be used to keep the area cleaner. The droppings and mud wash down through the gravel if it is deep enough. If you are lucky enough to have a natural spring or stream, small dams made of bricks and concrete or railway sleepers provide excellent pools; these need to be carefully maintained, as they become sediment traps. There are two great advantages to running

water; it stays cleaner, and, in severely cold winter weather, it does not freeze. Such a pool will become the favourite place for a goose to warm its feet in a cold spell.

FOOD AND FOOD SUPPLIERS

Grass

Geese are natural grazers; goslings instantly know that green is good. Grass is undoubtedly the cheapest way to keep and rear geese, as long as it is of a high quality. It is not, however, a complete food for the year. Grass is only a good food if it is kept short and sweet, less than 4in long.

The nutritional value of grass varies over the year. The protein content is high, rivalling that of starter crumbs, in the spring and early summer, but it declines rapidly after July, and remains low over the winter months. The high protein content therefore corresponds with the main growing season for both the grass and the goslings. Adult geese on farm range, grazed with sheep and cattle, need little, if any, supplementary food over the spring and summer. However, geese on restricted range, where they are the only animals eating the grass, need wheat and pellets if they are to stay healthy.

Wheat and Pellets

Wheat is a good basic food, higher in protein than barley and maize, although its protein content (9–12 per cent) varies with the variety and year of production. Barley is better used as a fattening food rather than a maintenance food. The whole grains are rather coarse and sharp, so it must be fed with plenty of sand available for the geese, or fed as rolled barley. Oats are said to be good for feather quality, especially in Sebastopols. The grains are rather thin and spiky and, if rolled, become floury. My birds have never been keen on cereal grains other than wheat, which seems more palatable.

Birds do not like change in their diet and it takes time for them to adapt.

If the grazing is good, wheat can be fed at the end of the day. The geese should eat as much as they want over a twenty-minute period before shutting up. If the grazing is poor or dirty, wheat should be fed ad lib. This is best done by putting roughly the amount the geese will eat in the water bucket. The wheat is softened by soaking in the water, and is milled up better in the gizzard. Wild birds cannot get at the food, although squirrels will learn about it and sit on the edge of the bucket and scoop handfuls out. Adult geese may eat up to 7oz (200 grams) of wheat in the winter, but less in the summer with the warmth and the greater amount of grass.

In general, geese prefer wheat to pellets, but Toulouse really seem to like manufactured food and keep weight on much better with a ration of pellets. Unlike Pilgrims, they have not been bred for a hard life, and are not such good food converters. In addition to the wheat under water, give Toulouse geese a few ounces of pellets each morning and evening.

There is no need to feed the geese in the shed overnight. They should not be left dry food without water and, if they are given a bucket in the shed, they will make a sloppy mess of the bedding. In hot spells of weather in the summer, make sure that too much wheat is not left under the water, as it will start to ferment and go sour.

Specialist wildfowl pellets are available, but if you search around for a local food mill, using the Animal Feed section of the *Yellow Pages*, you should be able to make some savings. For example, poultry grower pellets (at £2 a bag less than the specialist product) and layers' pellets designed for hens may be suitable for the goslings. Check that the use-by date has not been passed. Wheat lasts indefinitely and, even if you only use a small amount, is cheapest bought by the bag from a farm outlet, or direct from a farm.

Pellets may contain undesirable additives, so you need to read the label carefully. Egg-yellow colouring is added to hen-laying rations, for example, and you may prefer to switch to a waterfowl breeder ration in the spring. This will contain more protein (16 per cent) than a maintenance ration, achieved by the addition of fishmeal, which seems to do the geese good, although they are herbivores. Growers' pellets may include a coccidiostat, designed to reduce the incidence of coccidiosis in chickens. Geese suffer less frequently from this condition than chickens do, and the coccidiostat may be harmful for waterfowl. You must check with the company's nutritionist first; if there is some doubt about the additive's suitability, coccidiostat-free duck pellets may be available. Pellets also contain trace minerals such as selenium, copper and magnesium, plus added vitamins.

As long as the geese have access to green grass, they are unlikely to run into deficiencies. Only birds kept in yards, and for too long indoors, will suffer such problems.

Food Containers

Food is much better put in a container than thrown on the ground. The geese can pick it up more easily, and there is less wastage. Look for a receptacle that is heavy and has as broad a base as possible, as the geese will tread on the edge, and risk tipping it over. Non-tip dog bowls are good for small amounts of food. Eltex troughs are a good design for larger numbers of birds. Old saucepans with the handles removed are useful; never throw away old kitchenware, as it might come in useful for feeding and rearing.

SPACE FOR GRAZING

There is no set rule for the amount of land you need if you are to keep a pair of geese. It depends on how much food you are prepared to feed them, to supplement their diet of grass. The number you can keep on a space such as a large garden will also depend on the type of soil in your area, free-draining soils creating less mess than clay, which encourages water to lie on its surface. The smaller the space you have, the more important it is to shut the geese up at night, rather than leaving them loose in a fox-proof pen. Goslings, in particular, produce a lot of droppings. If the birds are confined to a shed overnight, the muck can be removed from the premises and the grass stays cleaner.

DIGESTION

Storing Food for Digestion

Unlike the chicken, the goose does not have a crop to store food, but its oesophagus and proventriculus (where the alimentary canal broadens before it joins the gizzard) fulfil a similar function. In the evening, geese will often stuff this long tube from mouth to gizzard before they are shut up, so that they have an overnight food supply. Some birds will stuff themselves so much that their neck can look deformed, and feel absolutely solid. This can temporarily impede their breathing. They do this especially when they are young, because goslings have such a huge food demand in order to keep up with their growth rate. Adults also do this in the winter months, when they know they have a long night ahead; the gut has a very rapid through-put of only two hours, and they are attempting to make their food supply last as long as possible.

Sand and Grit

As food passes through the gizzard, grains of wheat and blades of grass have to be ground up. To extract the maximum amount of food, this large, muscular organ has to be supplied with sand and grit. Mixed poultry grit is essential for chickens but, for geese, sand is equally important. If you live in an area of sandy soil, the birds will eat this, or they will help themselves from piles of builders' sand. This material must be available all year; if geese do not have access to it, they will not thrive. During the breeding season, from January onwards, the goose must also have access to mixed poultry grit containing flint, oyster shell and limestone chips. Flint is the insoluble grit designed to grind up wheat in the gizzard. It is made of Silica ($SiO2$) and, although the crushed material can have very sharp edges, this does not seem to affect the gizzard adversely. If you prefer not to give the birds flint, you can buy oyster shell alone, but sometimes the pieces are rather large and need breaking up.

The laying goose will pick up the bits of limestone and oyster shell for additional calcium for her eggs. This mineral can also be supplied in the form of baked eggshells, which the birds will relish. Do not, however, use eggshells from other people's birds, as this could import disease.

Goslings may also appreciate the mixed grit, as well as sand.

Cellulose and Cell Sap

The domestic goose, in common with many of its wild relatives, is a grazer and can be raised on grass alone, although wild geese actually have a much more varied diet. It was once assumed that the goose had a digesting mechanism, so that cellulose could be used as an energy source, and the cell contents contained by the cellulose walls would also be made readily available for nutrition. In ungulates, including cattle and sheep, food is allowed to ferment in the rumen for about twelve hours, so that the cellulose can be converted by bacteria and ciliates into material appropriate for absorption into the bloodstream.

Mattocks (1971) investigated the alimentary canal of the domestic goose to see if bacteria played any part in the digestion of the grass. Previous authors had thought that the extension from the large intestine, known as the caecum, might resemble the rumen functionally as a cellulose digester. However, after experiments, Mattocks came to the conclusion that this was unlikely. The caecum was a 'congenial place for anaerobic bacteria' but showed no evidence of using food, and, with a capacity of 20ml, could not handle the large volume of food required daily. He concluded that the bacteria of the caecum provided a source of stimulation in order to produce antibodies; the goose needs its caecal flora to stay healthy, because there are virtually no bacteria in its alimentary canal.

Goose droppings consist largely of cylinders of 'chewed' grass, which stay, on average, only two hours in the alimentary canal. The pieces of grass can easily be seen, and are apparently little changed by the bird's digestive processes. After the grass is snipped by the beak and its marginal serrations, the blades are swallowed whole. No grinding action takes place until the grass reaches the gizzard, where grit and sand puncture the grass cells, rather than grind up the blades, which emerge relatively intact.

The grass shows little evidence of the kind of grinding caused by a cow. The goose has to rely on the gizzard to mill up the food, so that the juices from the grass can be used in the gut.

Characteristically, about three-quarters of an ounce (15 grams) of sand and stones, together with fibrous debris, are found in the gizzard. Mattocks concluded that it is

Fig 80 The beak of the goose is serrated along its margin for snipping grass

Fig 81 The alimentary canal of the domestic goose. Unlike the chicken, the goose does not have a 'crop' for storing food overnight. Food is stored in the proventriculus. The gizzard is a large muscle which mills up the food with the assistance of ingested grit (Mattocks, 1971)

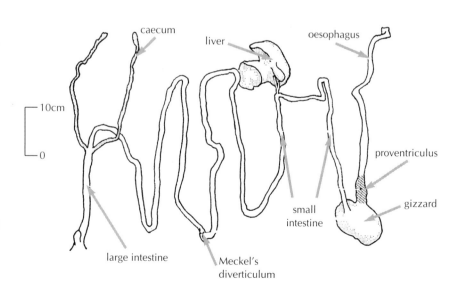

unlikely that cellulose digestion contributes significantly to food up-take. Cell sap appears to be the chief source of nourishment extracted from the grass. This makes the goose a very inefficient grazer, requiring a much larger pro rata intake of food than a ruminant. However, if geese are fed a readily assimilable diet of high calorific value, the rate of through-put is so high that the bird will grow very rapidly. A figure of 2.2lb (1kg) per day is cited for force-fed geese in France and Hungary for the production of *foie gras*.

HAZARDS

Aluminium, Glass, Nails, Lead Shot

Geese are inquisitive creatures, always on the look-out for something useful to do, and will pick up any bits of material for the gizzard. In the absence of grit, they will seek out almost anything hard, including dangerous substances. Bits of glass, nails, lead shot and aluminium foil can be ingested, sometimes with fatal consequences. Always collect any foreign bodies that have been discarded around the place before the geese do. Worms and moles are constantly turning the soil and its contents over, exposing new bits and pieces left by previous landowners, so keep an eye out.

String

Binder twine is the farmer's friend, and much used. Always use it sparingly, fix it well, and leave short ends. A goose will spend hours twiddling at something interesting, and can swallow the twine. If this happens, a short piece (if you know the length) can be removed by pulling gently after a squirt of medicinal paraffin has been applied down the throat. Sit and hold the bird and the twine, allow the paraffin time to go down the throat and lubricate it, then extract the string. If a large amount of string has been swallowed, you may do more harm than good if you try to pull it back through the gizzard and gut.

The best way to avoid the problem is to be tidy around the place.

Fig 82 An outwards overhang gives a 'floppy top' to deter predators from climbing. This is useful if you do not have access to electricity for additional protection. The over-hang will, however, collect snow and additional weight

Vehicles

Turning wheels seem to do something to annoy geese, particularly ganders in the breeding season. This does not matter so much if they are on a wheelbarrow, but it is quite common for birds to be killed in the farmyard, crushed when attacking vehicles. One of our birds hated the red postman's van so much that he would rush across the field, seeing it off in his imagination, as it drove up the lane two fields away. Do your best to separate geese from traffic.

Toxic Plants

Certain garden plants and weeds are toxic to geese. Daffodils, foxglove and ragwort should be avoided.

FENCING

Netting

If the birds are not to have free range on a farm and need to be confined, for whatever purpose, the most durable fencing, and the cheapest in the long run, is pig netting. Use the type with close-spaced wire at 6-in mesh, stapled to tanalized posts. Untreated wood is a false economy, as it will soon go rotten. Breeders often use lighter-weight rabbit or poultry netting, with a 1-in mesh, to separate breeding pens of birds. This has the advantage of keeping ducks in the right place if they are running with the geese, because ducks cannot get through the holes. It also avoids the problem of warring ganders fighting by grabbing each other through the holes in pig netting.

The disadvantage of chicken wire is that ganders may still try to fight through the wire, and end up with bloodied, skinned beaks.

A Fox-Proof Pen

Geese must be shut up every night before dusk to avoid predation by foxes. These predators can even be a problem in the daytime in urban areas, where they are not afraid of people, and do not confine their activities until after dark. When protecting the birds is a problem, a 6-foot (1.8-m) fence is the answer. With time and patience you can construct this yourself, but a tidier job will be done by a good contractor. Ask to see an example of his or her

Fig 83 A surprise 6–8in of wet snow in April 1998 clings to the upright fencing, showing how much can be collected

Fig 84 A single strand of electric wire on plastic insulators to deter climbers such as the polecat. This is not fool-proof, and a second strand, lower down and close to the fence, will be needed if the animals are known to be in your area

work before giving your specifications for an estimate.

Although chain-link fencing may seem to be the best material, it is extremely expensive, and has holes large enough for rats and stoats to pass through. The most commonly used material is heavy-gauge 1-in (2.5-cm) mesh in a 4-foot (1.2-m) roll for the bottom half and lighter-weight roll for the top half of the fence. The two rolls are clipped together on to a

Fig 85 A bottom strand of electric wire, mounted on plastic insulators supported on the posts, deters diggers. The grass will require maintenance, to stop it touching the electric strand

104

Fig 86 Geese and sheep graze up to the outside of the fence to keep the grass down. A fence in open ground minimizes maintenance and maximizes breeding pens for these Toulouse and Africans, because the outer 'pen' gives more flexibility for separating stock. The outside birds are driven in through a gate each night into sheds

middle straining wire, and the top roll is clipped to the top straining wire. The bottom roll has about 1½ feet buried under the turf, which is cut back and then rolled over the wire, to anchor it securely. The wire is supported by 4½-in (11-cm) thick posts sunk 2–3 feet into the ground and spaced at 17-foot (5-m) intervals.

If sufficient wire mesh is available, it can be turned outwards at the top as a 'floppy' wire to deter climbers. The disadvantage of this construction is that it will collect wet snow, and this will add weight to the fence. To deter

climbing predators and foxes, which sometimes try to run up fences, try a single strand of electric wire mounted on insulators around the top, instead of an overhang. To deter diggers, such as badgers and foxes, especially in areas of light, sandy soils, one or two strands of light-gauge electric wire should also be used. These wires can either be mounted on insulators on the fence uprights, or on independent supports.

Where an electric wire is necessary, the vegetation around it will have to be maintained by cutting or spraying so that it

Fig 87 Gates are weak points in your fencing, but are useful access points to extra grazing. The weldmesh of this gate is too coarse, and needs replacing. Ferrets can squeeze through or under this, and rats can enter

105

Fig 88 Gates and corners are strengthened by horizontal struts – a 'Yorkshire Corner' gives great stability

does not touch the wire and short-circuit the current. If sheep are grazing up to the fence, they will maintain the grass for you. A mains-operated electricity supply should be used rather than a battery, as it is more reliable, and gives a stronger current. Minimal electricity is used in operating the system. The mains supply is connected to a transformer to deliver the correct voltage to your length of circuit, and the whole lot is earthed.

When constructing a fox-proof pen, you also need to consider the following:

1. maintenance – this can be minimized by keeping the fence away from hedges that will grow into it and need clipping. There is also the risk of damage to the fence itself if machinery is used close to it;

2. maximizing breeding pens – if the fence is set in open pasture, maintenance is easier, and the grass on the other side of the pen becomes another grazing area for rearing or separating breeding stock;

3. gates – these are weak points in the fence; if predators are a real problem in your area, have as few as possible. However, access though a gate to pasture in the day and into the pen at night is useful for extra grazing for geese. Gates should be supported by extra posts and horizontal struts, and a good contractor will use this technique at gateways and at corners;

4. size – it may not be much more expensive to have a large pen built than a smaller one. Get the job done in one go; it will be much more expensive to get a contractor to come twice.

Fig 89 A pair of Africans appreciate the shade on a hot summer day. Geese pant when it is hot and must be given shade in extreme conditions. Goslings will stagger about and die if subjected to too much sun

Fig 90 Grass needs to be kept short for geese. Coarse grass is not nutritious and can cause a blockage in the proventriculus and gizzard. This old-fashioned mower, manufactured in Italy, is ideal for cutting longer grass on awkward slopes

SEVERE WEATHER CONDITIONS

Heatwave

When deciding where to keep your birds, if they are not to have free range, bear in mind that they will need shelter from bitter winds in winter and from hot sun in summer. If there is no shelter at all, plant some quick-growing evergreens that will not be eaten by the geese, and which can also be used in the future for nest screens. Extra deciduous trees for summer shade are also desirable; these could be fruit trees, although I have often been worried about large apples dropping off the trees in a gale and hitting the geese on the head. Geese do like to eat a few windfalls, which do them no harm. Do not, however, give them fermented apple waste.

Prolonged Freezing

If the birds live out in a fox-proof pen, you may like to give them shelter when temperatures drop below zero for several days at a time. Bales of straw as a wind-break and piles of straw on the ground can be used, although the birds may choose to ignore these. As long as the birds have access to water they suffer less in these conditions than in a heatwave. If running water, which does not freeze, is not available, I find it best to empty all buckets overnight, as the water freezes anyway. It is best to start with an ice-free bucket in the morning. Feed the birds well and they will be fine. They will sit on their well-insulated breast and tuck their feet securely into their flank feathers; their legs are well adapted to withstand cold temperatures.

MAINTAINING PASTURE

Geese will save you a lot of work on grass maintenance, especially in difficult corners and on steep slopes. They are excellent for grazing orchards, and have even been used to maintain a Christmas-tree plantation. However, the grass will probably need some attention, so that it remains short and sweet for the birds. In a wet summer it may grow too long and need mowing if you cannot get sheep to eat it. Sheep or mowing will be necessary at certain times for weed control, as the geese will not eat nettles, thistles and docks. Sheep reduce docks to some extent, and also eat plantain and other weeds such as mayweed and cow parsley. Thistles need to be mown and a herbicide is better in the long run for the nettles.

12 Goose Behaviour: Getting the Best Out of Your Geese

Geese that have been treated and reared well are a pleasure to keep. If you are out at work all day, they will be quite happy, as long as you let them out and do their water in the morning, and feed them and shut them up at night. However, if you like geese, and this is the main reason why many people keep these intelligent birds, they will certainly benefit from your spending much more time with them. If you understand their behaviour, and get to know what they like by observing them, your birds are likely to be more at ease, and, therefore, more likely to breed.

Wild geese live in pairs and family groups within the wild flock, because co-operation is essential for their survival. Well-paired geese will claim the best nesting sites because of their strength together. This is one good reason why geese normally stay in pairs for life. No time is wasted on courtship and display, because time in the short northern summer is at a premium. Birds that choose their nesting site and lay eggs first will produce early, strong goslings, well-feathered for the journey south. Late-hatched birds in migratory flocks stand a much lower chance of survival. With insufficient eating time, they may fail to build up their feathers, body weight and fat reserves for the long journey south.

BONDING

Imprinting

The family bond is an important one for geese. The larger the family, as well as the stronger the parents, the better the territory it can claim. Groups of goslings stick together. Other goslings are important to them for bonding; their constant peeping keeps them together. They 'imprint' on each other, as well as on their parents; being able to drive off smaller groups from their territory, they do better.

This imprinting of the gosling on the bird, or mother, that first looks after it is one of those attributes that make the goose such a sociable and interesting bird. Goslings that are hand-reared, or reared with a tame bird, will readily follow their handler. This makes them easy to manage and tame to show. Such birds also adapt to new owners. A group of goslings brought up by a human, by themselves or with a tame goose, will imprint partly on that human as well as each other. Treated well, they retain a confidence with people for life.

Greeting

Birds that know each other, and their human keepers, always use greeting as part of the family bonding process. A group of tame goslings will rush to their keeper with their necks outstretched and making a series of greeting sounds to establish their bond. To make the birds tame, the goslings need a response – bend down and talk to them; sometimes, the noisier your display the better. Chinese goslings, in particular, are very responsive and love to be treated in this way.

Birds that have been separated – for example, when one has been taken to a show

Figs 91–93 Geese that have been treated well are a pleasure to keep and can spot a bag of bread a long way off. Geese kept by the front gate learn that unloading shopping is associated with bread, and queue up – open the bag! Hurry up! Lovely!

Fig 94 These well-handled goslings will always be tame. Familiarity with people in the early weeks makes the biggest difference to behaviour

on its own – will make a big display to each other when they are reunited. This can happen even when the birds have become attached to humans. This attachment to humans is interesting. We were very flattered when we left our first two tame geese for ten days in the care of someone else; when we came back, the two birds spent several minutes in a greeting display of outstretched necks and calls, showing clearly that they recognized us and that they were pleased at our return.

PAIRING

Geese are very sociable creatures and cannot be kept on their own unless they are deliberately imprinted on one human. If a bird loses its mate, it is miserable. It may fret and not eat properly until it is given a new companion. Sometimes, however, after the death of a partner, a new goose may not be immediately accepted, as the gander is still pining for his old mate. Lorenz considers that 'animals are much less intelligent than you are inclined to think, but in their feelings and emotions they are far less different from us than you assume'. In grieving animals, the general

excitability of the central nervous system is reduced. 'Quite literally, a man, a dog, and a goose hang their heads, lose their appetites and become indifferent to all stimuli emanating from the environment.' A gander will sit by the body of his old goose in a miserable state; it is always best to find a new bird as quickly as possible if there is no flock into which he can fit.

Geese are curious about death. We once had a group of three sisters reared together with a tame goose, and one of them died when they were about one year old. This happened while I was out during the day and, when I found the body in the shed, the other geese were concerned about the dead bird. They were looking at it closely and talking about it in low, inquisitive tones, quite different from their greeting or danger calls. They certainly knew the situation was abnormal.

Just as geese pair in the wild, domestic geese also generally stay in pairs. In the breeding season particularly, ganders will fuss over and guard their goose, putting themselves between their chosen mate and any perceived threat. They will constantly stretch their neck out in front of their mate, and call if they think another gander is more attractive to her. The goose can become quite bored

111

by all this display, and stand demurely, or turn aside. A well-paired couple of geese will call in alternate voices when challenging another pair of geese in the next pen, and generally stick together. However, if there are trios or groups of geese around, you cannot trust domestic geese to stay with one partner in the breeding season, and the birds will need to be separated into their breeding pens.

If you want to keep a trio or quartet of geese (groups with one gander and two or three females), young birds may accept this, as long as all the females are introduced together. It is unwise to bring in a new female to an established pair, as she will be disliked by the resident goose. Never shut up a new goose with an old pair; she may well be picked upon, and even killed in a confined situation where she cannot escape. If you do have a trio or quartet of geese, you will probably find that, as the birds get older, the gander definitely has a favourite goose and that the other females become neglected, or even driven away by the dominant female. Larger sets only seem to work with young geese in the lighter breeds.

Unlike most drakes and ducks, and cocks and hens, a goose and a gander put together in spring will not necessarily breed. Sometimes there can be instant attraction, and it will happen, but a new bird will often take some time to adjust to a new place, and to accept a new partner. If you have several breeding pens of geese and want to switch the ganders between two pens of Brecons, for example, this can be disastrous. If the birds are able to see their previous partner, they will pace up and down all day and, even out of sight, they will call to each other. Then, when you think they have settled down, and are mating with each other, the breeding season might be completely wasted, with no fertile eggs. Back in the flock again in July, the birds will go straight back to their original partner.

It is definitely best to have well-established pairs, so, the sooner you can get your breeding pens together, the better. Geese are best left in their set all the time.

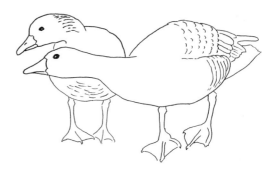

Fig 95 This is my goose! This gander is guarding his goose against the perceived threat of another gander being more attractive to her

Fig 96 Greyback preening after a good wash. A lot of attention is given to the coatings of newly sprouted feathers, especially on the wings. Feather maintenance is crucial for survival in the wild

Fig 97 Toulouse keep their feathers in good condition after a swim. Preening and oiling the feathers is habitual after a swim for cleaning them first

Fig 98 Behaviour in the breeding season: a gander will become much more possessive about his goose. A normally mild-mannered gander may hiss and stretch his neck out, while the female wonders what all the fuss is about

WASHING AND PREENING

Geese must wash and preen their feathers at all times to keep them in a good state of repair, and waterproof. These activities are especially important when new feathers are being grown, and as part of the activity and display in the breeding season.

The oil to waterproof the feathers comes from the preen gland, which is situated on the lower rump, just before the tail. Usually after a good wash, the goose will stroke and roll its head and neck over the gland, and then spread the oil over the whole of its plumage. The beak is also used to comb out the feathers and to nibble off the protective layer from newly sprouted feathers. Great care and attention is given to the wings.

Washing assumes a new significance in the breeding season. The birds definitely become more interested in water, and the ganders (in softer-feathered breeds, such as Brecon Buffs) proudly preen out their breast feathers by roughly combing them with their beaks. By late December, just as the days begin to lengthen, the gander may start to 'dip' to the goose on a pool. He will sharply immerse his head in the water and raise it with a sharply bent neck to attract the goose's attention. At this stage she is not usually interested, as she is not due to lay for several weeks; the gander is acting this way in order to ensure that the birds stay together as a pair. He will slowly pace about, his neck arched, as he keeps an eye on any competition.

13 Approaching the Breeding Season

Mating

When it is getting nearer to the time for the goose to lay, she will begin to take more interest in the gander's attentions. If the two birds are together on water and the gander dips several times, she will do the same, and they will synchronize their actions. When this has happened, she will flatten herself and spread her wings and allow the gander to mate. Her co-operation is essential; in fact, the gander usually falls off anyway, generally with a great cry, proud that he has succeeded in copulation, whether fertile eggs ensue or not.

If no swimming water is available, the birds will go through the same ritual on the grass, using the bucket for head-dipping first.

Fighting

Ganders may scrap at any time of the year, but fighting is much more frequent and serious in the breeding season. If the individuals are evenly matched and the geese are well paired, the scrap is usually just a quick flurry of feathers and a rapid separation. If there is great jealousy between the birds, one individual, using his beak, may hang on with great determination to the feathers at the

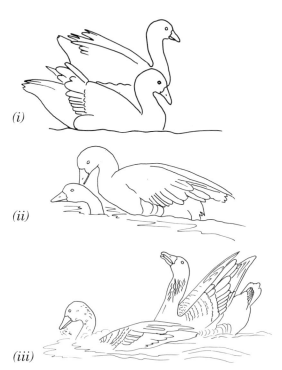

(i)

(ii)

(iii)

Fig 99 Mating. (i) Ganders arch their necks sharply when they are getting interested in the breeding season. This generally starts in January when the goose will probably not reciprocate. When she is coming into lay, the goose will arch her neck and repeatedly dip her head in the water, synchronizing her actions with the gander. Any gander which is not giving her enough attention will have his back feathers pulled and be generally beaten about until he shows interest in mating.
(ii) The goose allows the gander to mate by flattening her body and spreading her wings as he grasps her head to keep his balance. The gander's tail is bent down sharply as he copulates with the goose. (iii) The gander falls off with a characteristic cry. The goose dips and washes herself

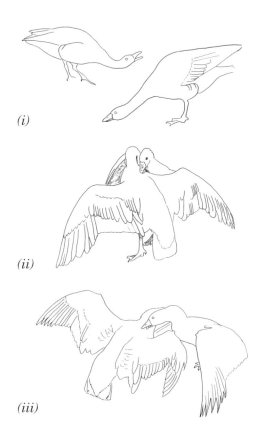

(i)

(ii)

(iii)

Fig 100 Fighting. (i) The gander in the background threatens the other as they approach each other sideways. The lowered neck posture becomes more and more exaggerated as they fix each other with their eyes. Eventually, the ganders may pause and slowly sidle off as if nothing has happened. Sometimes one loses his nerve and suddenly jumps away, or they approach each other, necks raised, to fight. (ii) Ganders grasp each other at the base of the neck, or where the wing joins the body. Their tail is used for balance and the wings are raised. (iii) The left wing is drawn back to beat the opponent with the carpal spur. This is quite a blow, which hurts and can numb. The scrap often ends with the ganders out of breath; the heavier bird is more likely to win, but it is tenacity that counts the most. Heavy Brecon Buffs can end up totally out of breath and hardly able to move, but still victorious, because they have hung on and pulled feathers out. Such a fight ends in a flurry of feathers where the lighter-weight beaten individual runs off. The victor will return in a triumph ceremony with his goose

nape of his rival's neck. At the same time, the opponent will grasp his rival in the same manner, and the birds will beat at each other with their wings. On the wing butt there is a hard, bony projection called the carpal spur, and this is used to flail the opponent, while the other wing is held back for better balance.

The ganders will continue to fight, sometimes adjusting their beaks to get a better grip, until one bird gives up, exhausted. The victor may hang on the back feathers of the loser, but usually he is allowed to escape. Fights can attract a ring of spectators, just as in the playground at school, but other birds will rarely join in, except vocally. As in their courtship and mating behaviour, the domestic geese mimic exactly the behaviour of the wild Greylag.

WHEN YOU HAVE NOT GOT A PAIR

Once people have bought a 'pair of geese', they tend to assume that that is what they are, but mistakes can be made. Only if you are experienced in observing goose behaviour, or if you take a particular interest in the geese, will you notice anything amiss if the birds are of the same sex. Ganders brought up together generally do not fight. Also, unrelated ganders can develop homosexual behaviour. In the absence of females, some ganders can be kept in 'pairs', and live together fairly amicably for most of the year. During the breeding season, they will start to go through the courtship ritual, but this usually breaks down at the point when one fails to submit to the other, and ends in a fight. This behaviour

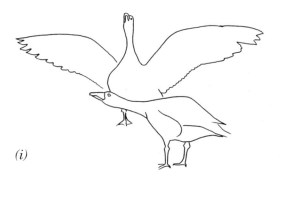

(i)

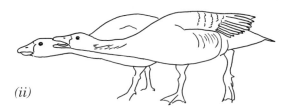

(ii)

Fig 101 The triumph display. (i) After a fight, the gander runs back to his goose, wings raised, in the triumph display. (ii) The pair finally vocalize together in an alternate cackling, bonding display

will indicate that you do not have a pair.

With a 'pair' of females, the situation may be more difficult. One friend complained that his new pair of Brecons had not bred; all of the eggs had been infertile. The goose had sat and had laid extremely well, producing an egg a day (when the laying cycle is about 34 hours). He was sure that only one of the birds had sat, and that they had mated. They probably did because, in the absence of a male, one female will pretend that she is the male, and the other will submit. Observing all the behaviour of the geese is important.

SEXING GEESE

In the first couple of weeks, Sebastopols and Embdens, as well as Pilgrims, should show autosexing colour characteristics (*see* pages 34 and 38). However, if you miss the opportu-

nity to see this, or are buying older birds, there are various other ways of telling the difference between the sexes.

Differences in Behaviour

Some breeds of geese are easier to sex than others. Africans and Chinese, in particular, show a marked difference in size between the sexes, and the ganders will stretch themselves much higher in a display pose than females (*see also* page 28 for details of differences in the knob and voice). Adult West of England and Pilgrim geese are autosexing, but it is possible to get a grey gander or a white goose, so observation of behaviour, and vent-sexing, are still both important.

With a new pair of adult geese, watch their behaviour and nesting habits and listen to their voices, for the mature gander and goose have different ways of talking, and use different tones. The gander will talk rapidly, in a high pitch with his head raised, whereas

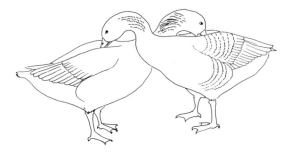

Fig 102 In the absence of females, young ganders can live amicably together until the breeding season. Then they may go through the courting ritual and attempt to mate. These two males try to rouse each other sexually by delving the beak into the back feathers. They will fail to submit to each other, and a fight will break out. A female can behave like this towards a gander too, if she is not getting enough attention, but then she will flatten her body and accept the gander

117

the voice and head carriage of the female is much lower. It is also the male who stretches up sometimes and gives a really high-pitched shriek. The ganders' heads are usually bolder than the females', and their body carriage is higher. The goose should have a heavier undercarriage, but do not forget that well-fed Brecon and Embden ganders also have dual lobes. This feature is not an 'egg pouch', as it has been mistakenly called.

As the breeding season gets closer, the female will start to lose feathers on her head. This happens when the gander has been mating with her, and trying to keep his balance as he 'treads'. This is, therefore, a good sign that all is well. The goose may also start to pick twigs and straw at random from the ground, and deposit the bits over her shoulder, as she thinks about nesting. I have rarely seen this behaviour in ganders.

Vent-Sexing

The easiest time to vent-sex geese is when they are about four weeks old (*see* page 180), but you may not get a chance to do this, of course. The birds may have been vent-sexed before you bought them, but mistakes can be made with juveniles.

If you have serious doubts about the sex of your birds, judging by their behaviour as the breeding season approaches, you might want to check them again. This is much easier with adult birds in early spring when the ganders have matured. The juvenile male penis is a tiny organ about 3–4 mm long in goslings up to16 weeks old; it can easily be missed, especially if the organ is the same pink colour as the area around it. Adult males, on the other hand, have a large, spiral penis, which cannot be mistaken.

Fig 103 When mating, ganders keep their balance by gripping the female's head and neck feathers. Missing feathers denote a female in the breeding season

118

Geese have only one 'vent', for bodily functions and for reproduction. To vent-sex the bird, you need to turn it over to open this vent, which is under the tail. This will not work if the bird is flat on its back. Instead, take the goose by the left wing and, with the other hand passed under the body, hold it by the upper left leg (this is your left as you face the bird). Holding it close to your body to support its weight, turn the bird upside down and hold it between your knees, breast facing you, while you lean on something solid for balance. Continue to hold the right leg in your hand and then use only the little finger to control the goose's leg. You now have several fingers and your left hand free to push the tail back (towards the bird's back), and depress the area around the vent in order to open it up.

The sphincter muscles are generally tighter in males than in females, so the female vent should open quite easily and be large and pink. The male vent should eventually open with more firm but gentle pressure, and a pale, rather corrugated penis should appear. Sometimes it is folded sideways and may not start to emerge easily, so do not be fooled by this. You must open the vent to expose the penis; it does not pop out on its own, especially in young goslings.

Once you are certain of the sex, discontinue the pressure. Make sure you always apply only gentle but firm pressure, otherwise the muscles may become bruised.

This procedure is as difficult and peculiar as it sounds, and it is best to get an expert to show you what to do the first time, because it does require a certain knack.

Although humans may have difficulty in deciding the sex of each bird, mature geese of normal behaviour do not. A goose may scrap with a new goose, and a gander will instantly challenge a new gander, and they will fight if the newcomer does not back off. Even though a gander may not like a goose, and may push her away, he will never seriously attack her. The only problem is if you get two young males 'pairing up', but they instantly give themselves away by their high-profile bossy behaviour with other groups of geese.

DIET

As the breeding season approaches, you will need to check that the goose has access to enough calcium (*see* page 101), and that neither she nor the gander is excessively fat. Overweight geese are said to be prone to damage to the oviduct, while overweight ganders find it difficult to mate. It is particularly important not to over-feed Brecons and Pilgrims. These geese are very good food converters on a largely grass diet, and they will rapidly become too fat if they become accustomed to eating too much manufactured food.

There are numerous opinions about the link between a goose's diet and the viability of fertile eggs. The consensus is that a higher protein content of 16 per cent, supplied by breeder pellets that contain fishmeal as well as added vitamins and trace elements, is beneficial, both for fertility of the egg and growth of the embryo. While geese fed with breeder pellets certainly produce more eggs than geese that get their living only from the land, there is some doubt that a higher-protein diet from breeder pellets is essential where there is good free-range grass, that is to say, on a farm with mixed grazing over several acres. In terms of fertility, the eggs of our grass-fed Brecons were as good as, if not better than, those of our birds that now have breeder pellets. Tom Bartlett has also noted that German breeders who run their Embden geese on pasture and oats enjoy a great deal of success.

Geese are meant to be grazers and, if the quality of the grass is good, it should supply sufficient vitamins and minerals for small quantities of eggs – a first clutch of twelve, for example – when the goose sits. Where geese are kept intensively, and a high number of eggs is required, there is benefit for both

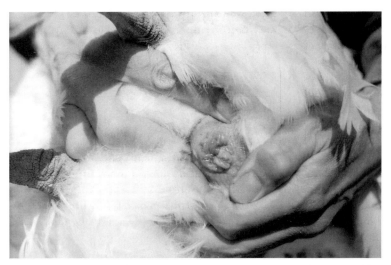

Fig 104 Vent-sexing: a mature Sebastopol female showing pink corrugations. The vent tends to be more easy to open in females, which is not surprising, as eggs have to pass through. In goslings, females show a pale genital eminence at the edge of the cloaca (the edge on the lower rim near the abdomen). This should not be confused with a male gosling's penis, which is a tiny, pale, pointed hook, originating a little deeper inside the cloaca

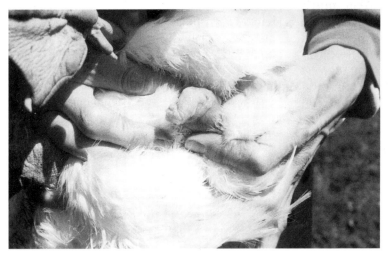

Fig 105 Vent-sexing: a mature Pilgrim gander is held upside down. The tail is bent backwards towards his spine and the vent exposes a pale, spiral penis

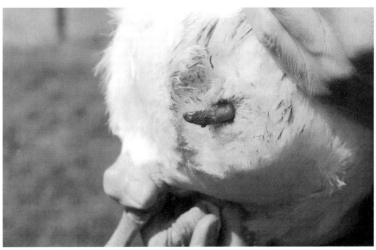

Fig 106 This gander has dropped his penis (a prolapse) and has not been able to retract it. The end dries and shrivels. If it does retract, the bird will be all right, as long as infection has not begun. In ducks, this condition makes little difference to fertility even if the necrotic end is snipped off at the vet's. However, avoid using a bird with an obviously damaged penis for breeding

adults and goslings from pellets containing fishmeal.

As long as the geese have a good diet, it seems to me that the most important factors in successful rearing are the happiness and genetic compatibility of a pair. If birds are well paired, and calm and happy in their surroundings, you should have a successful season. Birds harassed by farm dogs or children cannot be expected to lay well, let alone sit. The goose needs peace and quiet for the laborious process of laying.

AGGRESSIVE GEESE

During the breeding season, some ganders become much more aggressive than others. Birds that have lived quite happily together for most of the year begin to pick on one another, and a dominant individual can make life miserable for both gander and goose in another pair. If they were originally intended to be flock-mated, these dominant birds must

be given a breeding pen of their own, otherwise they will upset too many birds which need a quiet time to mate and lay.

Some ganders become more aggressive in spring with humans, too, but I have never had a bird that could not be persuaded to behave reasonably, using the right techniques. The worst birds are those that have been badly treated in the past, or those that are very tame and so have no fear. Lorenz also found this to be the case with the Greylag geese that he studied when he approached nests in the breeding season.

When a gander puts on a display of aggression, ignore it and carry on slowly, as normal. This gives him the opportunity to behave as if he has made a mistake, and give up, or pretend that he has seen you off and return in triumph to his goose. The worst thing you can do is to run away, as this is a clear invitation for him to follow and establish dominance over his terrain. Each time this happens, the habit becomes more ingrained, and it can lead to the bird making contact with beak and

Fig 107 The dominant gander is showing that he is the boss. The underling will be allowed to get up and run away eventually. This is what should happen when you hold down and dominate a troublesome gander, without hurting him

wings. Try not to touch a bird that threatens you. If you catch hold of an aggressive one he may join in with a fight, gripping with his beak and flailing with his wing butts, as if you were another gander. Striking a bird will have a similar effect. It will raise his adrenalin and make him even more eager to fight, while you risk injuring or even killing him with a random blow. He will also want another fight next time he sees you.

If a gander is obviously intending to make contact, try turning to face him, raising your arms. If the bird is used to being driven, this may have the desired effect. If this does not work, try bending and putting your head down and talking; this is a less aggressive pose, and the gander may respond by standing and arching his neck, and treating you as an equal. Head-to-head conversations take place between geese that are confident with each other, and you are showing him the same familiarity.

With a totally unresponsive bird that insists on going for your legs or face, your only recourse is to make contact; get the neck in one hand and a wing in the other before he is able to strike or bite. Still holding on, turn the bird around and flatten him on the ground by stooping down, and using the inside of your knee if necessary across his back to restrain him. Do not use your weight. You have now established who is boss by holding him like this for as long as you like. You are now the dominant gander, for a gander which is soundly beaten will lie prone on the ground in a submissive pose until he summons the energy to fly off. You can release him with a final stroke on the back and a tweak of the tail, which does not hurt, but represents a final ignominy. You might have to repeat this procedure a couple of times, but it will work; the gander should eventually treat you with respect. Geese are fortunately not like cockerels, some of which are never able to give up.

This extreme aggressive behaviour is unusual and should abate after the breeding season. If it persists, and the gander likes bread, you can try another ploy. Wear a glove while you hold some bread, and allow him to bite it in your hand. With persistence, the bird prefers the bread to aggression, and he will come to feed rather than to fight.

CHECKLIST FOR NEW BIRDS FOR THE BREEDING SEASON

- Make sure the birds behave as if they are a pair, not two of the same sex.
- Give them sufficient time to settle down together.
- If several birds are running together as a flock, make sure that the ganders are not interfering with each other mating.
- If you have more than one breed, make sure that the fencing keeps them separated, otherwise there will be cross-breeds. Clip a wing if necessary.
- Birds should have access to coarse sand, and poultry grit containing limestone and oyster shell.
- Birds should be fit, not fat. Their legs should be sound.
- The birds should not be too young (they will produce small eggs and goslings) or too old.
- Provide clean grazing, with short, high-protein spring grass, or breeder pellets, as well as wheat. Good nutrition is important for both male and female.
- Heavy breeds may need a pool for fertile eggs.
- Watch the goose for signs that she is starting to lay. Some lay in secret nests under hedges, or dump their egg in the pool.
- Make sure that eggs are coming at the rate of one every other day, or occasionally on consecutive days.

PART FOUR: BREEDING

14 The Breeding Season –

WHEN WILL THE GOOSE LAY?

The traditional saying about the goose is that a good breeder should lay by St Valentine's Day (14 February). Back in the early 1980s, we were assured by seasoned locals that this was the case; at that time, many farms and smallholdings had a pair of geese. The saying turned out to be true in the first year. Our young geese outdid the locals by laying on a snowy day on 29 January 1982. As time went on, however, the same ageing geese left it later and later each year. The time when the first eggs appear depends on several factors.

Geese can lay some eggs in the autumn. One breed to do this is the Chinese, which amazed their American owners when they first arrived from China, in 1788. These birds were accused of being 'the foolishest of geese . . . for they choose all times for setting but in the Spring' (Robinson, quoted in Brown 1929).

Owners of farmyard geese have also related how their birds have laid in October and November, but this is unusual, and the birds may have been brought into lay by artificial lighting. (It is the lengthening hours of daylight, even at the end of December and in the first week in January, which prompt the geese into thinking about spring, and encourage them to start laying.) One proud owner of such prolific geese had been keeping them in the yard by the house each night, with the outdoor light left on to deter foxes. The geese duly responded to the extra light. In these conditions, birds may pair, ganders may begin to get more aggressive with each other, and mating can start, even though it may be weeks before the eggs are due.

Probably one of the reasons why our local farmers thought that Valentine's Day was a milestone for their geese was that many of them were crossed with Embden stock, and Embdens are known for laying early eggs. Both young Embdens and three- or four-year olds we have kept have regularly laid like clockwork between mid-February and early March. Romans are also reported to be early layers, but other breeds frequently wait until March and even April before beginning. The older the goose, and the later the cold snaps in the weather, the longer you will have to wait for eggs. In the cold spring of 1996, some birds did not lay until May, and even then laid very few eggs.

WHEN WILL THE GOOSE SIT?

This is a frequently asked question; many people assume that every goose will sit after laying just the right amount of eggs and then happily rear her clutch of goslings. This is the ideal situation, since incubators are expensive, and a certain amount of expertise is needed in order to manage them success-fully. Unfortunately, the goose also needs careful management. Some breeds, like the Toulouse, are unlikely to sit, while others, such as Embdens and Africans, are happy to sit, but usually smash almost every egg because of their heavy feet and their weight. The best sitters are the medium-weights and lightweights, such as the Pomeranians, Brecons, Pilgrims and Sebastopols. The geese may not, however, sit when you want them to.

Brecons were developed to be the ideal farm goose. They were not over-fed on concen-trates, and were expected to find most of their own living on upland pasture. In these circumstances, they traditionally produced a clutch of 12–18 eggs and then went broody. If

these eggs were taken from the goose, a second clutch of about 10 eggs followed, with a break of about three weeks in between. Our first Brecons behaved like this. Over the years, however, there has been a tendency for some birds to produce more eggs, totalling up to 40 in some seasons. This may be due to less dependence on grass, and more wheat or pellets being supplied. In addition, the birds are not encouraged to go broody, since little of the brooding or hatching is done by the geese.

Many other breeds of goose also behave like this. Frequently, a bird will lay a dozen eggs, and then continue to lay without any sign of going broody. Sometimes she may stop laying, particularly if there is a cold spell in the spring weather. There is no rule about this. If you want a bird to sit, all you can do is provide the ideal surroundings to facilitate the process.

A PLACE TO LAY

Sheds

If the birds are kept in relatively small sheds – 4 x 4 feet for a pair, for example – there is not much room for a nest. The floor litter will need to be cleaned frequently to prevent soiling of the eggs if they are laid in the shed overnight. However, if the shed is inside a fox-proof pen, it is ideal for the sitting goose. If she chooses to lay there, the eggs will stay dry in spells of wet weather, and the open door of the shed can be screened off from marauding magpies by cypress branches. The goose will need protection from the sun in a heatwave. If the shed becomes excessively hot, or the goose is sitting out in the open in the blazing sun, a screen of branches should be used.

Nesting material will need to be provided, otherwise the goose will spend a great deal of time gathering it, even trying to strip off twigs from holly and hawthorn, if grass is in short supply. Clean, chopped barley straw or wheat

Fig 108 The goose has chosen a good, well-drained site under the hedge in a fox-proof pen. She has lined it with down from her breast and underparts. Another bird has recently laid the cleaner egg in her nest

Fig 109 The goose, a smooth-breasted Sebastopol, returns to her eggs on bare earth under the holly hedge . . .

Fig 110 . . . and settles down to cover them

straw is good for nesting, but not hay, as it tends to go mouldy more quickly. On a hardwood or concrete floor, the nest litter needs to be very deep, otherwise the goose will try to scratch out a hole in the floor, as she would do naturally in soft material. Eggs on a hard surface are readily broken, so a piece of old carpet, covered with plenty of peat, shavings or wood peelings, makes a good base. The edges of the nest need to be supported by bricks or heavy pieces of wood as retaining walls. Alternatively, if the floor in an old cowshed has been moulded, so that there are floor-level feeding troughs, these are an ideal place to add deep litter.

Outdoors

If the birds live out in a fox-proof pen and there is no shed for them to use, they will choose their own place; you may have to adapt to this, but you can encourage them to use sites that you think are ideal. You cannot move a goose from her chosen site as you can a broody hen.

The goose will tend to head for cover somewhere awkward, such as under a holly bush – good for concealment, but prickly for all concerned. I prefer to encourage them to use a dry site where the lie of the land is such that the eggs will not roll away. If the goose starts to make a scrape in the ground (just as wild birds do), you can facilitate this by taking out a shovel full of earth; the goose scrape will often have a lump standing up in the middle, from her efforts of turning round and tearing out the earth with her feet.

Eggs laid on the scraped earth can become very dirty, and the grit in the soil will abrade the natural protective coating of the egg. Also, in spells of wet weather, the soil will become compacted by the goose, and the nest will become a puddle. Build the nest up so that the eggs are at least kept above the water table. The best material I have found recently is bark peelings from a sawmill. They blend into the landscape, and eventually biodegrade.

The goose can use them to cover and camouflage her eggs, and water will drain through and leave the eggs relatively dry. Wildfowl nests are built up above the local level of the water, and the goose nest needs to be the same.

For additional cover from vermin and the rain, wigwams of cypress branches are ideal. The geese like the feeling of added protection.

CARING FOR THE EGGS

Collecting and Cleaning

You will need to know how to care for the eggs while the goose is laying. Most geese lay more eggs than they can brood, and it is not a good idea to leave eggs in the nest. They are likely either to be broken by the goose, or to be eaten by predators.

The eggs should be removed as they are laid, cleaned, and dated in pencil. If there are several to collect from different breeding pens, carry a bucket with some wheat in the bottom, or shavings, so that the eggs do not roll around. Label each egg in pencil as you collect it, because one egg looks very much like another, and they will become muddled up. If the eggs are *very* dirty, especially with droppings from a shed, they should be scrubbed well using a nailbrush. Take care not to keep turning the egg in the same direction as you scrub it, as this will affect the internal structure of the egg (*see* pages 144 and 146). Handle the egg gently, otherwise the germ may be damaged. Use running tepid tap water for cleaning; the particles and bacteria will be washed away, so there will not be cross-contamination. Some people recommend a drop of a bleach such as Milton and, for washing in a bowl of water, this would improve hygiene. An egg sanitizer may also be used.

The more hygienic the eggs, the better the hatches should be. However, if the eggs are not unduly dirty, and the mud or droppings are dry and will brush off easily, the eggs are

Fig 111 A wigwam of cypress branches constructed around a central pole. The geese feel secure, and predators do not find the eggs. There is also protection from rain to keep the nest site dry. Take out a shovel full of earth and fill the hole with shredded bark and shavings

Fig 112 Two Steinbachers share the same nest to lay eggs

best left unwashed, especially for natural hatching. The mucous from the oviduct, which helps the goose to pass the egg, also forms a protective, smooth coating that helps to exclude infection. In my experience, fewer goslings become ill from yolk sac infection if this mucous remains.

If the eggs are scrubbed, it is important to use warm water, especially if the egg is still warm. Cold water will cause the egg to contract, and draw in unwanted water and bacteria through the shell. This is why wet eggs in an outdoor nest are vulnerable. Any eggs laid in water are useless. When candling such an egg, water can sometimes be seen as a surplus droplet on the *inside* of the shell.

Storage

Temperature

While the geese continues to lay, the eggs should be stored in a cool place, such as an unheated room in the house, at about 12–14 degrees centigrade (53.6–57.2 degrees Fahrenheit). The longer the period of storage, the lower the temperature – for example 12 degrees centigrade (53.6 degrees Fahrenheit) if eggs are stored more than ten days. The egg is dormant at this temperature and will only begin to develop above 21 degrees. Prolonged exposure to these higher temperatures must be avoided on storage.

Water loss should also be limited. Water is lost through the pores of the shell in a dry atmosphere, especially if the air is moving. Low humidity is not usually a problem in Britain, where humidity tends to be around the optimum for storage, at 75 per cent RH. The humidity in a cool, north-facing room in the house should be all right; in Britain you are unlikely to have to resort to storing in polythene bags, which is recommended in drier climates.

Turning during Storage

Most sources recommend storing the eggs on their side and turning them once a day so that the yolk, which is lighter than the albumen and so floats upwards, does not permanently lie in the same position. The albumen acts as a shock absorber and suspensory mechanism for the yolk but, left in the same position for too long, the yolk can move upwards and stick to the shell's membrane. Storage on the side requires quite a lot of space, and turning is an extra job to do, so another way of storing is to place the eggs vertically. I prefer not to use old egg trays, because of the risk of any cross-infection. Some people use a bed of sand to

Fig 113 Storage: eggs are labelled and dated when collected. Store them in a cool place, propped up vertically against a wall. This will save turning them and is all right for a week

keep the eggs vertical, but it is far simpler just to prop them up in a corner against the wall. I have heard it said that, because this is not a natural position, it will affect the hatching, but if you are short of time or space it still gives good results.

I store the eggs with the air sac end uppermost, although some recommend the opposite way round. I prefer my way, as it has been said that pipping at the wrong end of the shell is encouraged by setting the eggs with the bulbous end in a low position.

The longer the period of storage, especially if it is more than a week, the greater the importance of turning the eggs. After that point they should be stored on their side and turned once a day through 180 degrees. Each turn must be in the opposite direction to the previous one.

Labelling

It is very important to label and date the eggs clearly while they are in store. Pencil is preferable to felt-tip pen, because the solvents in the inks could penetrate the egg and poison the embryo. Label on the bulbous air sac end if you must use felt-tips.

15 Incubation ——————

NATURAL INCUBATION

Selecting Eggs

Age

For natural hatching the eggs should be no more than 20 days old, but less than this is preferable. Geese do not lay every day. The cycle is less than 48 hours, approximating to 35, so that occasionally you will get an egg on consecutive days. To lay a clutch of 10 eggs will take 14 to 16 days, so this is about right for natural hatching.

Suitability

Not all of the eggs are suitable for hatching. In certain seasons a goose may lay thin-shelled eggs, eggs with a 'chalky' feel, which seem very porous, or eggs with an irregular, bobbled exterior. This may happen even if the birds have ample access to calcium, so it

seems there is little that can be done. We have had birds lay a succession of eggs with no shell at all in one season and yet lay normally the next, even though we could detect nothing different in the external conditions. Eggs with a poor shell may be fertile but readily go rotten and dehydrate too quickly. They are a waste of incubator space.

If there are more eggs than you need, choose eggs laid recently and of average size for setting. Reject small eggs, as they may produce small goslings. Large eggs are frequently double-yolked and will not hatch. This can be checked with the candler, where the yolks will appear as two shadows. Any cracked eggs will also show up on candling; these should not be set, as they will go rotten on incubation.

Some birds may lay eggs that are not typical in shape; they may be rather long and cigar-shaped. These are not ideal for

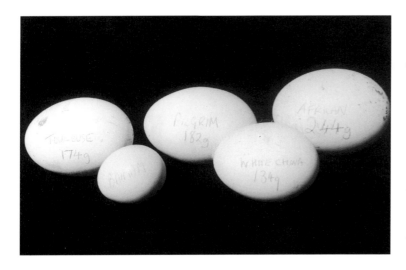

Fig 114 Selecting the eggs. The size of the eggs varies a great deal between the different breeds, as you can see from the weights recorded on the shells. Select eggs that are typical for your breed. If the goose always lays a very large egg, as does the owner of this African egg, hatching may be more difficult, owing to insufficient loss of water. Eggs of 190–200 grams are normal for Africans

hatching, and you will have to watch carefully to make sure that the gosling can get out. However, if the bird is a rare breed and a good specimen, it might be worthwhile putting up with this, but try to breed away from this undesirable characteristic in the offspring. Egg shape does tend to be inherited.

How Many?

A goose will usually cover about nine eggs well, and sometimes up to eleven in a large, deep nest. An odd number of eggs often seems to fit better than an even number but, whatever you select, it is best not to have the nest too crowded. Too many eggs will not only result in more breakages, but also lead to some eggs being too cool for part of the time. Make sure that the eggs that you have chosen are sound and not too old.

Getting the Goose to Sit

If you wish the goose to sit, she must have a nest where she feels safe, without interference from dogs or people. The nest litter must be clean and dry. To encourage her to go broody, after she has laid 12–15 eggs leave the oldest-dated egg in the nest. This will get dirty and can eventually be discarded; the first egg is often infertile, anyway. If the goose is ready to sit, she will line her nest with down

and then she can be given a couple more of the oldest eggs, to check if she is serious about the business. Frequently, a goose will not settle well. If the weather turns extremely cold, she may decide to have a break from laying rather than go broody. If she has messed about with eggs and sat on them at night and warmed them, and then gone off and left them to go cold the next day, they will probably still be all right. In the wild, the eggs would naturally be protected by the goose at night as she comes near to sitting. Some breeders think that there is an advantage to be gained in warming the eggs slightly on a daily basis, to mimic this natural process.

If you have two geese in the same shed, they may disturb each other. If they are close together they will steal each other's eggs, rolling them from nest to nest. Sometimes the two geese will want the same nest, leaving the other clutch of eggs to go cold in the middle of incubation. It is best to keep either a pair of geese or, if you have a trio, to have the sitting geese in different areas, and ensure that they go back on to the right nest.

Caring for the Broody Goose

More females are lost in spring through lack of care than at any other time. It is essential to make a note of the date when the goose first

Fig 115 Geese are good sitters! This Buff Back sat out a surprise 8-in fall of snow on the night of 14–15 April 1998. A Call duck, not surprisingly, deserted

131

Figs 116–118 Buff Back sisters share the nest. These birds were reared together and would sit together, but this set-up is not generally recommended, as one female will steal the other's eggs and disrupt incubation

sat seriously, both for the sake of her health and that of the goslings. Females that have been left to sit for more than 32 days often find it very difficult to revive their appetite, and sometimes die. This is especially the case if there are no goslings to stimulate them.

Worming

First of all, the goose (and the gander) should be wormed when she is definitely broody. The gander also tends to lose his appetite when the goose is sitting. The advantage of worming for the goose is that she does not lose so much condition while she is sitting and, if she becomes ill, one possible cause of disease is eliminated. Also, both birds will be free of worms when they lead the goslings out.

Feeding

The goose must be fed and watered once a day. This should not be too hurried an affair, as she will want to carefully cover her eggs with down, so that they remain warm in the nest for some time and are camouflaged. Wheat in a bucket of water is suitable, and the goose should be encouraged to swim if the weather is hot and dry, as this will give the eggs the correct amount of moisture.

If the birds are tame, the feeding and watering procedure is not a problem, as a tame goose will allow you look at the eggs and lift her off the nest, and a tame gander will not attack. In these circumstances, a goose can be fed twice a day if she is losing too much condition. With fierce birds it is much more problematical, and it is best to drive the gander to a place out of the way when you want to drive the goose off the nest, otherwise smashed eggs will result. Geese that are accustomed to sitting will probably look after themselves, but you must check. Young birds need more attention because they have not been through this process before, and can become very run down by sitting too tightly.

Egg Losses

Losses are most likely to occur in the first week of sitting because that is when the goose is heavy. As she loses weight, the eggs are safer. However, losses can occur at any time through vermin. Rats will take every egg from under a goose, so a rat-proof shed is needed. Magpies are adept at swooping in during the ten minutes when a goose is off the nest, so it is essential to leave the eggs well covered.

Checking the Eggs

It is pointless the bird sitting if the eggs are infertile. It is important to have clean eggs to start with, as it is virtually impossible to 'candle' eggs with a dirty shell. Candling involves shining a light through the egg to examine the contents, so that you can see if the egg is fertile and developing normally, or infertile (*see* page 147). If the eggs are 'clear' or infertile they will not go rotten, and a couple of clear eggs could be left in the nest with five fertile eggs, if they fill the nest well. Then there is a one in seven chance of the fertiles getting robbed or broken, instead of one in five.

As incubation proceeds, some of the embryos may fail. This is easy to identify with clean eggs in an incubator, but far more difficult in the nest. The eggs will acquire a good polish of goose grease and not become excessively dirty, and you should attempt to check them because eggs that have started, and then failed, go rotten. These need to be identified and discarded. If you cannot tell by candling, you can probably tell by smelling them. Bear in mind that, if an egg has broken in the nest, it can transfer quite a smell to the surface of the remaining ones. If the surface of the eggs seems to be extremely dirty by this stage, this does not matter. The natural oil from the goose feathers cleans the eggs and affects the permeability of the shell, preventing deterioration. The skin secretes a natural antibiotic and this is present in the oil and on the feathers and protects the egg (Anderson Brown).

If the eggs are so dirty you cannot candle them, but you think an egg is rotten, shake it. If it is seriously rotten, the contents will slop around inside; hurl it a long distance to break in a hedge, or bury it, immediately. If you are not sure, check again a few days later, or try candling again. If the air sac seems non-existent, the egg is probably rotten. If the egg is oozing a liquid, it should have been thrown out earlier.

Always keep the eggs well marked when they are handled. Re-do the labels in pencil, on the bulbous air sac end, as the label is less likely to rub off here than off the side of the egg. If you have to use a felt marker, *only* do so on the bulbous end adjacent to the air sac, away from the gosling's blood supply. Marking the eggs is perhaps more important if the goose is sitting on a batch of mixed breeds. However, a batch of eggs of uniform size and shell thickness is preferable to a mixed bunch.

Keep an eye on the size of the air sac and, after day 18, mark its outline in pencil, so that you can monitor progress. In dry weather in late May and June, eggs can dehydrate too rapidly under a goose, and are better finished in a damper incubator. In contrast, earlier eggs dehydrate much less readily. This may be as much to do with shell thickness as with the weather. Shell thickness in poultry and duck eggs as well as geese can decline as the season progresses and later eggs may simply be more porous. This makes later goose eggs easier to hatch in this respect. Conversely such eggs are more likely to go rotten in the nest. This may be a function of the more porous shell admitting more germs or of more bacterial growth in the environment in the generally higher summer temperatures.

Hatching in the Nest

As day 28 approaches, the eggs' shells will have become thinner as the embryos resorb some of the calcium for skeletal development. Healthy goslings will be able to use their muscle to chip and push at the inner membrane with their egg tooth, and burst into the air sac. It is essential that this sac is well developed, to about one-third of the

volume of the egg, so that the gosling can begin to use its lungs. The egg needs to have lost 13–15 per cent of its original weight by this stage, so you will have a good idea of the viability of the eggs by weighing them. It seems that the hatches are better if the eggs are slightly on the dry side, having lost 16 per cent of their weight rather than 13 per cent, which leaves them on the wet side.

At this stage, the goslings squeak. They continue to work at the shell, until they pip a hole in it at day 28–9. Then they seem to take a rest for at least a day before making the final effort to turn completely round in the shell, in a can-opener action, and prise off the end. The goose will often assist with this hatching process, nibbling off bits of shell and often devouring quite large portions of the discarded egg. If any eggs are broken during the progress of incubation, the remains can go this way too, and this may explain some disappearances.

This process may reach its desired conclusion with an idyllic picture of a contented goose with a clutch of goslings. All too often, however, rats may pay a visit, or the goslings will be squashed in the nest as they are trying to hatch, or just after hatching. The goose has enormous, clumsy feet, which she places squarely on top of the eggs during incubation. At this time, the eggs are quite strong enough to be stood upon, and it is often the turning of the eggs and their crashing together that breaks them, rather than the weight of the goose. However, as the gosling punctures its already thinned-down shell, crushing of the whole egg becomes more likely, as does suffocation of the hatchling.

Some females are adept at rearing their young, but others are hopeless. You may want to find out by experience, or avoid losses by finishing the goslings off from day 28 in the incubator. If the goose has reared goslings before, she will be happy to have these back from you (as long as she has had something to sit on in the meantime). If she has never hatched a gosling before, you cannot expect her to know what it is all about. Our very first goose, which was also very tame, hissed at her first gosling. She had been curious about the peeps from inside the shell, and about the tiny hole that was forming, but she was quite taken aback by the gosling that broke out and spoiled her perfect egg. She took some time to be convinced that this was the proper course of events.

With the excitement of the first gosling hatching, the sitting goose tends to lose concentration. After one or two have hatched, she will stand up and have a look at them. Once the goslings are on their feet (this takes about a day) the goose will want to lead them out, leaving any later hatchers to go cold. This is where the incubator is useful, as you can finish the goslings off inside it, and then return them to the goose at night by tucking them under her wings.

This method of returning goslings usually works very well, but we had one astute goose that could count. She had had four goslings for a couple of days and was very happy with them. Three more were added to the nest overnight, but when she came out in the morning she knew that this was wrong. She eyed up the goslings, which were identical in appearance, and identified the three that did not behave in quite the same way as the original four, and would have nothing to do with them. This is unusual behaviour. As long as the goslings are of the same age group, and look to the goose to be of the right sort, she is usually happy to accept them. A goose may, however, become worried by the responsibility of a large group, of twelve or more.

When there are No Goslings

When there are no goslings you may have problems. It is essential to note the date when the goose seriously sits and begins to incubate the eggs. The eggs should also be checked, to make sure that the bird is not carrying out the useless task of sitting on infertiles. The female loses a lot of weight over a 30- to 32-day period and the biggest problem, particularly if she has not been fed properly, is how to re-invigorate her appetite. This is particularly difficult if there are no goslings to stimulate her.

If the nest is removed, the goose will do her utmost to reconstruct another one on the same spot, even if you put something unpleasant in its place, like an orange feedbag, which will be removed, or even sat upon. If the nest was in a shed where the bird is shut up at night, moving the shed to another spot may do the trick. In the experience of one friend and her Brecon, the bird persisted in being broody on the spot where the shed had been. If your place is large enough, the best strategy is to move the goose to another paddock, or give her some goslings from another bird if she has reared goslings before. If she has not, someone else's goslings may be no use either, so moving the bird is the only option.

Why Go to all this Trouble?

The key to success in natural hatching is good observation. Since it is a natural process, many people assume that, left to get on with it, the birds will manage. However, these are not wild birds. They have not chosen their patch; their human keeper has. Nor have they been trained by their parents in the skills of survival. Also, they may be kept much more intensively than wild birds, so that the density of parasites may be higher. One similarity is that, in the wild, many eggs and goslings are lost to predators; yours will be too, unless you are vigilant.

Commercial rearers of goslings are not able to justify such a labour-intensive method of production, but hatching pure breeds is much more difficult than hatching a carefully chosen commercial cross. It is most satisfying to manage stock successfully without too much equipment, and many people are prepared to do this out of interest, rather than for commercial gain.

Broody Hens

Introducing Goose Eggs

I prefer to use broody hens rather than the geese for sitting. The hens can be persuaded to sit earlier, often shortly after the geese have begun to lay. Any type can be used, as long as she has the broody trait. We have used Silkies, Silkie cross Indian Game, and broody-type bantams. The smaller birds cover only three goose eggs, but a meatier hen can cover six. The hens are best started off on their own eggs then, when they are thoroughly broody, the larger eggs are substituted. Do not expect a broody hen to waste her energy warming up enormous stone-cold eggs. Give her warm eggs that you have started in the incubator and that you know are fertile. There is no point in wasting broodies.

Although a hen should sit for only 21 days to hatch her own, she can manage 28 days perfectly well if you keep an eye on her. Many breeders use the hens for even longer than this. The health of a hen can be gauged by her weight, if she is handled daily. Her well-being can also be assessed from the colour of the comb and her behaviour on feeding.

Feeding

Hens that are used to you become very tame when they are handled as broodies. If the weather is fine or hot, it is a good idea to lift

Fig 119 Broody hens are much more successful than the incubator at hatching goslings early in the season in dry straw nests. The eggs seem able to lose the correct amount of water in a nest better than in an incubator. A Silkie hen, like this one, will cover two goose eggs. She is on a turf nest on late-season eggs, which lose water more easily and are dehydrating properly

them off the nest twice a day to feed. Randomly hand-turn the goose eggs when you do this, in case the broody is having difficulty. Feeding once a day will do if it is raining, as the hens do not like being wet and wind-blown.

Wheat is usually recommended as a good broody ration; the droppings will be firmer, and the nest will be less messy if it is fouled. Birds do like wheat that has been soaked in water, so leave some in a bucket overnight, ready for the morning feed. It slips down more easily than dry rations and ensures that the hens do not get dehydrated in a heatwave. Water should always be made available, nevertheless. If household scraps are often used to feed the hens, these should be limited during sitting if they contain salt, as this will place more stress on the hen.

Parasites

During the broody period, a hen will become infested with northern mites. These are normally kept to a minimum with preening and dust-bathing so, while sitting, she will need help with a good dusting powder. It also helps if the nest litter is changed every couple of weeks, as it may contain blood-sucking insects. Before fresh litter is used, dust the nesting container, and the hen, particularly around and at the vent, where parasites accumulate for the moisture.

Rearing

Hens can hatch and rear goslings, and make a good job of it. However, because their feeding habits are so different from those of geese, I prefer not to rely on them for this. Hens can scratch showers of dust over the waterfowl, and often try to encourage the goslings to eat worms and insects while they try to graze. If no grass is available, the goslings may even graze the unfortunate hen and begin to strip her feathers.

Give the hen some chicken eggs that are on the point of hatching (from the incubator), and take the goose eggs away to a hatcher on pipping.

Reasons for Success

The truth is that the broody hen does the best job of sitting on the goose eggs. It is generally accepted that difficult eggs from pure breeds are best started under hens – natural conditions are better than incubators. Broody hens are, of course, in short supply when the goose eggs start to arrive in large numbers, and the small hens can cover very few eggs. The way around this problem is to start the goose eggs in the incubator (see pages 136 and 145), and give the broody hen the most precious goose eggs at 10–14 days incubation, or earlier, if there is space available. These eggs should have a better hatch rate than those that are wholly artificially incubated.

This improved success rate could be due to the fact that temperature conditions are optimum beneath the hen, allowing the embryo to grow well. However, I am inclined to believe, from observation, that the goose egg is able to dehydrate under the broody hen better than in the average still-air incubator. It is water reduction that can be a problem, not the delicacy of the embryos, especially with early eggs. The hen seems to provide the right conditions for this, despite research indicating that there are enormous variations in humidity in nests; the average is about 60 per cent RH. Variations depend on the nest site and on the prevailing weather conditions.

There are good nests and bad nests. Damp earth nests are not good in March; an airy wicker basket with plenty of straw is much more effective. However, in a dry May and June, the goose eggs might need a daily spray of water and a damper base, depending on the breed. However, it is still best to check by candling first. Eggs from chickens and Call ducks often seem to need this treatment, but not Pilgrim or Brecon eggs. Black out a window in a shed except for one corner, and use this as a 'candler', to see into the egg. This will work quite well, and will save you carting the eggs around and disturbing the embryo.

ARTIFICIAL INCUBATION

Which Type of Incubator?

Modern incubators run on electricity and have electronically controlled thermostats, which are excellent at keeping a steady temperature. They have the disadvantage of being out of action in a power cut, and this is why some people still prefer the older paraffin types, which now have to be obtained second-hand. These are, however, much more difficult to operate. There are two main types of electrically run incubator – the still-air machine and the forced-air (also called fan-assisted) machine.

Still-air incubators can only have one 'layer' of eggs, so this limits their capacity. An element in the insulated box heats the air, which convects naturally, so that it is cooler at the base of the box, and the warm air escapes at the top. The temperature is adjusted so that it is correct for the layer of eggs.

In the forced-air incubator, a fan circulates the air around the whole of the box, so there can be several layers of eggs inside a cabinet. The even flow of warm air around the eggs ensures that the incubator is the same temperature throughout. These incubators are generally much more expensive than the still-air models, because they tend to be larger, and some models incorporate automatic turning and humidity control. Some still-air incubators also have automatic turning gear, but I have not found an incubator of either type that turns goose eggs well. In a side-to-side roll, the eggs tend to march up on each other. In a forced-air cabinet, the automatic turn is only through ninety degrees, and this will do when turning is frequent. If you decide to opt for this type, make sure it is designed for goose eggs, otherwise the motor will not cope with the weight.

In a forced-air machine, eggs due to pip are generally moved down to the floor of the machine for hatching. The disadvantage of this is that dirty material is introduced into the machine, because eggs make a mess when they hatch. It is better to have a hatcher that is separate from the main incubator in either type of machine. A small still-air incubator is ideal as a hatcher, especially if it is made of sound materials that will clean easily. Plastic is better for this purpose than wood. Cheap polystyrene incubators are excellent for incubating the eggs, but are no use as hatchers, as the expanded polystyrene cannot be cleaned well.

Fig 120 A useful still-air incubator. The solid plastic is easy to clean and the base can be immersed in a bath. This is useful for a hatcher, which needs a good scrub after each hatch. This particular model has had the automatic turning removed

Fig 121 A larger still-air incubator designed for 150 hen eggs, which will hold about 50 goose eggs. Many may prove to be infertile, so it is useful to set quite a large batch at a time, and then transfer the fertiles to smaller incubators, or broody hens or geese. The seven eggs on top have a brief warm-up before being transferred to a broody hen

Still-Air Incubators

(The following information refers only to still-air incubators for small-scale production.)

I prefer the flexibility of more than one independent unit. Unless you will be happy with just one incubator full of eggs, going right through to hatching, and then cleaning before you start another batch of eggs, you really need two incubators. There are several reasons for this. Firstly, if large, cold goose eggs are added to a still-air incubator, they will take some time to heat up. They will reduce the temperature of the incubator, and it will take hours for the temperature to stabilize again. This adversely affects any eggs already started, for example, a week earlier. With two or three incubators, one can be used to warm up and start a new batch without affecting other incubated eggs.

Eggs also run at different temperatures. Eggs near hatching generate their own heat and are considerably warmer to the touch than newly added eggs; in a small incubator, some eggs can feel red hot, while others are not warm enough. Near to hatching, eggs are best transferred into an incubator to be used as a separate hatcher; the temperature can then be regulated better for these hot eggs,

which are 1–2 degrees warmer than newly set eggs. You must avoid a small incubator over-heating; 39 degrees centigrade (102.2 degrees Fahrenheit) is lethal if it is maintained. Hatching eggs also make a mess, so it is best to keep incubating eggs separate from them.

For a first incubator, I would not recommend a small automatic machine; these are usually extremely expensive for the amount of goose egg space they offer. Fertility with goose eggs can be poor, and it is better to have as much space as possible. Incubating goose eggs successfully is an art and it is better to start off in a small way. Instead of buying an automatic turner, you can buy two simple models, and teach yourself about hatching. One of them could be second-hand, as long as you have advice from someone who is familiar with that type, and it is a fairly recent electronically controlled model. Sterilize it thoroughly.

Generally, companies selling new incubators also supply spare parts, which are not difficult to fit.

If you are successful and wish to continue with the birds, you can graduate on to more expensive models for incubation and still use your basic machines as hatchers. If hatching is not for you, you will not have lost a great deal in capital outlay.

Even if expense is no object, reflect that fully automating everything to try to save time may not work. Observation is the key to hatching, and the most successful goose breeders are those who take time and trouble over their birds.

A Suitable Place for the Incubator

The following are ways of ensuring that the small incubator does as good a job as possible.
• Keep the incubator on a level surface.
• Keep as steady a temperature as possible, as recommended by the manufacturers.
• Keep it in the house, preferably in a spare, well-insulated unheated room; the incubator will heat the room itself. A suitable room temperature is 18.5–21.5 degrees centigrade (65–70 degrees Fahrenheit).
• A north-facing room is best, to avoid overheating from sunlight streaming through a window.
• The incubator will maintain a steadier temperature if covered by a folded woolly blanket.
• The blanket also has the advantage of keeping the eggs in the dark, which is considered to be beneficial.
• The room must have low humidity, so that you can control the RH in the incubator. If the room humidity is above 60–65 per cent, you cannot regulate the incubator very well, unless you get a dehumidifier for the room. If you live in a stone cottage without a damp course, it is unlikely that the incubator will hatch goose eggs. Choose a room away from sources of damp air. Avoid the kitchen and the bathroom, and make sure that moist air is vented from the house rather than into the incubator room.
• If you have young children, make sure that they cannot get into the room and change the controls.

Humidity

Measuring Humidity

Air contains water vapour as a gas. The amount the air will hold depends on its temperature. The easiest way to measure this is not by its weight per cubic metre (its total humidity), but by its relative humidity (RH). The amount of water vapour the air could hold

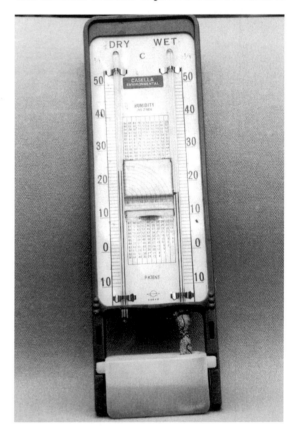

Fig 122 Hygrometer – wet and dry bulb thermometers. The dry bulb measures the air temperature. The wet bulb is sheathed in a damp cotton gauze, which wicks moisture up from a reservoir. Evaporation cools the wet bulb; the difference in temperature allows the relative humidity to be calculated. The reading from the instrument can be used to check the less accurate hair and bi-metallic meters. In the incubator, the bulbs should be at the level of the eggs for checking RH at the egg temperature

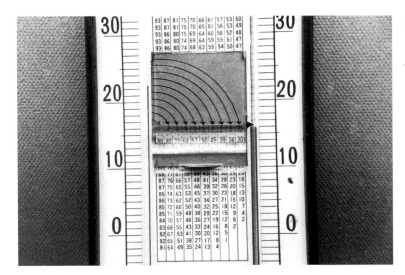

Fig 123 The sliding scale shows the relative humidity by comparing the wet bulb temperature with the dry bulb. In this case, the RH outdoors is 50 per cent

at a certain temperature (if enough water were available to saturate the air) is compared with what it is actually holding. This can be calculated by using a wet and dry bulb thermometer. Evaporation from the cotton gauze at the wet bulb causes heat to be taken from the adjacent thermometer. This causes a drop in temperature, similar to the effect of wearing wet clothes. The drier the air, the greater the rate of evaporation, and the greater the difference in temperature between the wet and dry bulb. Using a sliding scale, the difference in temperature allows the RH to be calculated.

Although quite expensive, a modern electronic humidity gauge will allow spot checks to see if conditions are right for the egg both in storage and incubation. Cheaper hair hygrometers, where the value is read straight from the dial, are quite effective. For a check on the accuracy of these hygrometers, use a wet and dry bulb hygrometer; this is unwieldy to use, but accurate.

Humidity and the Incubating Egg

Eggs are porous, so, in an incubator at RH 38 per cent, eggs should lose water more rapidly than at RH 55 per cent. As the egg gradually loses water through its pores, the air sac at the bulbous end increases in size. The gosling breaks into this air space and breathes in air just prior to hatching; the space also gives it enough room to manoeuvre to get out of the egg. After that point, no air sac is seen on candling.

Small incubators always arrive with a water tray and it seems obvious that waterfowl need high humidity for their eggs. The standard recommended humidity for hatching waterfowl is 55 per cent, which is lower than a room's normal humidity, of 60–70 per cent (warm air is able to hold more moisture, so RH drops in the incubator). In a dry house, in dry weather, water will generally have to be added to the incubator in order to achieve that 55 per cent. The egg has to increase the volume of its air sac and lose about 13–15 per cent of its water by weight before it can hatch.

In my experience, most pure-breed goose eggs will not do this at RH 55 per cent, so you should not expect to hatch goose eggs (other than Chinese) in the same incubator as duck's eggs. As a general rule, you should never add any water to a still-air incubator, unless the air sacs look enormous and you begin to worry about dehydration. With a room RH of 60–65 per cent, the incubator will run at about 38 per cent, and early Brecon and Pilgrim eggs will still not hatch because they will be too wet. Sufficient weight loss is unlikely to happen, except in a dry spell in late May or June, when eggs seem to dehydrate more rapidly because of their own changing properties. The eggs of Chinese and Africans are different; they dehydrate much more rapidly and by mid-season are generally best run at 55 per cent.

The best weather for early incubator hatching is when there is a cold north wind in spring. This cool air stream often has low relative humidity and, because it is cool, its total moisture content is also low. Once the air is warmed up in the house, the RH drops even further. The worst weather is continuously wet conditions, when the incubator meter stubbornly stays at 55 per cent even though you have added no water. The old tale that a thunderstorm ruins a hatch is true. Humidity rockets and the goslings do not stand a chance of taking a breath. The difficulty of tightly regulating humidity in a small still-air incubator derives from the fact that RH is mainly dependent on external atmospheric conditions.

The ideal RH for the correct weight loss varies between different breeds of geese, and is also different for a specific breed at different times of the year. The commonest problem in hatching goose eggs is their failure to lose sufficient water over the incubation period. Although this can be monitored visually, by checking the size of the air sac on candling, weighing the egg gives a much more accurate assessment of its progress, and indicates how it is responding to the ambient humidity (*see* pages 158–59).

'Dead in Shell'
Goose eggs that fail to lose enough water result in 'dead in shell' goslings – goslings that have tried to pip the membrane to breathe, but have failed, due to excess liquid. This is such a problem for early eggs that it is necessary to resort either to low-tech broody bantams or to expensive high-tech forced-air incubators and dehumidifiers. The middle way is to use a reliable still-air

incubator, combined with broody birds.

Some incubators have variable vents at the base. Read the operating instructions for your incubator carefully. There needs to be balance between carbon dioxide build-up and oxygen supply if the embryo is to grow correctly. You can open up the vents during the last week to get a flow of air through; this also seems to improve dehydration. Old text-books, worrying about hatchlings getting too dry, used to recommend closing down the vents when the 'felts' were wetted near pipping, to increase humidity for hatching. Higher humidity is still desirable on hatching, particularly if hundreds of eggs are being produced. However, in small-scale production, you can keep an eye on those that seem to need help and allow the hatcher to remain fairly dry if some eggs are still struggling to lose weight. Ideally, you should have two incubators – one kept dry for development, and a second one used as a hatcher, where the humidity can be increased after 'pipping'. Remember, however, that a wet incubator is a breeding ground for bacteria, which can infect the umbilicus; if you do not need the water, do not add it.

Spraying Eggs
A fine spray of warm, clean water once a day is often recommended for goose eggs. The idea is that this prevents the internal membranes from being desiccated and impeding the gosling from escaping from its shell. While this seems to be good practice when using a forced-air machine, there seems to be little point in this procedure if weight loss of the egg is a problem. It may be useful for Chinese and African eggs that are dehydrating too quickly.

Temperature
Temperature is important but not, in my experience, as crucial with goose eggs as water content. With a still-air incubator, manufacturers usually recommend 38.4 degrees centigrade (101 degrees Fahrenheit) for the thermometer 2in (5cm) above the floor of the egg tray for hen eggs during the first

Fig 124 A useful thermometer on a stand. The bulb is just above the centre of the eggs and should read 37.2 degrees centigrade (99 degrees Fahrenheit)

week, rising to 39.5 degrees centigrade (103 degrees Fahrenheit) for the third week. Anderson Brown recommends 38.4 degrees centigrade (101 degrees Fahrenheit) for goose eggs, the thermometer being level with the top of the egg. This will give a correct core temperature of 37.2 degrees centigrade (99 degrees Fahrenheit). The thermometer bulb should not rest on the egg, because it is the *air* temperature that must be read.

You are unlikely to be able to regulate the temperature so closely in a small still-air incubator. For example, if you place three or four thermometers at different positions around the incubator (at the same height), you will find that there will be 1–2 degrees of difference in temperature between the sides and the middle. This does not matter; conditions in the nest vary too, and, as long as you shuffle the eggs around the incubator from time to time, they will come to no harm. Alternatively, if the eggs are from different geese and are of different sizes, the larger eggs should be in the middle and the smaller ones around the outside, depending on the heat source. In my incubator, designed for 150 hen eggs, the edges are the hottest and the centre is the coolest. This is because the element is located around the edge at and just below egg level. Because the hot air rises inside the incubator, the higher levels are warmer than the floor; the eggs that stand the highest have a warmer top, and their increased height compensates for the fact that they are further from the edges. The temperature difference between the base of the egg (on the floor of the incubator) and the top of the egg will be as much as 2–3 degrees for a large egg.

Incubation temperatures for goose eggs compared with other species

Species	degrees F	degrees C
Goose	99.0	37.2
Duck	99.2	37.3
Hen	99.5	37.5
Pheasant	99.75	37.6

(figures taken from Anderson Brown, The Incubation Book)

Curfew supply a very nice mercury thermometer on a stand designed to show the incubation temperature above poultry eggs. As it happens, the mercury bulb is just above the centre of the goose egg, in an ideal position. When the thermometer reads 37.2 degrees centigrade (99 degrees Fahrenheit) at about 3in (8cm) from the edge of the incubator, conditions are ideal for goose eggs.

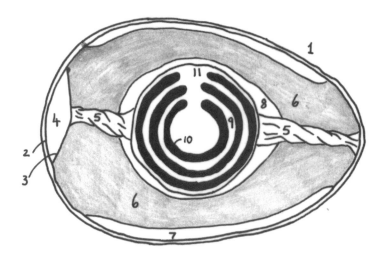

1 shell   2 shell membrane   3 egg membrane   4 air sac/cell   5 chalazae
6 dense albumen   7 outer liquid albumen   8 inner liquid albumen   9 white yolk
10 yellow yolk   11 blastodisc /germinal disc

The egg is covered externally by a **porous shell** formed from the **external cuticle** and the chalky **testa.** This chalky layer gives the egg its strength and provides the calcium to be partially absorbed by the embryo.

Inside the shell is a **membrane.** It has two layers. These separate at the broader end of the egg to form the **air cell** or **sac.** The outer membrane is attached to the testa and the inner membrane to the albumen. Gases are exchanged between the albumen and the blood supply of the embryo and the exterior through the porous shell structure.

The **albumen** is held within the membrane and within this are two twisted cords, the **chalazae.** Their function is to suspend the yolk in the albumen. These cords are coiled in opposite directions so that when the yolk rotates in the albumen one coil is wound up as the other unwinds. Turning the egg in the same direction all the time will therefore destroy the egg's structure. Most of the albumen is formed from **dense albumen** which extends to the ends of the egg where protein fibres are attached to the shell. The chalazae are within the thick albumen. The inner and outer part is **fluid albumen,** the inner fluid layer allowing the yolk to rotate on turning. The albumen is a store of protein and water and is used up during incubation.

The **yolk** is rich in fats and proteins and is surrounded by a thin membrane. The yolk itself consists of alternating light and dark layers which are laid down by night and day respectively. The centre of the yolk contains a ball of protein-rich yolk and a narrow column of this extends to the surface where it broadens into a cone. The blastodisc sits on top of this. The majority of the yolk is not used during incubation; it is drawn into the abdominal cavity of the gosling just before hatching.

Whatever position the egg occupies, the **blastodisc [germinal disc]** occupies the upper position. This is a small, white spot [about 4mm across] from which the gosling will grow. The part of the yolk next to the germinal disc is less dense than the rest of the yolk so it tends to float upwards, rotating the yolk so that the germinal disc is always on top. In the early stages of development the embryo can only use the nutrients in contact with it; turning the egg gives it a new source of food and oxygen from the inner liquid albumen.

The yolk and the germinal disc originate in the ovary. The albumen, shell membrane and shell are formed by the oviduct.

(adapted from Charnock Bradley, 1950, Brooke & Birkhead, 1991)

Fig 125 Structure of the unincubated egg

It is important to achieve a steady, correct temperature at the start of incubation. Some allege that this is why broodies produce better hatch rates than incubators. Marginally high temperatures late on produce earlier hatches, but core temperatures above 39.4 degrees centigrade (103 degrees Fahrenheit) are lethal. Slightly lower temperatures delay the hatch and resorption of the yolk sac. This feature is particularly bad if humidity has also been high. The goslings that do manage to hatch are large and soft, and slow on their feet.

Unfortunately, mistakes with temperatures cannot be corrected by compensating the other way once a mistake has been made. Instead, try to keep as steady a temperature as possible for the remainder of the incubation period. If, however, the eggs have been severely heated for a short period, take the top off the incubator and allow them to cool for fifteen minutes, to get the core temperature back to the correct level as quickly as possible.

Setting the Eggs

Timing
When setting the eggs count on to, and make a note of, the optimum hatching date. This should be a day when you are likely to be around to keep an eye on things.

Cleaning and Age of Eggs
The eggs should have been cleaned first (see pages 126–28). For development in an incubator they should be no more than 14 and preferably less than 10 days old.

Labelling
All eggs should carry the date laid and indicate the parent; that way, you will soon find out which birds are going to have a successful season and which are infertile, for one reason or another.

The eggs will have to be turned manually in a small still-air incubator, so they are traditionally marked with a circle on one side and an 'x' on the other. This is to check that every egg has been turned.

If you are to have more than one setting in the main incubator at a time, it is wise to mark them differently – for example, a double circle on one batch or different coloured crayon marks – so that you can see at glance which batch you are dealing with when candling and observing development.

Preparing Eggs for Incubation
The following points are very important.

- The eggs should have been stored at 12–14 degrees centigrade (53.6–57.2 degrees Fahrenheit).
- They should not be transferred immediately to an environment at 37 degrees centigrade (99 degrees Fahrenheit). A rapid rise in temperature can cause the membrane around the yolk to burst, making the egg useless. Bring the clean eggs into a warm room overnight to raise their core temperature to about 20 degrees centigrade (68 degrees Fahrenheit), then transfer them to the incubator.
- The incubator should have been pre-heated to 37.2 degrees centigrade (99 degrees Fahrenheit) for a couple of days.
- Having noted the position of the dial for that temperature, turn down the indicator, and then gradually raise the temperature over the next 24 hours. This should only be done if you know the behaviour of the incubator well, otherwise you may find it difficult to stabilize the temperature. There is nothing to gain by heating the eggs rapidly. They warm up very slowly in a nest.

Turning
- Eggs need not be turned for the first 24 hours in the incubator.
- After the first 24 hours, turning is essential. The germinal disc (the white spot on the yolk of the unincubated egg) is where the incubated cells will divide and grow.

This disc is located on a part of the yolk that is less dense than the rest so that, when the egg is turned, the disc floats upwards. It is, therefore, in closest contact with the body temperature of a sitting bird. Turning the egg not only prevents the disc and yolk sticking to the outer membrane of the egg, but also places the disc in contact with new nutrients. In the early stages, when the embryo has scarcely developed its own blood supply, it needs an immediate source from adjacent fluids.

- Eggs are turned frequently by broody birds, once recorded as every 35 minutes on average. In automatic incubators they may be turned once an hour, but only through 90 degrees where the mechanism rotates the whole tray.
- Turning twice a day by hand is an absolute minimum, and the turn should be through 90–180 degrees. A small turn is acceptable in automatic incubators, because turning is more frequent. Hand-turning three or five times a day is more effective. If the time intervals are not equal, the odd number of turns will compensate for this on each second day.
- Geese can turn their eggs end over end in the nest but, more frequently, they just stir them about. Religiously turning the eggs left, then right, seems to work well. It is important not to keep winding the egg in the same direction as the chalazae – the rubbery strings supporting the yolk in the centre of the egg – as they will gradually become tightened up at one end, and too loose at the other; this should also be taken into account when washing the eggs.
- Insufficient turning of the incubating egg will result in the embryo dying. However, turning is unnecessary in the two days before hatching.
- It is best to get into a routine for turning the eggs. Always write down what you have done. List the dates, indicating the date of incubation and the likely date – 28 days later – for pipping. Opposite each date, write down the left/right/left turns when you do them each day, then you can be certain whether you have turned the eggs or not.

It may be a nuisance turning the eggs, but it allows you to check frequently how things are going. We once lost a number of goose eggs in a forced-air cabinet incubator, because we relied completely on the thermometer. The temperature seemed to be too low, so we turned the heat up. This happened again. Too late, we realized that the alcohol thermometer had a hair-line crack, was losing liquid and under-registering. The eggs had been cooked at a lethal temperature. This cannot happen if you are handling the eggs more than once a day for turning, as you will quickly become accustomed to the feel of the correct temperature. The eggs in an incubator should feel the same as, or slightly warmer than, eggs from a bantam's nest, if the temperature is correct.

As incubation progresses, the embryo begins to generate its own heat. By 14 days, the eggs often feel a bit warmer that those in the bantam's nest. They seem to do better in the incubator like this. However, you may need to regulate the temperature dial downwards, to prevent the incubator from over-heating. Although the incubator is always needed to keep the eggs warm, after two weeks the egg's own metabolism raises its temperature above that of the air in the incubator. It is this raised temperature that allows the broody goose to know which of her eggs are fertile. An experienced goose often turfs dead eggs out of the nest.

If there are two batches of eggs in the incubator, spaced at two weeks apart, the newly incubated eggs should be placed in the warmer part of the incubator, and the two-week eggs in the cooler part, otherwise the temperature differential between them will increase. This is another advantage of having a heat gradient across the still-air incubator.

There is no need to worry about the eggs and incubator cooling off while the eggs are turned. The eggs maintain their internal heat

Fig 126 A candling device can be made quite cheaply. This wooden box has an oval hole on the opposite side. Use a low-wattage bulb, otherwise too much heat is generated. There is no need to rest the egg on the box; hold the egg above the hole

quite well for at least five minutes. Some people even recommend cooling the eggs during the mid-incubation period once a day for 5–10 minutes, to mimic natural conditions and hence improve hatchability. This may improve dehydration.

Candling Eggs

Candling not only saves you wasted incubator space, but ensures that rotten eggs are not kept. It is essential that incubators are kept clean, and that rotten eggs are not allowed to explode. If you have your incubator in the house, you will certainly smell bad eggs before this stage anyway, and remove them before they become even more offensive.

A torch can be used for candling, but the beam is not really bright enough to shine through the egg. A good candling device is essential and will save money in the long run because you will be saving incubator space. Proprietary brands can be purchased but, if you have the time, a simple device can be made much more cheaply out of a standard light fitting, plywood and a light bulb.

If the eggs are clean, successful candling may be done, with experience, at 4 or 5 days. A bright light is needed in a dark room; the

goose egg's shell is very thick in comparison with the duck's, which is very easy to candle. A fertile goose egg will have a yolk that appears to 'glow' at 4 days, whereas an infertile looks just like any unincubated egg, with the yolk casting a dull shadow. If you think an egg is infertile, check it against an unincubated egg. If you are unsure, check again at 6 to 7 days, when the eye, which develops early, should appear as a definite spot and veins are visible. Eggs that have started, and then died, will not show an eye, and appear to slosh around in the shell as the egg is rotated. In duck eggs, degeneration of the veins after the death of the embryo goes through a 'blood ring' stage, but this is hard to identify in the goose egg because the shell is so much thicker. Sometimes there are black patches inside a transparent egg, but no veins. These are probably bacteria colonies and the egg needs to be removed.

Candling should not take place unnecessarily, as the heat from a light bulb is quite excessive; a rapid inspection is best. However, the eggs will need to be checked again. As incubation progresses, the whole of the egg will darken between day 10 and 14. There should be a clear dividing line between the membrane of the air sac and embryo. An indistinct line and a pale band adjacent to the

In a fresh egg, the embryo can be seen as a small white spot 4mm in diameter. It has a clear centre. There are two layers of cells: the upper layer or **ectoderm** above and the **endoderm** below. The **mesoderm** forms in the middle within a few hours of laying. The ectoderm will form the skin and nervous system; the mesoderm the heart, skeleton and kidneys; the endoderm the liver and lungs.

Further development will only take place on incubation when a groove forms along the centre of the disc in the ectoderm. During the first day of incubation the primitive streak is formed from linear thickening in the ectoderm. The sides of the disc then fold and join to become the neural tube [at 38–48 hours] from which develop the brain and spinal cord.

Diagram of chick embryo at 38 hours drawn from Charnock Bradley

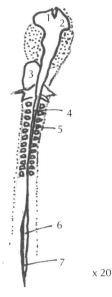

x 20

1   Fore-brain
2   Optic vesicle from which the eye is produced
3   Heart
4   Neural tube
5   Mesodermal segments (somites)
6   Notochord – the primitive stiffening rod of all vertebrates
7   Primitive streak

(Note that the times given are from studies of poultry. There do not seem to be any specific references to geese. Incubation is a week longer in geese, so 25 per cent should be added on to each time stated.)

It will not be possible to see this detail on candling but after about 3 days incubation, the blastodisc (egg nucleus) has grown to a cap of about 25mm in diameter. It is an area of blood islands (the *area vasculosa*) and by day three these have formed a network of blood vessels which radiate from the embryo rather like a spiders web. It is these blood vessels which make the yolk appear to glow on candling at three to four days. When you are experienced at candling, it is possible to reject the infertiles with a high degree of accuracy at this stage. Do not do this if there is any doubt; wait until day 5–7.

Fig 127 The embryo during early incubation

line indicate that the egg has died. If the egg is cooler to the touch than the other eggs, this is another confirmation of your suspicions. If you are not sure if an egg is dead, leave it in the incubator, as long as it is not smelly. Eggs that have started and then died are the dangerous ones; they will go rotten and could explode, infecting the whole incubator and its contents.

Development during Incubation: Hints for Candling

The size of the air sac should not appear to change a great deal up to 18 days, even though there has been a fairly steady loss in weight, but, after that, regular and more rapid change should occur visually. If you have candled the egg, mark the extent of the air sac with a pencil line at and after day 18,

By about the fourth day the embryo has grown its extra-embryonic membranes: the yolk sac, the amnion, the chorion and the allantois. These are the embryo's life support systems. Blood vessels linked to the heart transport nutrients from the yolk to the embryo. The allantois contains waste products from the kidneys and is eventually left behind. The amnion is a fluid-filled bag to protect the embryo. The chorion is at first surrounded by albumen, but as the albumen is absorbed, the chorion eventually contacts the inner shell membrane. Between day 4 and 7, most of what can be seen on candling is the brain and a large rudimentary eye. This shows as a central spot within a system of radiating veins.

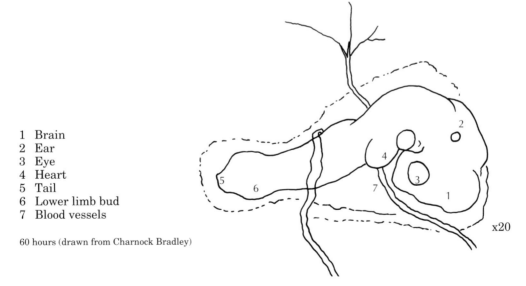

1 Allantois
2 Amnion
3 Yolk sac
4 Chorion
5 Albumen
6 Air sac

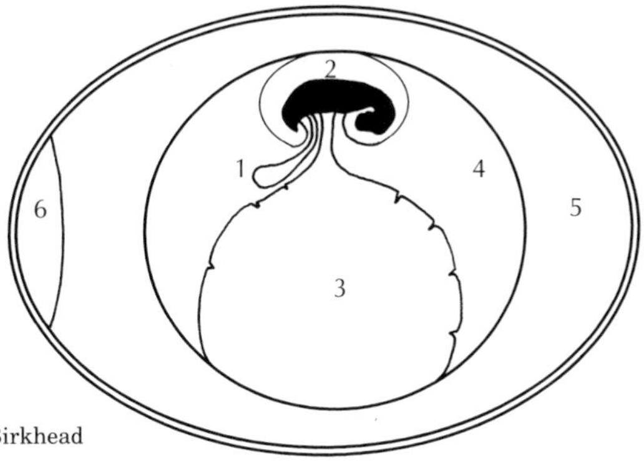

Adapted from Charnock Bradley and Brooke & Birkhead

Fig 128 The Fourth Day

1 Brain
2 Ear
3 Eye
4 Heart
5 Tail
6 Lower limb bud
7 Blood vessels

60 hours (drawn from Charnock Bradley)

x20

Fig 129 Development of the embryo showing the eye and radiating blood vessels

so you can see how it is developing. Usually the eggs with the best development of this feature are the early hatchers. However, if the weather is dry and you are incubating eggs that need higher humidity, such as African and Chinese, you may have to intervene with a higher-humidity incubator even before this stage.

149

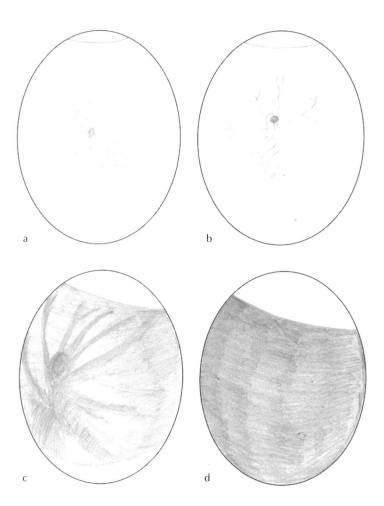

a **Three to four days**: the egg yolk appears to glow, as a network of blood vessels develop. If you look carefully, a small dark spot, about 4mm long will be seen, formed by the embryo and its large eye. In duck eggs, the blood vessels will clearly be seen at this stage, but the goose shell is too thick to see this.

b **Seven days:** the embryo shows up as a dark spot and the radiating blood vessels are clearly seen. This is the best point at which to candle as you are least likely to make a mistake.

c **Twelve to fourteen days**: the egg has darkened considerably. The embryo itself can scarcely be distinguished, but the blood vessels can be made out. The air sac has grown and, at the opposite end of the shell, the candler's light passes through some un-absorbed pale albumen. At the air sac end, the membrane margin is clearly defined.

d **Eighteen to twenty days**: the whole egg has darkened and there is a sharp margin between the membrane and the air sac The embryo has absorbed the albumen and the air sac has grown considerably. There is a rapid change in the size of the air sac which the embryo can control to some extent by using the amniotic fluid[1]. The change in weight is steady. This is a healthy egg which stands a good chance of hatching.

[1] Anderson Brown, Dr A F

Fig 130 Candling eggs during incubation

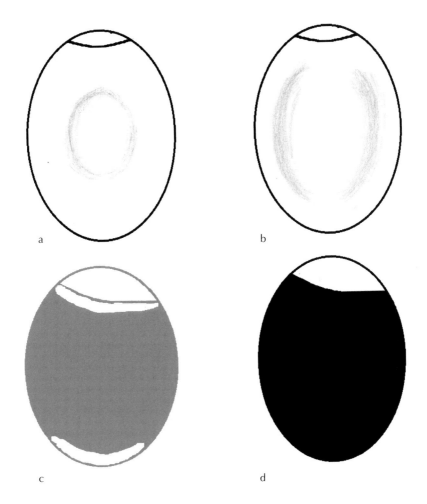

a **Incubator clear:** infertile egg with only a faint shadow of the yolk. Reject at any stage after day five. This egg will not go bad.

b **Fertile egg which has died**: the 'blood ring' stage where the veins have degenerated. There is no eye and no network of veins. The egg sloshes around in the shell when it is rotated. This may happen after day seven so candle the eggs again around day 12–14 to identify these. This egg will decompose. The air sac does not change as much as in good eggs and it may even disappear – a bad sign.

c **Fertile egg which has died:** at a later stage of development than b. The margin of the membrane and air sac is not sharp and there is a band of slightly translucent egg instead of solid black on candling. This egg will also go bad.

d **'Dead in shell':** the egg has failed to lose enough water by day 27. If weighed, it will have lost less than 12–13 per cent of its initial weight. On candling, the membrane may have been moving feebly on days 24–27 as the live gosling moves. However, the gosling will fail to break the membrane and cannot pip the shell. Always give these eggs plenty of time; a few may hatch. They will be sticky goslings and are often not healthy.

Fig 131 Incubation failures

151

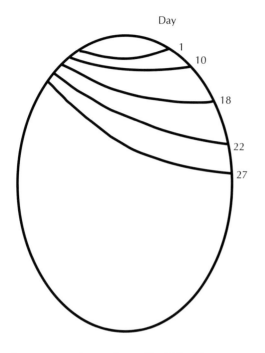

Day

1
10
18
22
27

An egg must lose at least 12–13% of its water to hatch. The most accurate way of monitoring this change is to weigh the egg, but this is time consuming. A quicker way is to monitor the air sac visually by candling. The rate of change of the air sac is greater between day 18 and 22 than prior to that period.

Fig 132 Ideal air-sac development

Hatching in an Incubator

Cleaning and Fumigating

It is preferable to keep one incubator separately as a hatcher and to give it a thorough clean every time it is used. It can, of course, be used as an ordinary incubator in between hatches. The hatching incubator can be a smaller model than your main incubator. A cheaper, second-hand incubator is ideal. The pre-requisite is that is must be easy to clean. Make sure you can immerse the whole of the base of the incubator in the bath, and scrub it with detergent; a drop of Milton can also be used afterwards as a disinfectant. The interior of the lid should also be wiped

down with a damp cloth and disinfectant. Although removing the motor leaves a hole at the base of the incubator, this does not seem to make much difference. Regulation of air flow is also controlled by the vents in the lid.

Incubators can be disinfected by fumigation, but the main benefit of this is in large hatcheries, where there is continuous setting and hatching. Eggs can be fumigated quite safely at certain stages, so there is no need to interrupt the process of production.

Formaldehyde gas is generated by introducing formalin to potassium permanganate crystals in a large ceramic or glass container placed inside the warmed incubator. There is quite a violent and immediate foaming reaction as the gas is generated. As well as being lethal to micro-organisms, the gas is also lethal for you, and everything else alive. Unless you have had many problems with goslings suffering from infections shortly after hatching, stick to liquid disinfectants. For fumigation, check the quantities of chemicals needed for your incubator capacity with a chemist first, and ask for advice about the use of the chemicals and about protection in using them.

Suitable Hatching Materials

Rolls of hatching paper are available from incubator stockists and are useful because they help to keep the incubator clean. Perforated aluminium and wire mesh are rather harsh on the raw umbilicus of a newly hatched gosling, so special paper or textured paper kitchen towels can be used. Newspaper is no good, because it is too smooth and will only encourage spraddled legs. If there are any old clothes available, cut these up and use them as incubator cloth; they are better than paper, as long as there are no loose strands to get tied around legs, or eaten.

Regulating the Temperature

The temperature of the hatcher will need to be watched carefully. Active hatchlings generate a lot of heat, and the incubator temperature will therefore rise to unacceptable levels if you do not regulate it downwards. Maintain the hatcher at a core egg temperature of 37.2 degrees centigrade (99 degrees Fahrenheit). Eggs that are active will feel very hot and can be 2 degrees higher than their recommended core temperature because of their exertions. They should be allowed to cool. Those that are having a rest (or are dead) will feel cooler. On the whole, it is better to have the hatcher on the cool side rather than on the lethal hot side. Go by the feel of the eggs as much as by the thermometer.

Pipping

The embryo breaks out of its membrane by twitching movements of the neck, which cause the tip of the beak to jab upwards. The beak tip has an 'egg tooth', which is quite noticeable on hatching, but is then resorbed. This tooth breaks the internal membrane, so that the bird breathes from the air sac to take its first breath into its lungs. As the neck muscles twitch, the yolk sac in also withdrawn into the body cavity. The twitching also breaks or 'pips' the eggshell, so that the bird has access to fresh air and, once this is achieved, the hatchling often rests. This pause varies in duration, but during this time the yolk sac should be fully withdrawn, and the blood vessels of the egg are shut down.

If you have achieved the correct temperature in the incubator, the smaller eggs of the more active breeds, such as Sebastopols and Chinese, should pip on day 28 and should then be transferred to the hatcher. If the air sac looked the correct size before the goslings penetrated it, a small amount of water can be introduced into the awaiting hatcher. Leave the larger, slower goose eggs in the main dry incubator until they too have pipped. It is no use going by 'rule of thumb' hints, such as adding water on day 25 if the eggs are still too wet. You must candle or weigh the eggs to decide what they need. If the eggs have become too dry, you can halt dehydration completely by filling all the water containers in the incubator and adding wet cloth spread out on vacant floor space. It is the *area* of evaporating water that controls the humidity.

Hatching

After the customary rest, for about 24 hours after pipping, the gosling should rotate in its shell and complete the hatching process. It is worth keeping an eye on them, as a few unfortunate individuals fail to flip off the lid, and then suffocate. This would not happen in a nest, where the goose will nibble at the eggs. If, after a day, the gosling has made no further progress, inspect the egg to see what is happening. Remove the next bit of shell. If the membrane bleeds, the bird is not ready to hatch. It may well be that its development has been retarded by too low a temperature, or the egg is too wet because of lack of dehydration. Such goslings may get no further. If they die at this stage, check the dead hatchling to see if there is excessive moisture, which will run out if you tear the inner membrane. Usually, in such a case, the yellow yolk sac remains attached to the umbilicus externally, so the bird would have stood a poor chance of survival.

Late Hatchers

Sometimes, a gosling will hatch a day or two after the main hatch. Keep an eye on stragglers. If the membrane no longer bleeds when more shell is broken away, and the inside merely looks pink, hatching is due soon. If the inner membrane is dark brown and the gosling is getting smelly, hatching is overdue and the yolk sac should have been resorbed. You can then proceed to hatch the gosling.

Deformities

Eggs that take a long time to hatch frequently have something wrong with them. Retarded development is one cause, and deformity in the gosling is another. Twisted toes or a crooked neck make it more difficult for the

Fig 133 Pipping on day 28–29. Repeated twitching of the gosling's neck causes the 'egg tooth', seen here on the end of the bill, to puncture the shell. After this has occurred, the gosling rests, to recover and build up its oxygen supply. Oxygen demand is much higher in the later stages of development and hatching than during the early stages of incubation

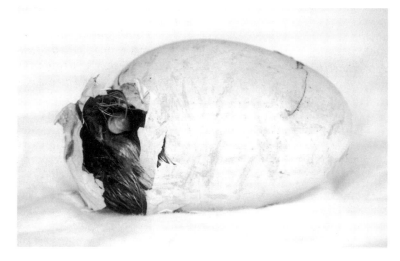

Fig 134 The gosling rotates in its shell about 24 hours after first pipping. This one had not made a big enough 'lid' to flip off, so its shell was broken further to release it. Geese assist with this in the nest

Fig 135 A wet gosling emerges. It is still attached to the membranes of the shell by a shrivelled umbilical cord. It pulls itself away and breaks the cord. The down of each plume is still enclosed in a sheath, which splits and falls away as the gosling dries out. It is this material that forms the yellow particles of fluff left behind in the incubator

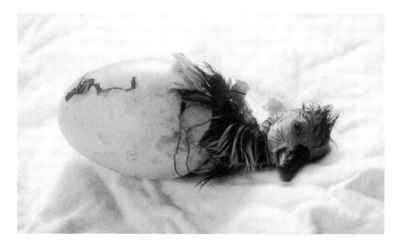

Fig 136 Some eggshell and membrane is still attached to this gosling, which was a little too dry. As the down of the modified feathers fluffs up, the bits of eggs will drop off

Fig 137 Two Africans on the first day of hatching. They have not started to eat or drink yet. The droppings are dark green meconium – waste products from nutrition inside the egg

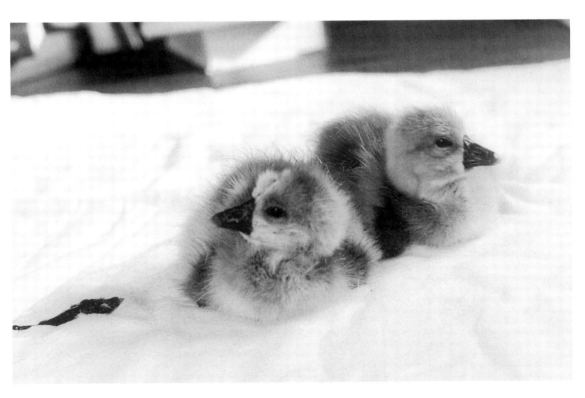

gosling to hatch. These deformities may be genetic, but incorrect incubation temperatures can allegedly cause curled toes, for example. If such a gosling does hatch, curled toes, and even ankles that are turned back out of place, can be corrected by using masking tape as a shoe (top and bottom of the web) or ankle reinforcer. These birds should not, however, be used as breeders. In a large commercial hatch, they should undoubtedly be put down, if they hatch at all.

Occasionally, a gosling seems to be stuck like glue to its shell and membrane. No excessive moisture runs out of some 'dead in shell' eggs, but the albumen does not appear to have been properly used up. Some of these occur as an odd gosling in an otherwise normal hatch, and can be helped out. They sometimes need a wash in warm water to get rid of the 'glue' and the membrane, which may stick to their eyes. Anderson Brown attributes this condition to too little moisture in the early stages, giving excessive shrinkage of the egg contents. This condition is unusual compared with eggs that are simply too wet.

Malpositioned Goslings

A few goslings pip at the wrong end of the shell. They should always break into the air sac at the bulbous end, but some attempt the pointed end. The goslings that insist on doing this the most frequently with us are the Toulouse. They need help, because there is no air sac for them to breathe, and they may suffocate. Always clear a small air space for them to breathe, even if they bleed; they tend to bleed more at this end of the shell. They do not have enough room to manoeuvre and perform the can-opener action of correctly positioned goslings. Consequently, you must give them help, if you want them. Leave them alone, except for checking the air supply, and only hatch them when other birds that pipped at the same time have hatched themselves normally, and the membrane is no longer bloody.

This problem is alleged to occur if the eggs have been set with the air sac end too low, but it also seems to happen when the eggs have all been set in the same normal way. To guard against malpositioned goslings, always

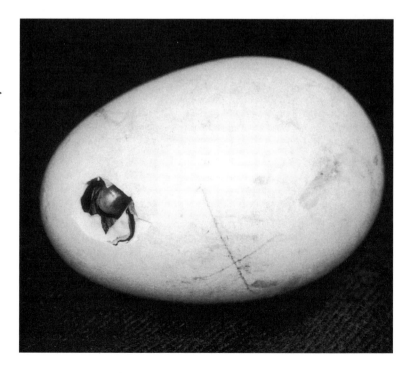

Fig 138 This gosling has pipped at the wrong end of the shell – the opposite end from the air sac – and may need help in getting out later on. Keep the air space clear but do not hatch the gosling until others in the same batch have hatched. If hatched too early, the yolk sac may not have been completely withdrawn into the body, and the blood vessels will not have closed down. Goslings that pip at the wrong end often do so before those that choose the bulbous end. However, they often need longer than the correctly positioned goslings before final hatching

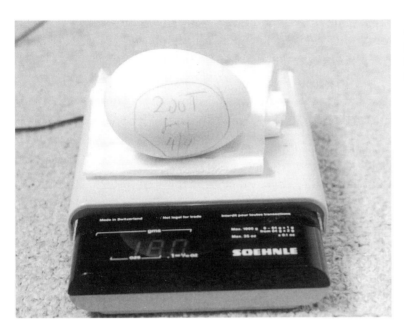

Fig 139 Weighing eggs: a fairly accurate balance (indicating each gram) is needed

handle eggs slowly and gently, and avoid vibration and jarring. Turn eggs as frequently as possible.

Power Failures

Fortunately, many power failures are preceded by a warning, but the majority do seem to be in spring. In such an emergency, I once transferred a clutch of incubating duck eggs to an incubator in another area, but most of the embryos died as a result of being moved by car. One strategy is to stuff as many eggs under the broody hens as possible for the day. Otherwise, cover the incubator with a duvet when the power cut occurs (not before, or the incubator may over-heat), and leave everything alone until the electricity comes back on. Remove the duvet shortly after, otherwise the incubator will over-heat. Eggs that seem stone cold are remarkably resilient and often survive.

SUCCESS RATES

Hatching the eggs of Indian Runners and Rouen ducks in incubators is relatively easy compared with hatching goose eggs in the same conditions. A common experience is that very few, if any, eggs will hatch when set in March to hatch in April, but that hatchability improves in May and June. One experienced breeder I know never bothers with early goose eggs both because of the low success rate, and because of the higher number of ganders you are more likely to get from early eggs.

Until 1997, I had always believed that the problem was high humidity in the earlier months, unless there was a cool north wind, resulting in a low RH. However, 1997 produced a heatwave and drought conditions in April. Room humidity was typically 61–65 per cent and the incubator ran at 38–40 per cent RH with no water added. As in the usual June heatwave conditions, the eggs were tending to go rotten. As you can see from the first graph), the Sebastopol and large cross-breed eggs lost only 10–12 per cent of their weight, and were far too wet. They failed to hatch. The African eggs lost 18.5 per cent and

Fig 140 Weight loss in goose eggs in grams during a 28-day incubation period 1–28 April, 1997, in a still-air incubator

Egg	Day 0	2	4	6	8	10	12	14	16	18	20	22	24	26	28	% loss	hatched
Large cross breed	234	230	229	228	225	223	221	219	218	216	214	212	210	208	206	12	no
African 27.3.97	190	186	182	179	176	174	171	168	166	164	161	158	157	156	155	18.5	yes
African 19.3.97	202	197	192	190	185	182	179	176	173	170	167	164	163	162	161	20	no
Sebastopol 18.3.97	188	185	183	182	181	180	179	178	177	176	175	174	172	170	168	10.6	no

(* extrapolated weight)

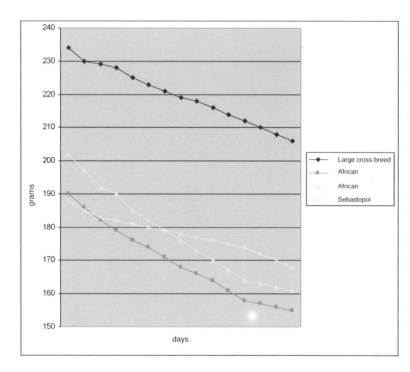

Fig 140 Graph of loss in weight of goose eggs during a 28-day incubation period 1–28 April 1997, in a still-air incubator. Egg storage 75 per cent RH; incubator room 61–65 per cent RH; goose incubator 38–40 per cent RH; duck incubator maintained at 50–55 per cent RH.

An egg must lose at least 12 per cent of its initial weight in order to hatch; 13 per cent is usually regarded as ideal, but some authorities recommend 16 per cent. Eggs have been known to hatch when weight loss has been 20 per cent [Anderson Brown].

20 per cent, and one hatched. These two eggs had to be put into a wet incubator before the other eggs, to try to rescue them from rapid dehydration at the end.

During incubation, the duck-egg incubators were maintained at 50–55 per cent RH by adding water. The room's RH was typically 60–62 per cent and that of the goose egg incu-bator typically 38 per cent. Eggs were stored at 75 per cent RH before setting.

Another set of eggs was monitored under broody hens during the same period in 1998.

This small set of results reflects what seems to happen regularly over the years, and we have drawn the following conclusions from them:

Fig 141 Weight loss in goose eggs in grams in a 28-day incubation period using broody hens, 1–28 April 1998

Day	0	2	4	6	8	10	12	14	16	18	20	22	24	26	28	% loss	hatched
Egg																	
Large African 30.3.98	226	222	220	220	218	216	213	211	209	207	205	203	202	198	196	13	yes
Pilgrim 26.3.98	200	197	195	194	192	189	187	185	183	181	179	178	176	173	171	14.5	yes
African 25.3.98	196	192	189	186	183	181	178	176	174	171	169	167	166	164	162	17	no

* removed to wet incubator

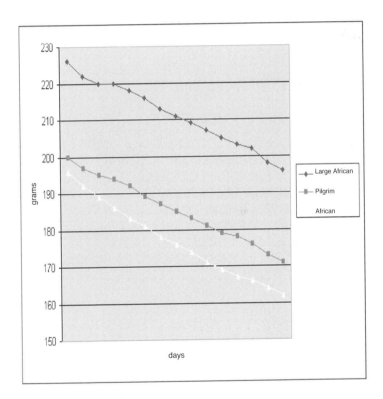

Fig 141 Graph of loss in weight of goose eggs over a 28-day period of incubation 1–28 April 1998, under broody hens

- The main reason why goose eggs are difficult to hatch is because of insufficient water loss.
- Eggs of different breeds often need different treatment; Chinese eggs, in particular, and African eggs hatch more easily in incubators because they lose water more readily than the eggs of European geese. These Chinese and African eggs can become too dry both in incubators and under broodies.
- The figure of 55 per cent humidity quoted for the incubation of eggs is correct for mid- and late-season duck eggs and mid-season white Chinese eggs, but is far too high for Pilgrims and Brecon Buffs. The European goose eggs need to be incubated with no additional water. Some Pilgrim eggs that did hatch went for 28 days at 38–40 per cent humidity. Humidity even lower than

38 per cent is needed early in the season for these eggs.

- Large eggs are more difficult to dehydrate than average eggs; the large African egg needed 100 per cent of its incubation time in the broody nest, while the average African egg became too dry.
- Later eggs were much more successful at dehydrating than the earlier ones, despite

the humidity being the same.
- It is probable that later eggs have a thinner shell and membrane, allowing easier dehydration.
- If you want early goose eggs to hatch, use broody hens that usually get everything right, especially early in the season, whatever the weather.
- The incubator will beat the broody hens

Fig 142 African and Chinese eggs hatch more easily in incubators than Brecon and Pilgrim. These early-season 1998 African were incubated at 40 per cent RH in early March and needed 55 per cent RH for finishing in the last two weeks. Five out of six fertile eggs hatched. Marking the air sac in pencil from day 18 onwards allows you to monitor its progress; you will get to know the correct rate of change for a good hatch. This is quicker than weighing the eggs, but less accurate, especially in the early stages, when visual change is barely detectable. As is clear from the results of the preceding graphs, it is possible to lose African and Chinese eggs by too-rapid dehydration

later on in the season, probably because it is cleaner than the nest.
- Forced-air incubators seem to be slightly more successful than still-air models at hatching goose eggs. They are also more successful later in the season.
- Weighing the eggs and comparing their weight with an ideal weight-loss chart is probably the only reliable way of charting an egg's progress, and making correct adjustments to humidity. Many breeders of valuable wildfowl now do this.

Commercial goose producers must be successful at using incubators otherwise they would go out of business. So, what are the secrets of their success? Firstly, commercial geese are usually white Embden crosses, sometimes crossed with Chinese. Cross-breeds are easier to hatch than pure breeds. Secondly, Embdens were originally praised, in the nineteenth century, for being early layers and producers of good hatching eggs. When we bred Embdens, we found them relatively easy to hatch in the incubator compared with Brecons and Pilgrims, which are the most difficult. In general, white geese lay eggs that are easier to hatch in this way than coloured geese, except for Africans and Chinese. These also do relatively well in incubators.

Thirdly, commercials often lay smaller eggs than exhibition birds. Small eggs are easier to hatch than large ones, because their surface area is greater in proportion to their volume, and so they dehydrate more easily. This is why people sometimes get better hatches with first-season geese than with older birds. The goslings, however, do not make the best breeders. Finally, commercial flocks are bred for uniformity; most of the eggs will require the same conditions. In addition, the large-scale forced-air incubators can be much more tightly regulated for temperature than small table-top models. The humidity can also be regulated by a dehumidifier.

CHECKLIST

Incubation is as much an art as a science, and there is no substitute for observation and experience. If you are successful the first time, it may not last, as there are so many variables over which you have little or no control. If you are unsuccessful, run through the following possibilities:

Infertile Eggs

- Old eggs set;
- ruptured membrane – pre-warming neglected;
- gander infertile – behavioural problems; fighting with other ganders; bad feet; over-weight; dropped/withered penis;
- poor diet of breeders, for example, insufficient vitamins for the goose and the gander;
- congenital defects, especially from very inbred birds carrying lethal genes;
- rough handling of eggs.

Bad Eggs

- Eggs dirty when collected, especially from wet, muddy areas;
- eggs washed in cold water, germs drawn in;
- cracked eggs set;
- dirty incubator;
- embryo starts to develop and dies.

Embryonic Mortality before Day 26

- Incorrect storage, for example, too warm, causing some embryonic development prior to incubation;
- insufficient turning;
- fluctuating temperatures in incubator, causing embryo to die;
- poor diet of breeders, causing embryo to die;
- congenital defects;
- infections (*see* above).

'Dead in Shell': Mortality in the last 2–3 Days of Incubation

- Early-season eggs; things may improve;
- humidity too high; insufficient air sac – liquid runs from torn membrane, yolk sac not absorbed;
- humidity too low – air sac very large, membrane tough and leathery;
- malpositioning of gosling: chance factor or incorrect storage of egg;
- deformed gosling – congenital defect;
- over-heating – a lot of heat is generated by hatching eggs; watch the air temperature of the incubator.

Early Hatching

- Incubator temperature too high; goslings may have bloody umbilicus, because of insufficient time to resorb blood from veins of egg;
- smaller eggs of young geese or smaller breed – no problems.

Late Hatching

- Old eggs; fresh eggs hatch earlier;
- large eggs can take up to 32 days, but 30 is ideal;
- incubator temperature too low;
- deformed gosling.

Deformities

- Inadequate diet of breeders – mineral and vitamin deficiency;
- crooked toes and turned ankles can result from temperatures that are too high;
- if eggs from the same goose also produce deformed goslings when hatched under broodies, this is a genetic defect, and the same pair of geese should not be used again for breeding.

16 Rearing the Goslings –

REARING WITHOUT THE GOOSE: THE FIRST THREE WEEKS

Heat

I prefer to get the goslings out of the incubator as soon as they have fluffed up. This will be quicker if the incubator is being run fairly dry. The umbilicus on some of the goslings can be a bit raw and it is best to get this dried off quickly, to prevent infection. Transfer the goslings to a cardboard box with crumpled old clothing or towels or chopped straw, not newspaper. This box can be put against the hot-water tank in the airing cupboard overnight, but you must monitor the temperature. This is safer than leaving the new goslings under a heat lamp overnight, when there is always the possibility of the bulb popping. Newly hatched goslings would probably die of the cold, especially if there were few of them, or they were still wet.

Do not over-heat the goslings. They soon die if over-exposed to the lamp and they must have access to a cool end of the box. Watch their behaviour – they pant if they are too hot. When they are first hatched they do not have the energy to move far, or the knowledge that there might be a better position. Keep an eye on them until they are mobile.

Suitable heat lamps come in two types, glass and ceramic. The easiest ones to obtain are the 250W infra-red glass bulbs used by farmers for lambs and piglets, and available from most agricultural stores in spring. If you buy a cheaper type, make sure that the fitting for the bulb is ceramic, not plastic, which will over-heat. Bulbs are either clear glass or ruby. The colour does not seem to matter for goslings, but the ruby light is less intense for them. These lamps feel as if they have a higher heat output than the ceramic bulb for the same amount of energy, but they are easily broken, and the element can blow quite unpredictably. Also, the glass can shatter over the goslings. The ceramic bulb is more expensive, but lasts longer and gives the goslings a quiet night. If they have started to pull at each others' fluff, the darkness is a big advantage. Always make sure the lamp is suspended safely. If it falls on the goslings with the power still on, they will be killed by the heat, if not by the weight of the lamp.

Prolonged exposure to heat lamps is particularly bad for goslings. They will grow quickly on a 24-hour feed regime, and develop rather soft bones. Weak hocks can result, and toes start to curl, rather like poultry over-exposed to infra-red lamps. It is better to use the dull emitters if these have a sufficient heat output for the time of year, and to get the goslings out on clean grass and exposed to daylight.

Heat Required

Floor temp. first seven days	30–32 degrees centigrade/86–89.6 degrees Fahrenheit
Second week	27–30 degrees centigrade/80.6–86 degrees Fahrenheit
Third week	22–27 degrees centigrade/71.6–80.6 degrees Fahrenheit

Sometimes a cold, wet spring makes this extremely difficult. If the goslings have to be kept in longer than this, they benefit from greens and the addition of brewer's yeast to their diet (*see* page 187 on vitamin deficiencies).

Early Familiarity

Many hobby breeders, who hatch only a few birds, like to rear them in the initial stages in the house, out of security and interest. Goslings can be kept in the house longer than ducks because they are less messy; they do not play with water so much. To avoid the carpet going rotten under a goslings' cardboard box, stand it in a plastic tray from a garden centre (known as a 'planter'); these can be scrubbed out and disinfected.

It is advantageous to keep a close eye on the goslings during the first few days, and for them to have an eye on you. We like our birds to be tame. Many are sold as pets as well as breeders. The best birds will eventually be shown, and they perform far better, and are under less stress, if they are used to people at close quarters. If you are only rearing a small number of goslings each year, rather than hundreds, it is also useful to get the birds accustomed to being handled at an early stage. The goslings will then consider it to be a normal activity when they are picked up to have their weight checked, and, when they are adults, they will not fight you off, either when being caught for showing, or when being checked for health.

When you are approaching all birds, especially those that cannot see you, in coops or sheds, remember to speak to them first to let them know that you are there. This avoids a panic when a door is unexpectedly opened. Always move slowly, to give them confidence, and talk to them. Geese are great communicators, and goslings in particular need to greet each other and their handler in order to feel secure.

Early familiarity with people seems to produce calm birds; this opinion has been confirmed in *Poultry World*. It is of economic importance to have birds that are unstressed by their handlers, otherwise they will panic and press into corners, and perhaps suffocate each other. Early exposure to humans prevents this sort of stress.

Mortality Rates

When keeping goslings in the house, you can keep an eye on their health. However hygienic you have been with eggs and the incubator, some birds will become ill. It is possible to hatch two hundred ducks and only lose five or fewer in the first two weeks after hatching, but with geese the mortality rate can be higher, depending on how easily the goslings were hatched. In a healthy hatch you may lose none. Where there are 'dead in shells' and late hatchers, two or three out of fifteen may die. These losses can be reduced by sterilizing incubators thoroughly, watching the birds carefully, and treating them appropriately.

First Food and Drink

Exhausted goslings do nothing much for 24 hours. They do not need to eat for up to 48 hours after hatching, because they are using nourishment from the yolk sac. However, when they are under a heat lamp, offer them water on the first day and food on the second. A cylindrical egg cup is a good first drinker, as it is too small for the gosling to drown in. To get them drinking, offer water on a teaspoon if they seem hot or dehydrated. Always make sure part of the box has a cooler temperature, away from the lamp, so the goslings can escape if the height of the heat lamp is not correct. The food and drink should be placed in the cooler part. This avoids splashes of water on the lamp, and keeps the food cooler. Vitamins deteriorate rapidly in the direct heat.

Chick starter crumbs may not contain sufficient Vitamin B for waterfowl; a 'rubbery beak' condition in ducks kept on chick crumbs for too long has confirmed this. A waterfowl ration is preferable in any case, if you can get it, as it will not contain a coccidiostat. Brewer's yeast is a good source of Vitamin B, so it can be sprinkled on food that has been slightly moistened to make it stick, or put in drinking water. Deficiency in the diet is unlikely to develop if the birds are outside and on greens early enough.

If a few birds are not keen to start on chick crumbs, they can have their appetite stimulated with greens. The best for this are tender dandelion leaves, which can be finely shredded with a bread saw on a board, or tied securely in a bunch for the goslings to pull at. This satisfies their instinct to pull, and may prevent them from pulling the fluff off each other's backs. Some batches of goslings become dreadful chewers, while others behave impeccably. The worst ones may need separating from those they pick on, or given something like a piece of turf. At this point, they must be moved out to a shed for more space.

Problems

Failure to Eat
Any gosling that fails to eat must be checked. Poor doers will have thin legs, will start to

Fig 143 Dandelion leaves are good for goslings. Having something to pull at stops them from 'grazing' each other!

Fig 144 A group of day-old Pilgrim goslings (one Brecon Buff in the middle); the four paler ganders are on the left and the two dark females on the right. Pilgrims are the worst breed for pulling each other's fluff; they need to graze

Fig 145 Heat lamps shared between groups; each group preferably has two lamps, so that if one bulb goes, the other acts as a back-up. This is essential for early hatches, when temperatures in sheds can be very low

drop their wings, and will have little energy to move around with the rest. Isolate any such gosling, which may have an infection, then put another one with it to keep it company. Treat them with a soluble antibiotic powder, in the drinking water, for eight days. The antibiotic must be obtained from a vet. This will usually do the trick if you can persuade the gosling to eat. The antibiotic in the water can be mixed with chick crumbs into a porridge, with brewer's yeast added for Vitamin B. This enhances the flavour and encourages the birds to eat. We have also successfully used concentrated liquid Horlicks for feeding birds that refused dry food.

Single Goslings

If you are unlucky enough to have a single gosling, you will need to get it a companion if there is no goose to look after it. Goslings need something on which to imprint. This will be its keeper if nothing else is available. It will cry if it is left on its own, and will fret and not eat properly. To prevent this, get hold of any other bird of the same age. Another gosling is best but, failing that, ducklings are good companions for a while. Eventually, you may be able to get the single gosling to join another group of younger or older goslings, but this takes care.

'Spraddled Legs'

Large, soft goslings that have retained too much moisture are too heavy to support themselves, and their legs may splay out to the side. They should not be encouraged to eat, as losing a little weight will help them. However, do not let them dehydrate if they are unable to get to a drinker. These goslings need a rough surface to help them get a good grip; a crumpled old woolly jumper is the best, and chopped straw is also good. In bad cases, the goslings may need to have their legs hobbled together around the ankles with double-strand soft wool. A bad case may not be able to stand up and, unless helped, will dislocate its hip joint and have to be put down. Remedial swimming in the kitchen sink in warm water can solve this, if you have the time and patience.

Transferring to an Outdoor Shed

After a few days indoors, depending on your level of interest and the family's tolerance, the goslings can be moved to a rat-proof shed with a reliable electricity supply.

Heat

It is safer to have two heat sources rather than one, in case one breaks down; the heat

166

sources can be shared between two groups separated by low partitions. When the goslings are small they can be kept in groups of up to fourteen, but I prefer a maximum of eleven. If more than this huddle under one heat source, the one in the middle may be suffocated. If the shed is at all draughty, a cardboard box laid on its side, with all of the flaps and the top cut off, makes a nice warm spot beside or under the warm spot of the heat lamp. There is no 'roof' to the open-sided box, so the cardboard should not over-heat and present a fire risk.

The heat source should gradually be raised as the goslings grow. They require less heat as they become bigger, and, of course, their backs move nearer to the heat source as their legs get longer. Your aim should be to 'harden them off' a bit before they go out. You will have to gauge from the behaviour of the goslings whether the lamp is at the correct height. If they crowd underneath it, it is too high; if they disperse to the edges of the area, it is too low. Bear in mind that overnight temperatures may be significantly lower than at those times when you observe the birds.

Fig 146 A warm spot in the cardboard box, away from draughts. This is important for early hatched goslings in a cool or windy April

The Shed Floor and Litter

The floor of the shed should be concrete, to prevent rats entering. Mice should also be excluded or dispatched because they will contaminate the food. They can be trapped or poisoned, but do this away from the gosling area to avoid accidents. The floor should be thoroughly scrubbed with lots of water and hosed out and dried before the goslings are transferred to the shed.

Wood shavings are sometimes used as a litter for young birds, but I find these unsatisfactory as the goslings always eat them. Chopped barley straw is good, because the smaller pieces are easier to handle than full stalks, and the amount that can disappear down the goslings' throats is limited. They will undoubtedly pick at the wisps of leafy material that come off the stem, but this does not seem to matter. Do not attempt to pull out long lengths of straw from a gosling's mouth.

It is best left where it is and just broken off. The litter keeps them occupied and, if coarse builder's sand or concreting sand is supplied in a cup, any roughage will be broken down in the gizzard. The floor litter can be topped up with more straw as it gets messy; you will have to decide when it needs completely removing and starting again depending on the smell and amount of ammonia that builds up. Moulds will be developing in the straw and a clean layer has to be maintained above this if the goslings are to be kept healthy.

I have seen goslings reared on weldmesh wire; this way is commonly used to keep young ducklings well supplied with water, but clean and dry, but it does not work so well with geese. If the weldmesh is the wrong size, they will get their hocks stuck in it, and they suffer from sore feet because of their greater weight.

Fig 147 Chopped barley straw is ideal litter. The pieces are quite short, in case some of them are eaten. These Africans are a few days old and they have already started to 'graze' each other's tails. This can become a serious problem, especially with Brecons and Pilgrims; the birds must have something green to pull, otherwise they will even draw blood by pulling each other's fluff

Partitions

Partitions to keep groups of goslings separated need be only about 12in (30cm) high. Hardboard bent into a circle is frequently used. If your floor space is limited, squares are more economical; I use interlocking pieces of thin plywood, which can be scrubbed down and re-used between batches, and from year to year. It is important to make sure that a gosling cannot get its head and neck stuck in any joins.

Water

It is safest at first to provide water in a drinking fountain, but, because the rim is near floor level, the water is easily fouled by droppings. A deeper water container seems to work better for goslings. They need to be able to wash their eyes and a good heavy pie dish or casserole, which cannot be turned over, is ideal. The goslings should be able to get out of it if they choose to get in, or fall. A stone can be placed in the middle to dissuade them from bathing and getting soaked. The kitchen is a good source of containers – a casserole dish also functions as a foot bath. The goslings inevitably get in it from time to time, and this stops the droppings on the floor setting like concrete on their feet and toenails.

Fig 148 Partitions made from interlocking plywood. A notch is cut half-way through each piece of board, the notch being the thickness of the board itself. The boards then interlock and support each other. They form useful partitions to separate groups of different ages, or to keep the groups to a suitable number, so that the birds do not crush each other

Fig 149 A suitable drinker for young goslings – a washing-up bowl anchored by a brick. This avoids casualties from drowning

A further advantage of young goslings getting wet from time to time is that they learn to condition their fluff and feathers early by using the preen gland. Well-oiled feathers repel the rain better and the gosling is less likely to get waterlogged in a water container.

Diet

If you only have one or two goslings, clipped grass, chopped dandelions and not more than 20 per cent crumbled hard-boiled egg repre-

sent a good starter diet. Gosling appetites soon become enormous and it is much easier and less time-consuming to feed chick starter crumbs, or a waterfowl starter ration if you can get it.

Chick Crumbs

During their time in the shed, which can be up to two and a half weeks old if the weather is bad, chick crumbs are the goslings' main diet. It is preferable to choose a brand specially manufactured for waterfowl. Chick crumbs contain a coccidiostat that has been tested for poultry, but not necessarily for geese. My

Fig 150 Older goslings graduate on to wide, shallow buckets. Deep buckets are death traps; goslings, even at ten weeks old, may up-end in the bucket and drown

locally produced rations – with the additive Ethopabate as an aid to control coccidiosis – have always been all right, but other additives may not be safe. If in doubt, buy a ration designed for waterfowl or wildfowl. The protein content of the starter diet is high, often 19 per cent, so this should not be fed for too long a period. Fishmeal is generally used to boost the protein level. The crumbs are the ideal size for tiny beaks, but the birds like to move on to a larger-sized pellet as they grow.

Growers' Pellets

The larger pellets for rearing are called growers' pellets, and these also contain more protein than maintenance rations. Again, check for any coccidiostat. Ethopabate may be all right in the early weeks, but waterfowl probably need a coccidiostat less than poultry. If there is any doubt, you are better off without the additive. The pellets should be mixed in with the crumbs, so that the goslings can choose the size they want, until they have moved on to pellets alone (depending on the size of the particles) at about three and a half weeks.

The goslings should also be given as much green stuff as you have time to collect and chop. Some people keep a patch of trimmed lawn for the express purpose of providing lawn clippings for the birds. Chop dandelion leaves and feed them in a dish several times a day – goslings have such an appetite for these that they must be beneficial.

Coops and Runs

On warm days, the goslings can be transferred to a coop and grass run, where mesh will protect them from cats, crows and magpies. Make sure that the birds cannot escape where the ground is uneven; block any holes up with a brick. Put plenty of straw on top of a paper sack liner in the coop (remove all string), and show the goslings this warmer area. They are slower to recognize this than ducks.

If the weather is cool and wet, cover the run with polythene, or leave the birds in the shed for longer. If the weather remains poor, put them out in the covered run for a short time. If there are several goslings, they will huddle up and keep each other warm when they are not grazing. If there are only two or three, they cannot be left out for long. They must be warm and dry at night and in bad weather you will need to put them back under the heat lamp in the shed. It is important to keep the backs of downy goslings dry. They will catch pneumonia if left wet and cold for prolonged periods, and need protection from heavy rain for this reason. If goslings are caught in heavy rain or have got stuck in a drinker, and seem nearly dead with cold, they should be blotted dry immediately and put under a heat lamp to dry and fluff up. Birds that seem about to expire can pick up again.

The grass for the runs should be short and sweet. It must also be free from bird droppings. The best place to use is an area that has recently been grazed by sheep, as this will reduce the incidence of gizzard worm. If you can rear goslings each year on ground that is otherwise unused by geese, so much the better. The best lawn in the garden is also ideal for this short period of time, and the goslings will improve the texture by biting off the grass really low and fertilizing it. They consume enormous amounts of grass, so the runs will need moving on three times a day by the time the goslings are three weeks old.

REARING WITH THE GOOSE

If you are a good enough shot to keep magpies and crows at bay, and they are wary of your area, you might let the goose take the goslings out by the house where you can keep an eye on them. It is, however, still best to keep them in a shed on chick crumbs for the first few days until they are all well on their feet.

Fig 151 A coop with plenty of shelter from wind and rain. Make sure you buy a design that is comfortable for the birds, rather than pretty for you to look at. The open part should be covered in polythene, well anchored, by the coop itself, or by bricks, if the weather is wet and windy. Make sure ventilation is adequate; extra holes often have to be bored in the wood

Fig 152 A different design with more grazing, which is excellent for goslings. The 'hay box' end also has a weldmesh floor, which provides better ventilation and dries out the bedding better for waterfowl than a solid wood base. The weldmesh is best covered by a paper sack, followed by straw. If the lid of the coop lifts, tie it down with string at night. Foxes have been known to flip up the lid and eat the contents

Fig 153 Goslings of different age groups do not mix well – the older ones may persecute the little ones, given the chance

Problems

Most geese brood their goslings well and will protect them from showers, but they are not very good at protecting them from predators. There are other problems in letting the geese have the goslings back early after you have finished hatching the late ones in the incubator.

Firstly, the adults will eat all the food. Goslings out on grass will not grow very quickly without crumbs, and you want them to grow quickly so that certain predators will take less interest in them. One way to stop the adults stealing the crumbs is to make a gosling creep. A circle of pig wire into which the goslings can run, to get at the food, is usually effective. This has to be of sufficiently large diameter to fit the food and water bowls, so that the adults cannot reached them with outstretched neck. This usually works well, but we had one goose that was smart enough to reach the rim of the feed bowl, grasp it, and pull it towards her. Then she would eat all the contents.

Secondly, the adults must be wormed if you have not done this already when the goose sat. More goslings are lost through ignorance of gizzard worm than through any other cause.

Thirdly, the water containers are a problem. A bucket is suitable for adult geese which are too big to up-end in it, but goslings must be started off with shallow trays and graduate on to washing-up bowls. These should be anchored down with a brick, to stop the receptacle turning over, and also to provide an escape route. Containers with smooth surfaces, like a bath sunk into the ground in the garden, are a death trap for small goslings, which cannot get a grip on the smooth surface to get out. If they fall in, they become waterlogged and exhausted, and then drown.

Observation

The first three weeks require close observation, otherwise you will lose stock. One good system has the goslings where they can be seen by the parents inside the coop; they are then allowed to join them. In this way, the geese are familiarized with the offspring and want them, so that, when the goslings are released, there are no problems. In general, this can only be done with a goose that has hatched and reared goslings before, so if you have a young goose that is new to this, she will have to hatch something first. Geese unfamiliar with goslings, and especially females, can be thoroughly nasty to them, and even attack them. On the other hand, most ganders (unlike drakes) make excellent fathers. They are more careful with their feet than the females and less likely to tread on goslings. Some take guard duty very seriously and will stand head up, on watch, all day. Showing a behavioural trait noted by Harrison Weir, one particularly good gander would summon his goslings by paddling his feet up and down on the spot. This movement does indeed seem to attract them; you can mimic it by doing it with your hands.

Initially, you will need to confine the geese to a relatively small area. Do not allow the goose to march off over the whole farm with week-old goslings. They will get lost in the grass, stuck in a ditch, fall foul of some machinery, or be devoured by crows. They need to have an obstacle-free area at first.

REARING AFTER THREE WEEKS

After three weeks, the goslings are much more robust and, depending on the weather and the size of the breed, can be put out in paddocks on their own, or with trusted, tame geese. The smaller breeds may be four weeks old before they are left outside all day. In general, when the goslings are this old, the crows are more interested in the bowls of pellets than in attacking the birds, but there is still the possibility of a rogue crow having a go. At this age, the goslings should not be grazed with larger animals. Inquisitive lambs may chase them and there is the risk of trampling. When herding sheep, take care not to get geese of any age into the same confined area, for the same reason.

There are two different routes you can take for rearing the goslings after this point, depending on the amount of space and pasture you have, and the kind of growth rates you require. Each method has its own benefits and problems.

Rearing on Grass

Grass Quality

From this point, the goslings can be reared without much supplementary food, depending on your conditions. If they are to be grass-reared, the stocking density of the birds must be low. This means that they must be grazed after or before other animals such as sheep and cattle, which bite the grass down and keep it short. Short, succulent spring and early-summer grass is up to 16 per cent protein, but this drops by mid- to late summer, and when grass is longer. Geese, and goslings in particular, do not thrive on long, tough grass. They like to strip the seed heads off mature grasses, but growth of the birds in spring is achieved by eating young shoots.

If the grass is coarse, it can cause impaction in the tract before the gizzard. Unlike a chicken, geese do not have a 'crop' in which to store their overnight food; instead, they can stuff their whole oesophagus full of food. Blockage can occur in this lower part before the gizzard (the proventriculus) if the gizzard is not working very efficiently, or is finding the food difficult to pass through.

The Gizzard

If grass rather than pellets is the main diet, it is particularly important that the geese have access to hard grinding material for the gizzard. The gizzard is a giant muscle, used to mill down the food and make it suitable for the intestine to extract the nutrient. Since the beak only snips off bits of grass, the gizzard, in the absence of teeth, has to comminute the material. The goose does not have the complex digestive system of a ruminant, so all the gizzard does is to break down the cell walls of the grass by physical action, so that the juices are released in a useable form.

Wild geese spend time at the river finding suitable material for the gizzard, and goslings a few days old will sieve sediment in puddles to find the right grade of material for them. Kept geese are sedentary, so the right material must be provided if your local soil does not have the raw materials. In an area of sandy loams, the soil may well provide the correct nutrients and particles, but in most areas the geese will benefit from having access to coarse builder's sand all year.

If geese have been without grinding material for some time, they will devour large quantities of it very quickly, and it is probably better to ration it in these circumstances.

Birds seem to suffer less from gizzard worm if they have access to proper grinding materials in the gizzard. The gizzard lining is quite coarse and horny due to the action of grinding materials, and this layer is known to slough away and re-form periodically. This may well keep the gizzard healthy, and is a process that will be helped by regular access to sand.

Supplementary Food

This is best given in the evening, to save wastage and to encourage the geese to range for grazing in the day. How much you decide to feed will depend on your economics, the state of the grass, and the health of the birds. There is no point in feeding wholewheat in bits over the day if the birds are eating large quantities of grass. The grains get wrapped up in the plant fibre and pass through the gut unmilled. Whole grain can be fed at the end of

Figs 154–155 Familiarizing geese with goslings before they are released together. This goose wanted the goslings, but the gander needed more contact with them before he would accept them. When they had grazed together for a couple of weeks, the goslings then joined the adults in the same shed at night

the day and, with sand available, will be broken down in the gizzard. Pellets are made of a ready-milled material and are easier to digest. The usual maxim for feeding is to give the geese what they will clear up in 20 minutes, with access to water. There is no need to leave food and water in the shed overnight. The water will end up making the shed a soggy mess.

174

Problems in Grass-Reared Birds

If grass is the main part of the diet, it must be clean and free from parasites. Breeders who stock ducks and geese intensively only manage to stay fairly free from the trouble caused by parasites through good management, and by feeding up to 100 per cent from bags.

Parasites causing the most problems in grass-reared birds are gizzard worm, throat worms and coccidia. These problems can arise in birds fed on concentrates and should be borne in mind if the birds seem ill, although they are relatively uncommon in well-fed birds.

Gizzard Worm

Infestation of this worm is one of the most common causes of death in goslings. Its incidence would be a great deal less if all geese were wormed whenever they were sold and moved on to a new property. Once the disease is recognized, it is too late; the parasite is already there. Problems are therefore best avoided by grazing geese only on clean pasture, at a low stocking density, so that they do not pick up more worms in the egg stage from droppings. The goslings should also be picked up regularly to see if they are of the right weight. They should feel fat and heavy. If they seem light, always worm them as a precaution.

If the infestation is reaching an advanced stage, you may notice a change in the goslings' behaviour. If birds are listless and too easy to catch and pick up because they have no energy, they are very ill. With gizzard worm they are literally starving to death, because the gizzard cannot function to prepare their food. Goslings that have deteriorated this far are very difficult to save. They lose their appetite, and just sit and die. They can sometimes be saved by forced liquid feeding, but it is better to avoid this eventuality by carrying out regular inspections.

A suitable liquid feed that I have used on thin goslings has been instant Horlicks, because this contains milk and other nutrients. Mixed up as a strong, sticky liquid, and squirted down the throat with several refills of a 2.5mm syringe, it has revived the appetite. The gosling must also be wormed with a single drench of a suitable wormer *see* page 188). Flubenvet powder on the food is not effective if the bird is hardly eating.

Throat Worms

These are picked up by birds grazing on areas well frequented by other birds. I have not found them to be a problem in goslings; probably, following routine treatment for gizzard worm, the throat worms are dispatched before they become a problem. A bad infestation of these worms will cause geese to cough in an effort to dislodge them from the throat. In an extreme case, they will asphyxiate the bird. This is more likely to happen with adult geese that have not been wormed for a long period.

Coccidiosis

Coccidia live in the gut and in small quantities probably do little harm. If the grass is covered in droppings, and this is the only food available to the birds, the infestation will build up. This is particularly the case in hot, damp weather. Goslings are especially vulnerable. They become thin and listless, and can hardly drag one foot after the other. The outward signs are similar to those of gizzard worm.

If coccidia are suspected, the most recent droppings should be examined first thing in the morning to see if there is any obvious blood, which is a sign of infection. A sample taken to the vet could be used, both for a coccidia count and for a worm egg count, which would give a better idea of what treatment to give. The best policy is to worm the bird anyway, and then treat with a prescribed coccidiostat if the sample dropping indicates this.

Coccidia are said to be species-specific, so there is no need to worry about sheep getting coccidia if the geese have an infection, or vice versa.

Rearing with Supplementary Feeds

At the three-week stage, the goslings should be graduating on to grower's pellets, which are 16 per cent protein, and it is also wise to start adding a few grains of wheat. In no circumstances should they continue on just chick crumbs. Not only is this wasteful, as the birds will scatter the dry powder, but it also makes a condition called 'dropped tongue' much more likely. Also, the protein content of the crumbs is higher than necessary.

The goslings do not particularly like wheat at this stage, but you may need to cut down the protein levels in the diet. There is a fine line to choose between feeding birds really well to grow to exhibition size, and getting them grossly overweight with leg problems. The best way to avoid the problems is to give them food ad lib, but to cut down on the protein. The diet has to be watched particularly carefully where birds are reared with no access to grass. Where they have plenty of grass and exercise, their legs are stronger, and there are fewer problems with vitamin deficiencies, weak legs or wings turning outwards ('angel wing').

While the goslings are on deep litter, they should have access to sand so that the gizzard can break down any straw ingested. While pelleted foods are easy to absorb, and the birds can get by without grit, I prefer to continue to make sand available for the health of the gizzard. Once hard grains are fed, grit is essential for the gosling to make use of this food.

Amounts and Types of Food

Poultry grower's pellets frequently contain the same coccidiostat as chick crumbs. This is not a treatment for the disease if birds become ill, but helps prevent the disease occurring. Rations containing coccidiostat are generally not recommended for waterfowl, or for any birds over 8 weeks. This time may be stated on the bag, because most commercial birds are culled by that age, and there is a with-drawal time between feeding these rations and slaughter. However, there is no advantage in feeding this additive to birds at 8 weeks; the goslings should proceed with a maintenance ration.

It is preferable to obtain a food specifically for waterfowl, as layers' pellets are designed for laying chickens, and contain sufficient calcium for shell formation, as well as undesirable additives such as egg-yolk colouring. If waterfowl food is not available, you could try a fattener pellet, which should contain no additives – check the label. Remember to cut the protein content by mixing it with wheat.

Goslings with no access to grass will eat enormous amounts of food. For example, between 8 and 16 weeks of age, growing Embdens will eat at least 1lb (450 grams) and Brecon Buffs up to ¾lb (350 grams) of mixed wheat and pellets per day. This compares with 4–8oz (110–225 grams) for most adult stock birds (depending on the time of year). So, considering that the birds have to be fed until Christmas, it is clearly not economic to produce geese under a zero grazing regime for the table. The only way of producing 'broiler geese' with zero grazing is to manage them like other poultry and slaughter them at 7–8 weeks, when the food conversion figures are much more favourable.

Problems – Angel Wing

Intensively fed goslings must be watched carefully at the stage when, at about 3½ to 4 weeks old, the blood quills start to sprout and grow quickly. If growth is very rapid, the weight of these growing quills cannot be supported by the final bone of the wing, which is distorted outwards. In a few cases, this can be an inherited weakness, but it is mostly caused by over-feeding at this crucial stage. This is why it is important to accustom the goslings to some grain in the diet at 3 to 4 weeks, to cut down on the protein. If there is a mixed diet of grass and pellets, under-feed the pellets at this stage, until the feathers are safely sprouted and set in place, by about 7 weeks. This condition is far less likely to occur

176

Fig 156 Wing problems – the eight-week-old Pilgrim gander has grown his primary feathers very rapidly, but the secondary feathers are delayed. The lack of secondaries means that there is nothing to tuck the primaries under, so the wing tends to drop. The feathers will not set smoothly, and the bird may be permanently 'rough-winged'. This particular batch of goslings wanted to grow very quickly and it was difficult to hold growth back by under-feeding pellets to control wing problems. The birds responded to a lower-protein diet by feather picking and raising blood from each other at the blood quill stage. Even when the feathers had sprouted, they still persisted in feather chewing at night, as you can see from the wet breast feathers on the male, and the female in the next photograph

Fig 157 The dropped-wing condition can be helped by taping the wing up to take the weight and setting it in the correct position. The smaller, slower-growing goose in the background does not have the problem. This Pilgrim goose is too young to show the characteristic white face markings which develop later

Fig 158 Chinese seem particularly prone to developing heavy blood quills which drop and may also fall outwards. The quills should fit snugly in the thigh coverts or under the wings, but are starting to fall outwards on the left wing. If such a condition is left, it can develop into 'oar wing' where the outer joint sticks out at right angles to the body and sets in this position. This is more often due to rapid growth and over-feeding than genetic disposition. Africans and Chinas develop their wing feathers slightly later than Greylag types

Fig 159 It is easy to prevent this condition becoming a problem if you act promptly and cut down the protein by feeding more wheat, or making them eat more grass:
(i) Set the wing in the correct position

(ii) Bind it securely with a light tape as shown. The tape should not go into the crook of the joint where it will nip the flesh. You need two people to do this: one to hold the bird, the other to do the tape

(iii) Taped and ready to go

(iv) The bird's first reaction to hold out its wings, but it will soon settle and tuck the wings correctly. The sticky part of the tape usually starts to come undone after about three days. You must cut the tape and remove it after three days, because the birds are growing rapidly and the tape will tighten. Also, the joint needs exercising. Usually, one application of tape is enough. This gosling was five weeks old

in grass-fed goslings, because their rate of growth is not so fast.

Grass or Bag-Feed?

The method you choose will depend on the space you have available and the type of birds you wish to rear. I prefer to mix the two methods. The grass provides essential vitamins that the pellet food may not. The pellets provide the added minerals and extra protein and easily-digested milled food without which the geese will not grow. If the cost of production is crucial and the birds are destined for the table, grass rearing with later fattening is cost-effective. This method will not, however, increase the size of the birds where this is desirable, for example, in producing the heavy breeds for exhibition and in producing breeder-quality heavy geese. Birds with high nutrient demand, such as the Toulouse, which require careful management, will not do well on range alone. Remember, it is essential to choose an appropriate breed for your purpose.

Fig 160 Vent sexing goslings – the gosling should not be held up-side down like the adults because the bones are soft. Sit down and place the bird across your knee, and tuck it into your body to stop it struggling. Its head will also be supported. Bend the tail gently backwards (downwards). The vent should not be forced open; wait until the bird is more relaxed, otherwise you will cause bruising of the sphincter muscles. This gosling is a male. The penis is, as yet, a tiny organ only 2–3mm long. It is paler than the cloaca and also curved. If you cannot see this, you need to open the vent a little more than shown in the photograph to make absolutely sure there is no penis, only crinkles of pink flesh denoting a female

SEXING THE GOSLINGS

It is much easier to sex young goslings than adults. Although it can be done at a day old, I prefer to leave it until 3 to 4 weeks. At this age, you catch them before they have sprouted quills, which get in the way, but they are a little larger. It is easier to see what is there, and there is less likelihood of damaging the bird, which is more robust. If the goslings are accustomed to being handled it is a relatively stress-free operation.

Sit down and put the bird across your knee, resting it on its back and holding it against your body. The tail can be pushed downwards and the sphincter muscles gently opened, using the forefingers of both hands, to reveal the sex. Males have a small 2–3mm long, curved, pale penis in paler-coloured breeds. It may be darker in fawn Chinas. Take care that this is not confused with the genital eminence in the female, which is a small pale raised blob on the outer edge of the vent.

The legs of the birds are surprisingly large at this stage, and they can be given spiral rings, which will be all right for several weeks. Only ring one sex, the one in the minority.

With practice, you will get 100 per cent accuracy using this method of sexing. You can confirm by behaviour, size and voice that you have got it right as the birds grow up. If you are unlucky to have hatched nearly all ganders, you can at least sell them as table goslings at this stage if you wish.

Checklist for Breeding Exhibition Geese

It seems to be a common complaint that geese are not as good as they used to be. This may be looking back at the past with rose-tinted spectacles, but there could also be some validity in this view. In the earlier part of the century, geese were more commonly kept as farm birds, or as exhibition birds by professional breeders. Only the latter were frequently seen at the shows. Now that geese and ducks have become more popular on smallholdings and as pets which do not get to the exhibitions, stock bred and reared in a far greater variety of ways is appearing. The birds reared by the professional breeders with years of experience still make the size they should but, quite often, stock in the medium and heavyweight breeds is too small. Unless good practice in breeding and rearing is followed, then geese do get poorer by the generation. The checklist that follows is a summary of the recommendations in the text for breeding quality birds.

- In-bred birds may produce smaller offspring; use unrelated stock. This is not true in certain lines where the pedigree is known and breeders selectively in-breed to produce size from a genetic trait.
- Feed the goose and gander a nutritious diet of good quality grass, supplemented with breeder pellets if they wish to eat them. The heavier breeds such as Toulouse benefit more than lighter breeds such as the Pilgrim and Brecon. Breeder pellets should contain fishmeal and be at least 16 per cent protein.

- Do not use yearling females for breeding. The eggs are below the weight typical of the breed. Wait until the goose is two years old or more.
- Choose eggs of average weight with a good shell.
- Use clean, unwashed eggs. The goslings are less likely to get a yolk sac infection and will grow well.
- Use eggs stored for ten days or less. Old eggs may hatch but can produce small birds.
- Eggs hatched early and mid-season will, in general, produce larger birds than late season eggs. This is especially true of Chinese and Brecons where late goslings are a waste of time. You may have to use the goose or broodies to hatch these early eggs. Note also that early hatches (apart from the first couple of eggs) tend to produce more males; later season eggs are more likely to have a higher proportion of females.
- Feed the goslings clipped greens if you cannot get them out on grass. This avoids leg problems.
- Graze the goslings on clean grass unused recently by adult geese.
- As well as grass, provide *ad lib* grower's pellets (except whilst the blood quills are sprouting). These pellets should contain fishmeal.
- Always have coarse concreting sand available for the birds to eat to break down food in the gizzard.
- Worm the birds if they seem light – pick them up frequently.
- Heavy breeds of geese continue to grow until at least two years old and must be fed on quality food during this period.

Appendix
Diseases and Ailments ——

If you only have a few geese, and follow a few precautions when you buy new stock, you are unlikely to have many problems with the birds. The commonest ailments are gizzard worm, infected leg joints, and egg binding in females in the laying season. Other problems do occur and a consultation with the vet can be useful, although many do not specialize in birds. The list of ailments that follows is not intended to be exhaustive, but it is a result of our first-hand experience, and of that of other breeders.

It is often quite impossible to tell why a bird has died, unless your vet does a post mortem, and then, if necessary, sends off a tissue sample to the local Ministry of Agriculture pathology laboratory. This is a time-consuming and expensive procedure and, unless you have several birds dying inexplicably, not worth doing. By the time you have the result, it is either too late, or antibiotics have resolved the problem anyway. In contrast, your local vet can usually do a quick check for TB, gizzard worm or the likelihood of coccidiosis.

Any bird that is ill should be wormed as a matter of course. Getting rid of these parasites will always help recovery, even if they are not the prime cause of any problem. Unwell birds frequently appreciate coarse sand, and it is worth checking that they have had access to this, and to enough mixed poultry grit.

---

[1] Pearce, *Waterfowl* 1979

CONDITIONS

Air Intake Beneath the Skin

This peculiar condition caused two of our Toulouse geese literally to inflate with air trapped beneath the skin. The vet had previously seen the condition in pigeons. In one bird it was confined to the head region and neck, in the other, it affected the whole body. Both birds had to be put down. There seems to be no explanation, other than some trauma initiating the damage, which then spreads.

Aspergillosis

Spores of various fungi proliferate in damp, mouldy bedding, particularly hay. Only buy straw that smells sweet and has been dry-baled. The spores cause 'farmer's lung' in humans, and also lead to respiratory distress in birds. The fungus grows inside the respiratory system and gives the symptoms of pneumonia. Unfortunately, the fungal disease does not respond to antibiotics.

You should be able to avoid cases of aspergillosis by using rough sawdust for bedding, straw plus shavings in the breeding season for nests in a shed, and bark peelings for damper places outdoors. Nesting material must be clean otherwise *aspergillae* can be transferred to the incubator and affect the goslings[1]. There is no treatment, so make sure bedding is not a problem.

Avian Tuberculosis

TB can be carried by wild birds[2], and it can be very persistent. We have only ever had one case in a bird bought in, which transferred the disease to only one other. The disease takes a long time to develop, and causes the bird to become listless and thin, and then die. A post mortem of such a case will quickly reveal infected joints and an enlarged liver, studded with small white or yellow nodules. All associated birds should be subjected to a pin-prick test to the skin, applied to the side of the bill at the fleshy base where it is attached to the head. Do not allow the feet to be used, as the test can cause the birds to go lame. Affected birds react by a swelling at the test point, and must be culled and burned. Further testing is necessary at one- to two-month intervals until the flock is clear. The birds should preferably be moved on to clean ground and the housing disinfected.

Botulism (or 'Limberneck')

This is caused by a species of *clostridia*. An affected bird rests its head on the ground because of paralysis of the neck, hence the alternative term 'limberneck'. Toxins are ingested from boggy areas with rotting vegetation, particularly in warm spells in summer. Make sure that birds do not have access to these. There is no treatment for the disease[3] other than removal of the source of the infection, providing clean drinking water to flush out the system, and hoping for the best. Antibiotics help stop further deterioration of tissue.

Bumblefoot

This is a colloquial term referring to a swelling on the foot caused by bacteria entering through a bruise or injury. Antibiotics may help, but there is no really effective treatment. The condition will ease if the bird has access to plenty of clean swimming water.

Coccidiosis

Coccidia are species-specific[4]. These organisms live in the gut and damage it so that the bird becomes thin and looks miserable, and will fail to grow. Continued damage results in further infection and death. Symptoms are lethargy and loss of weight and, particularly, blood in the droppings. This cannot be seen easily if the birds are eating grass. Look at droppings passed in the morning, just before the birds are released from the shed. A good vet can gauge the level of infection from a sample, and the birds may be treated with a coccidiostat. The coccidiostat added to some poultry grower's foods is not a treatment.

Geese are less affected by the disease than poultry, but it is a problem if the geese are grazed on dirty grass covered in droppings, particularly in the summer heat in damp weather. *Coccidia* oocysts are highly resistant and, given warmth and moisture, will proliferate. Oocysts are present on all poultry farms and even the healthiest birds are likely to be affected with a few parasites. These birds are resistant to further attack. Fatal disease follows in birds that have failed to acquire the resistance that follows light infection. In geese, the disease will also affect the kidneys. Young geese are much more likely to be affected than adults.

Avoid problems by using feed from bags or clean grazing. Oocysts take two days to 'ripen' after they have passed through the gut, so that moving coops on to clean ground each day keeps down infection in young goslings.

---

[2] ADAS leaflet 1, 1980

[3] Curtis, P., 1987

[4] ADAS leaflet 16, *Coccidiosis in Chickens,* 1979

Co-ordination Loss

When ill, geese will often sit down and may lose their balance if they try to move around. Sometimes this will improve with the use of antibiotics if there has been a bacterial infection of the gut. In other cases, the antibiotic makes no difference. This is sometimes because *listeria* have caused permanent damage. In other cases, a viral infection of the spinal cord is said to be the cause. Other than patience in looking after the bird, there is little to be done, and the goose often has to be put down.

Crooked Toes

This can be a genetic defect, or may be caused by incorrect incubation temperature.

Crop Binding and Sour Crop

Unlike chickens, geese do not have a crop to store food. Food is stored in the gullet and proventriculus in a similar way to the crop, hence the term 'crop binding' when things go wrong. Avoid problems by making sure that the birds have access to coarse builder's sand for grinding grass in the gizzard. Also, keep the grass short so that it is tender; long, stringy grass will cause problems.

Toulouse are more prone to this condition than other breeds, probably because of the shape of the keel and the proventriculus, which is carried low down. A lump develops at the base of the keel if the food is not passing through properly, and this develops into 'sour crop' when the proventriculus begins to swell and the keel distends. You can try to treat this with massage to break up the lump, while holding the bird out, or its neck downwards. The bird will have difficulty in breathing in this position, so do not persist. If you are successful, also treat the bird with an antibiotic in the water. The bird may also be operated upon by the vet to clean out the impacted debris, but the condition usually results in it having to be put down.

'Dropped Tongue'

I have only seen this in Toulouse, but it can occur in other breeds. The floor of the mouth sags and the tongue drops into the hollow. This causes problems in eating and drinking for the bird, and the hollow becomes full of food which needs cleaning out. The condition can develop with a poor feeding regime, for example, if birds are fed a dry mash with insufficient water to clear their mouths. It is also alleged to develop if grass is too fibrous. Whatever the cause, it can be cured by stitching the loose skin (not the inner membrane of the mouth), then drawing the stitches together. This strangulates the blood supply so that the skin withers and falls off.[5] This does work, but fluid can bubble around the stitches for a while and look unpleasant. Another remedy is to put a marble or appropriate-sized pebble in the hole inside the mouth, and tie it off tightly. Again, the skin atrophies.

Eye Problems

Geese occasionally get a bacterial eye infection. The eye looks sore and runny, and they rub it against their plumage. Treat the eye with an antibiotic cream at night when there is no access to water. Allow the bird to bathe freely in the daytime. Toulouse are rather prone to slight foaming of the eye, particularly in spring. This condition may not respond to antibiotic treatment, and there may be no abnormality there; no pathogen was found in a sample I once sent off to the path lab. The condition may be due to physical irritation, such as mud or mites, or to a poor diet. If the bird is having problems, make sure there is no

---

[5] Soames, B., 1980

northern mite on the bird, provide plenty of clean water and feed a good-quality pelleted diet.

Gapes

Worms in the throat (*Syngamus trachea* in poultry) cause birds to gasp for breath. This is less a problem in geese than in chickens, but has been known to kill geese that are not treated. The infestation is indicated by birds shaking their heads, and by a rattling in their throat, as they have difficulty breathing. The birds otherwise behave normally and do not seem ill. Humphreys[6] says that the eggs of the gapeworm *cyathostoma* (which is one species, among others) can be picked up directly from the grass. Some birds seem more prone to it than others, possibly because of eating soil to aid digestion. Treat using a proprietary wormer (*see* the section on worms).

Helminth Parasites

See the section on worms.

Listeria

We had some young Chinese geese that became ill with this problem in a hot spell one summer. The birds were eating soil and presumably picked the disease up from the ground. They lost co-ordination, ran a high temperature and, although their condition improved slightly with antibiotics, they eventually had to be put down. They continued to eat and drink throughout the illness. Path lab analysis confirmed *listeria*.

Maggots

During spells of hot, damp summer weather when flies proliferate, eggs may be laid around the vent of a goose. This is more likely to happen with Toulouse than other breeds, which stay cleaner. Birds with access to plenty of bathing water will not suffer. The flies are more likely to settle on a bird that is already ill, or injured. Pick the maggots off, use an ointment if the skin is raw, and treat the affected area with fly spray.

Mineral Deficiencies

As with vitamin deficiencies, these are unlikely to occur if birds receive a mixed diet. Calcium is added to poultry pellets in the correct amount for growers, maintenance and layers. Extra calcium should always be made available in the breeding season as limestone chips and oyster shell so that the females can help themselves to the amount they want for egg formation. Excess calcium is not necessary for goslings and the calcium content of layer's pellets is higher than they need and can be harmful as it will then increase their demand for phosphorus.

Other minerals such as magnesium, manganese, copper, iron, iodine, potassium, sodium, selenium, zinc, and so on, are needed in trace amounts and the feed label on the bags of pellets will indicate if these have been added. If the goslings are suffering recurrent problems with wobbly legs and slipped tendons, despite a good diet, and it happens with more than one pair of geese, it would be worth while checking if the soils in your area are deficient in particular materials. Deficiency in certain minerals as well as vitamins can result in leg problems. Farmers are often aware of local deficiencies because of sheep and cattle nutrition and agricultural services may be able to give advice.

A particular gosling with wobbly legs could be given a course of multivitamin and mineral pills; this does help in some cases.

---

[6] Humphreys, P.N., *Waterfowl* 1975

Mites: Red Mite and Northern Mite

Northern mite is a red, blood-sucking mite that lives on the bird. In waterfowl, it seems only to infest the head and neck. It causes the bird to scratch, and may be a contributory factor in eye-foaming in Toulouse, and in air intake under the skin. It is difficult to keep birds completely free of the parasite, as it is transmitted quickly from bird to bird. The parasite is difficult to see on coloured birds. It is more easily discovered on white birds if the feathers are parted on the crown of the head. If birds are scratching, they should be treated with a pyrethrum powder, ruffling up the feathers when the bird is dry, preferably when it is shut in for the night. The process should be repeated ten days later, as pyrethrum is a contact killer, and is not persistent. These mites die without a warm host.

Red mite commonly infests chicken houses, but can also get in the goose house. If the birds are scratching for no apparent reason, try spraying the shed with insecticide. Duramitex used to be recommended, but it is a very persistent chemical. Alternatively, try a pyrethrum spray on the woodwork first, and repeat ten days later. This infestation is rare with waterfowl. Mites live in the cracks in the shed and are not permanently on the bird; they can live for months without food. They look virtually the same as northern mite when they have eaten – they are red. If they have not eaten for weeks, they are grey.

Newcastle Disease

This is a highly infectious viral disease, causing respiratory problems, diarrhoea and high mortality. It occasionally visits Britain from the continent, as it did in 1996–7, probably carried by migratory starlings. It seemed to affect large commercial establishments rather than a few birds. When a case in reported, zones of exclusion are drawn and poultry movement halted. This is a notifiable disease in the UK, with compulsory slaughter for highly pathogenic strains[7]. Chickens and turkeys are much more susceptible than waterfowl, which are reputed to carry the disease but not suffer from it. A vaccine is available.

Pasteurellosis (Fowl Cholera)

Birds suffering from this may have watery green droppings, difficulty in breathing, discharge from the mouth and nostrils, and be unable to get up. They lose control of their neck muscles in the later stages. Isolate sick birds. Treat with antibiotic; if the disease is caught very early, you may save the bird. The disease can be spread by wild birds and may occur at any time of the year.

Pseudotuberculosis (Yersinia)

In dirty conditions, birds can develop internal white growths in the liver that resemble TB. Infected birds are thin and infectious. As with many diseases, this cannot be readily diagnosed except by post mortem. Antibiotics can help. It is uncommon, but it can affect humans[8].

Pneumonia

This is supposed to be common in goslings up to six months of age, but yours will not get it if you keep them warm and dry at night, and on clean bedding. We have only had it in one adult bird. Symptoms are laboured breathing and lack of appetite. This is difficult to cure with antibiotics unless it is caught early. Make sure that sheds are well ventilated.

---

[7] Curtis, P.
[8] Curtis, P.

Reproductive System Diseases

Egg Binding

Birds may sometimes have extreme difficulty in passing an egg. If it is low down in the oviduct and the eggshell can be seen as the bird strains to pass it, the bird can be helped. Squirt olive oil into the vent with a syringe (no needle), and try to aid the passage of the egg by holding the egg from the outside of the bird (beneath the abdomen) and gently easing the egg outwards. In a bad case, the muscles are tight and will not allow the egg's passage. A calcium injection may help to relax the muscles; ask the vet. Sometimes, the egg may have to be broken and the bits extracted by forceps. This is best done by a vet, as any tearing will cause infection. Always give the bird a course of antibiotics to prevent infection of the oviduct.

Egg Peritonitis

Egg peritonitis and associated abnormalities of egg-producing organs are one of the most common causes of death. The abdominal cavity can become inflamed due to the presence of egg yolk, or even eggs with shells. Birds in lay should always be treated quietly to avoid such problems.

Impaction of the Oviduct

The tube carrying the eggs from the ovaries to the cloaca may become impacted with cheesy material, and often broken eggshell, and may become infected.

Prolapse of the Oviduct

The lower part of the oviduct may protrude from the vent as a result of egg binding or straining. This can gently be replaced in some cases, but it is likely to be a persistent problem and the bird may be best put down if the prolapse is bad, or if the problem recurs.

Birds suffering from acute oviduct problems in the spring can die quite quickly, for no obvious external reason. In chronic cases, death may be delayed for several days or even weeks. The abdomen may become swollen.

Birds obviously suffering from oviduct problems are best put down.

Sinus Infection

This is much rarer in geese than in ducks. If a swelling develops at the base of the bill, so that the bird's 'cheek' swells out, do not assume it is a tumour. Treat first with an appropriate antibiotic, from the vet. The rather hard swelling should soften as it responds to the antibiotic and, after about a week, should have gone. Watch the bird to check that the infection does not re-occur in susceptible individuals.

Staphylococcus Infections

These occur as localized infections of the tendon sheaths in the legs, and in the feet. The affected area is hot to the touch and swells; the bird limps. Infection can follow as a result of sprain injury or skin damage. Treat the bird with antibiotic injections. Infection is less likely in adults than in young birds. Avoid problems by having clean grazing and feeding the birds well. We have had fewer problems with this, as we have used pelleted feed with extra vitamins and minerals rather than just wheat and grass.

Tumours

Tumours can arise in quite young geese, even at two or three years old. They appear as round, bloody tubercles on the wings, head and neck. These may bleed and make the bird look in a worse mess than it actually is. The bird should eventually be put down.

Vitamin deficiencies

These are unlikely to develop where birds are given some pelleted foods and are kept in natural conditions i.e. grazing on clean pasture. As with humans, a mixed diet including fresh food is best. Green foods supply vitamin A and K; sunlight allows the bird to use vitamin D; B vitamins and vitamin E are provided by cereal grains. Fish meal and oils, added to starter and grower pellets, are especially important sources of vitamins. Deficiencies are most likely to occur in intensively reared goslings kept indoors and reared on starter rations designed for poultry.

Leg weakness is the most likely manifestation of vitamin deficiency. It may show as weak hocks in 1–4 week olds, or wobbly legs leading to difficulty in balance. If some goslings, perhaps breeds or strains with a particularly high vitamin demand, are not given greens in the first two weeks, they develop bowed legs and slipped tendons. These conditions cannot be cured and so the problem is best avoided. Adding niacin or brewer's yeast to the diet prevents the condition, as does simply getting the goslings out onto grass[9]. Sunlight also allows the birds to utilise vitamin D. If a particular bird, despite having a good diet, becomes unsteady, there is no harm in giving it a course of those multi-vitamin and mineral pills for the over-forties, plus a course of antibiotics if you are not sure what the cause of the problem is.

Wing problems

Oar Wing/Angel Wing

This occurs between 3½–5 weeks when the blood-filled quills of the gosling are sometimes too heavy to be supported by the final wing joint. It may happen in some seasons and not others in goslings bred from the same breeding pair. Its occurrence is therefore more often controlled by environmental factors than genetic disposition. See the section of feeding goslings and correcting Angel Wing; treatment must be immediate to stop permanent deformity.

Dropped Wing

The gosling, between five and even eight weeks, allows its wing to fall below the normal position, but the quills do not rotate outwards. The muscles merely seem too weak to hold up the wing, which the gosling frequently hitches up. This often corrects itself, but can also be helped by taping the wing.

Rough Wing

The primary feathers do not fold snugly under the secondaries. This is a result of earlier wing problems (as a gosling), but can also develop in older birds after a summer moult. Toulouse seem particularly prone to developing this as adults and it may well be in the breeding of these birds. It can sometimes be corected by taping.

Worms

Caecal Worms (Heterakis gallinarum)

These are generally harmless unless in large numbers.[10]

Acuaria

Humphreys[11] refers to this particular roundworm being a problem in waterfowl. The worm damages the proventriculus so that the organ ceases to work, and the bird gets thin and dies. This worm has a stage in its life cycle when it lives in the body of the water flea *Daphnia*, which is common in ponds. A good strong flow of water is recommended as it stops the *Daphnia* from multiplying.

Gape Worms

See under Gapes.

---

[9] *Magazine of Ducks and Geese*, Spring 1954

[10] *Poultry World Disease Directory 1994*
[11] Humphreys P.N., *Waterfowl*, 1975

Gizzard Worm (Amidostomum anseris)

This is the only commonly harmful worm that attacks geese. Like the gape worm, the gizzard worm is spread directly on to the ground via the birds' droppings. The eggs grow into an infective stage to be swallowed with the grass. The hair-like worm burrows under the horny lining of the gizzard and sucks blood. If the droppings of goslings are reddish rather than greenish, this is a bad sign. Large numbers of worms are sometimes found in the gizzards of adults that have died from other causes. Adults may carry an infection with no obvious effects. For goslings, a heavy infection is fatal; prevention is better than cure.

Worming Geese

The approved wormer for birds is flubendazole, found in the product Flubenvet. Follow the approved dosage on the label. The Flubenvet powder is mixed with dry food, preferably pellets, and is fed to the birds for a week. This is often not a suitable wormer for geese when their main diet is grass, as insufficient worming powder is consumed. Also, when a bird is really ill, it does not eat. It is possible to administer Flubenvet as a single drench; ask the vet for details. Flubenvet is also available from agricultural stores and other licensed retailers such as *Interhatch*.

Levamisole is a single-dose, liquid wormer which can be obtained from a vet and used with their advice. The dose for Levamisole 7.5 per cent solution (out of a Vet's handbook) for cage birds is 0.13–0.26ml per kg. The dosages multiplied up for geese are given below. The upper limit for geese is too high; as an animal increases in body weight, the dosage for medicines does not increase pro rata. Do not allow more than 1ml of Levamisole 7.5 per cent solution to be used. An overdose can kill. Levamisole should not be used on goslings less than 10 weeks old.

4kg goose	8.5lb	0.52 – [1.04 ml]
5	11	0.65 – [1.3]
6	13	0.78 – [1.56]
7	15.5	0.91 – [1.8]
8	17.5	1.04 – [2.1]

Always dilute the dose with at least an equal part of water. It saves the bird distress; neat doses can cause them to shake their head and neck about. They will fall about if the dose is too high. Levamisole is also good for controlling throat worms which can cause geese to cough and choke if neglected.

This wormer can be given in drinking water over a period of about half a day. The container has to be securely anchored, fairly small so the geese do not use it as washing water to throw over themselves, and the only drinking water available. It must also be completely cleared up to make sure that they get the correct dose.

Panacur 10 per cent solution (for cats and dogs, and cattle) could be used for goslings instead, with the advice of a vet. *Panacur* will kill gizzard worms but not their eggs. However, it is much safer than Levamisole and can be used on young goslings. If *Panacur* is used, the goslings will require a second dose two weeks later to kill off any more gizzard worms which have developed from the egg stage in the meantime. Check that you do have the 10 per cent solution as it is also manufactured at 2.5 per cent strength. The manufacturers note that *Panacur* is not licensed for use in geese; it is sold for cats, dogs, horses, cattle, sheep and goats.

Problems with worms are best avoided by good management. Goslings should always be grazed on short, clean grass. If they are accompanied by adult geese, the adults should be wormed first. This is preferably done when the goose sits, so that if she gets ill or too light you know gizzard worm is not the problem. The gizzard worm cycle is about three weeks from egg to adult, so if the goslings have not been allowed on grass until two weeks old there should be no initial problem. Always keep a check on goslings by picking them up frequently to check their weight. Any bird that seems slow or sluggish should be examined and wormed. Goslings rarely get ill if they are fed crumbs, then pellets with wheat are introduced ad lib. It is those expected to survive largely on grass that are more likely to suffer.

The effectiveness of various wormers on parasites affecting geese is shown on the table opposite.

188

Useful Addresses

Allen & Page
Small Holder Feeds
Tel 01362 822900
www.smallholderfeeds.co.uk

Ascott Smallholding Supplies Ltd
Tel 0845 130 6285
www.ascott.biz

Blackbrook World of Birds
BWA Conservation and Education Centre
Winkhill
Near Leek
Staffordshire
Tel 01538 308293

BOCM-Pauls (Mardens Game Feeds)
Tel 01379 742007

Brinsea Incubators Ltd.
Tel 01934 823039
www.brinsea.co.uk

British Waterfowl Association
Tel 01892 740212
e-mail info@waterfowl.org.uk
www.waterfowl.org.uk

Fancy Fowl
Tel 01728 622030
www.fancyfowl.com

Humane Slaughter Association
Tel 01582 831919

Interhatch, Chesterfield
Incubator specialists
Curfew spare parts
Tel 01246 264646

Marriage's Poultry Feeds
Tel 01245 612000
www.marriagefeeds.co.uk

Smallholder Magazine
Liz Wright Tel 01354 741538
www.smallholder.co.uk

The effectiveness of various wormers on parasites affecting geese

Wormer	Amidostomum	Syngamus	Heterakis
Fenbendazole found in Panacur	No, eggs not killed	yes	yes
Levamisole found in Nilverm, 7.5 per cent	yes	yes	yes
Flubendazole	yes	yes	yes
Piperazine	no	no	partly

Note that Piperazine, which has been recommended as a wormer in some texts, is not very effective for goose parasites. Ivomec has been used for waterfowl in recent years as a systemic treatment for all internal and external parasites. It is not licensed for poultry. It may be administered in tiny amounts on the skin, or injected. Ask your vet for details.

References

Acheson, H. V. C., *Modern Goose Keeping* (Crosby, Lockwood & Son, 1954)

Ambrose, *The Aylesbury Duck* (Buckinghamshire County Museum, 1991)

Appleyard, R., *Geese, Breeding Rearing and General Management* (Poultry World Ltd, 1940s)

Bowie, S. H. U., 'Shetland's Native Farm Animals – Shetland Geese', *The Ark* (1989)

British Waterfowl Standards, reprinted from *British Poultry Standards* (fourth edition, 1982)

Brooke, M. & Birkhead, T., *The Cambridge Encyclopaedia of Ornithology* (CUP, 1991)

Brown, Dr A. F. A., *The Incubation Book*, World Pheasant Association (Wheaton, 1979)

Brown, E., *Poultry Breeding and Production* (Caxton, 1929)

Browne D. J., *The American Poultry Yard* (1853)

de Bruin, 'The Steinbacher Fighting Goose', *Avicultura* (1995)

Brown, E., *Races of Domestic Poultry* (1906)

Charnock Bradley, O., *The Structure of the Fowl* (Oliver & Boyd, 1950, revised by T. Grahame 1950)

Curtis, P., *A Handbook of Poultry and Game Bird Diseases* (Liverpool University Press, 1996)

Gordon, C. D., 'Sexual dimorphism in the down colour and adult plumage of geese', *Journal of Heredity 29:335–337* (1938)

Grow, *Oscar, Modern Waterfowl Management* (American Bantam Association, 1972)

Hawes, R. H., 'The origin of Pilgrim geese', *Fancy Fowl* (1996)

Hoffmann, *Fancy Fowl* (1991)

Holderread, D., *The Book of Geese* (1981)

Humphreys, P. N., 'Worms in Waterfowl', *Waterfowl* (1975)

Irvine, Lynn, *Field with Geese* (The Country Book Club, 1960)

Ives, P., *Domestic Geese and Ducks* (Orange Judd, 1947)

Jerome, F. N., 'Inheritance of plumage colour in domestic geese', Proc., 14th World Poultry Congress (Madrid) 2:73–76 (1970)

Johnson, Lt. Col. A. A., *Chinese Geese* (1950)

Llewellyn, R., 'The Brecon Buff Goose', *Fethered World* (Oct 26 1934)

Lorenz, Konrad, *The Year of the Greylag Goose* (Eyre Methuen, 1979)

Lorenz, Konrad, *Here I am – where are you? The behaviour of the Greylag goose* (HarperCollins, 1991)

Mattocks, J. G., 'Goose feeding and cellulose digestion', *Wildfowl 22* (The Wildfowl Trust, Slimbridge 1971)

Ministry of Agriculture, Fisheries and Food, *Ducks* (MAFF Publications PB0079, 1990)

Nolan J. J., *Ornamental, Aquatic, and Domestic Fowl and Game Birds* (1850)

Owen, M., Wildfowl of Europe (Macmillan, 1977)

Parr, J., 'The Embden geese in Germany', *Waterfowl* (1996)

Pearce, 'Sorting out problems with geese', *Waterfowl* (1979)

Poultry Club Standards 1997

Poultry World Disease Directory 1994

Roberts, M. & V., *Domestic Duck and Geese in Colour* (Domestic Fowl Trust, 1986)

Robinson, J. H., *Ducks and Geese for Profit* (1924)

Robinson, J. H., *Popular Breeds of Domesitc Poultry* (1924)

Soames, B., *Keeping Domestic Geese* (Blandford, 1980)

Schmidt, H., Letter in *The Magazine of Ducks and Geese* Vol. X, No.1 (1959)

Schmidt, H., *Puten, Perlhuhner, Ganse, Enten* (Neumann–Neudamm, 1989)

Stoll, Andreas, 'Autosexing Geese', *Waterfowl*, (Autumn 1984)

Todd, F., *Waterfowl: Ducks, Geese and Swans of the World* (Sea World Press, 1979)

Weir, H., *Our Poultry* (1902)

Wright, Lewis, *The Illustrated Book of Poultry* (1880)

Wright, Lewis, *The New Book of Poultry* (1902)

Index